ROYAL DATES WITH
# DESTINY

# ROYAL DATES WITH
# DESTINY

## ROBERT EASTON

AMBERLEY

First published 2010

Amberley Publishing
Cirencester Road, Chalford,
Stroud, Gloucestershire, GL6 8PE

www.amberley-books.com

British Library Cataloguing in Publication Data.
A catalogue record for this book is available from the British Library.

ISBN 978-1-84868-830-8

Typeset in 11pt on 11pt Venetian301 BT.
Typesetting and origination by Amberley Publishing
Printed in Great Britain

# CONTENTS

✻ *Frontispiece*     *viii*

✻ *Preface*     *ix*

✻ *January*     *1*

✻ *February*     *23*

✻ *March*     *41*

✻ *April*     *59*

✻ *May*     *77*

✻ *June*     *95*

✻ *July*     *113*

✻ *August*     *131*

✻ *September*     *151*

✻ *October*     *167*

✻ *November*     *185*

✻ *December*     *203*

✻ *Cause of Death*     *221*

✻ *Index*     *233*

*S.M.E.*

*1928-2009*

*M.W.R.*

*1917-2009*

*In Memoriam*

Ars moriendi, *woodcut 7 (4a), Netherlands, c. 1460.*

# PREFACE

*Pallida mors aequo pulsat pede pauperum tabernas regumque turris.*

Horace, Odes I.4.13-14

In the middle of the fifteenth century, a rather unprepossessing book with the rather unprepossessing title of *The Art of Dying* found its way into print. *Ars moriendi* was little more than a pictorial of eleven woodcuts of a man on his deathbed, attended by two sets of individuals pursuing two diametrically opposed agendas. While one group is praying that the man will 'die well' and begin his ascent to heaven, the other group hopes that he will put his own needs before those of God and take his first steps down the primrose path to hell.

Ten of the woodcuts were to be considered in pairs, with the first of each pair detailing one of the five temptations that a man in his last hours faces – despair, impatience, spiritual pride, avarice and faithlessness – and the second promoting the appropriate, godly response to that temptation. The frontispiece to this book is an example of the former. Here we see some ugly little demons pestering the feeble *Moriens* ('the dying one') to accept their gifts of crowns, in the hope that in his vulnerable state he will focus on earthly success rather than his failure towards God. To one side, behind some cherubs, we see a pensive God the Father, God the Son, and Virgin Mary, silently egging him on to resist temptation and 'make a good death.' In stark black and white, the eleventh woodcut presents the reward that awaited the man who made the grade; *Moriens* is welcomed into the eternal bliss of heaven, while the defeated demons slink back to hell, their tails between their legs.

*Ars moriendi* sold like hot cakes. For literate and illiterate alike, reeling from the Black Death and debilitating effects of war and drought, here was a simple, no-nonsense 'conduct book' on how to prepare for the unavoidable at the end of the perilously unpredictable. With real religious ministers in short supply, this book provided a 'pictorial priest', offering spiritual comfort and hope to a laity desperate for a modicum of assurance in a fickle world.

Publishers kept the new-fangled printing presses busy in their attempt to cash in on Europe's new obsession with death, but nothing came close to the success of *Ars moriendi*. No book since, in fact, with the possible exception of Jeremy Taylor's devotional masterpiece *Holy Dying* of 1651, has addressed the somewhat taboo subject of preparing to meet one's maker and come close to being on the bestseller list. Perhaps, then, the time is ripe for a contemporary *Ars moriendi* — a new, thoughtful analysis of morality and mortality in the post-modern age, a consideration of how, modern medical advances notwithstanding, one should prepare for a 'good death' in the twenty-first century.

Well, *Royal Dates with Destiny* isn't it. Yes, there are deaths within these pages that are undoubtedly dignified and highly admirable, but this is a work that focuses ostensibly on deaths of nobles rather than noble deaths. From the machinations of stepmothers (January 1) to the effect of eating too many Austrian snails (December 31), this is a book that concerns itself primarily with the circumstances in which aristocrats have met their maker, rather than the state of their soul at their moment of departure from this mortal coil.

Unlike *Ars moriendi*, *Royal Dates with Destiny* does not purport to be spiritually uplifting. With its vast time frame, spanning ancient Egypt and modern-day Kuwait, and global subject matter (Aztec warriors vie for space with Australian cricketers, Sarawak ranees with Zulu kings) it is a diffuse, secular panorama of the eccentricities of fallible humanity rather than a concentrated work of 'moral thanatology.'

That said, this wide-ranging calendar of royal dates with destiny might just have a smidgen of instructional value. Perhaps the ways in which the daily blue-blooded *Moriens* meets his or her end will help the red-blooded readers of today ready themselves for the Grim Reaper's arrival. After browsing through some four hundred stories of noble (and sometimes sticky) ends, readers might come to the following eleven conclusions about death:

## ❀ 1) Death can be noble

One cannot but be impressed at the composure with which Holy Roman Emperor Charles VI (October 20) or Queen Blanche of France (November 26) met their ends. Granted, Charles's obsession with etiquette, which remained with him to his dying breath, was a little alarming, and the nature of the accident that ushered Blanche to an early grave was rather weird, but their self-possession at their very end is a lesson for us all. Admiral Byng (March 14) and John Andre (October 2) meanwhile, both faced their executions with astonishing grace and dignity.

## ❀ 2) Death can be decidedly ignoble

Down in a sewer (February 21), surrounded by one's own filth (September 13), or on the toilet (October 25) are hardly surroundings in which royals would have hoped to leave life's stage, but such were the environments for three of Europe's most powerful monarchs (James I of Scotland, Philip II of Spain and George II of England respectively). Nor are embarrassing exits a European preserve; Moghul and Japanese emperors taking a tumble (January 27 and February 10), an Ethiopian King paying the price for ignoring good advice (October 4), and the Prince of Ghor ending up a dishevelled heap on a San Francisco sidewalk (October 21) all attest that the undignified death is universal.

## ❀ 3) Death can strike at any time

Death can come as suddenly to the great and the good as to common folk. The unsuspecting Henry of Castile, walloped by a roof tile (June 6), or poor Simon IV Montfort, decked by a lucky mangonel missile (June 25), had no chance to put their affairs in order. Anne Boleyn (May 19), on the other hand, knew all too well that her death was imminent, but, thanks to an executioner at the height of his powers, not as imminent as she thought.

On the other hand, dying can be long drawn-out process. Princess Charlotte of Belgium (January 19) took nearly half a century to complete a life that seemed over when she lost her beloved husband and left her beloved Mexico. Her saving grace was that she was imprisoned in her own mind for most of that time. The life force of King Ludwig I of Bavaria, meanwhile, evaporated when the luscious Lola left him for pastures new, but it took him another twenty years to die (February 29). Far more disturbing are the miserable existences eked out by such aristocratic prisoners as Peter, Count Griffenfeld (March 12), and James, Earl of Bothwell (April 14), 'living' in squalor, simply aching for their last day to arrive.

## ❀ 4) Death can strike at any age

Friedrich of Hesse tipping out of a window when just a toddler (May 27), the body of Angelino, the infant son of Marchioness Osoli washing up onto shore (July 19), and prince Albert of Hawaii succumbing to brain fever at only four (August 27) provide heart-rending evidence that capricious death pays no heed to youth or innocence.

In contrast, some members of the nobility have lived to a ripe old age. Sir Provo Wallis (April 26) and Elizabeth the Queen Mother (March 30), for example, are members of a select club of centenarian aristocrats, the former bemusing the British Admiralty with his longevity, and the latter receiving a congratulatory telegram from her own daughter.

## ❀ 5) Death can be invited

If you go into a mosquito-ridden swamp ripe with malaria, (as did King Mongkut of Siam on October 1), wear a top hat into battle (Sir Thomas Picton on June 18), or travel unaccompanied in bandit-infested scorching deserts with a gammy leg (Emmeline, Lady Wortley on October 30), you are simply asking for trouble. Likewise, if you sport an obvious identification mark at a masked ball when assassins are two-a-penny (like King Gustav III of Sweden on March 29), run around in a shower of infected feathers (Charles, Duke of Orleans on September 9) or go for a stroll during a lightning storm (Emperor Jiaqing on September 2) you are recklessly chancing with death.

And the same goes for wanton over-indulgence. Wolf down too many puddings like Adolf Frederick of Sweden (February 12), drink two gallons of wine a day (Frederick II of Denmark, April 4), or spend an inordinate amount of time between the sheets, as did Dagobert, King of the Franks (January 19), then you only have yourself to blame.

Tragically for some royals, inviting a doctor to one's sickbed was tantamount to issuing one's own death warrant. The woeful diagnoses and outrageous 'cures' of clueless doctors make one deeply grateful to live in a time of kinder, gentler medical care. Mercifully, we don't live in an age when the brutal practice of 'lowering', such as that borne by Charlotte, Princess of England (November 6) is common. And although quackery still abounds, the savage blistering and bleeding and cupping that doctors once thought restorative is thankfully no more. Certainly the humiliation of being made to bathe in ice cold water, as endured by Ethiopian Princess Zewditu (April 2), or having a pigeon placed on one's head, as undergone by Henry, Prince of Wales (November 6), are no longer deemed textbook procedures

## ❀ 6) Death cannot be avoided

There's nothing you can do to halt death's progress. You can try everything you like – you can try bathing in blood of tortoises from the Cape Verde Islands like

Louis XI of France (August 30), or gulping down mercury like Chinese emperor Shi Huangdi (September 10). You can try mouth-to-mouth resuscitation as did the Hawaiian Queen Emma on her husband (November 30), or you can try coffee enemas like 'King' Steve McQueen (November 7). But if it's your time to go, it's your time to go.

## ❧ 7) Death can come in different sized packages

Sometimes the seemingly inconsequential can have terminal consequences. The midge that felled Lord Carnarvon (April 5), the stone that toppled Aztec emperor Montezuma (June 29), the ear of barley that choked young Baron Lucas (July 21), and the flea that did for Emperor Justinian (November 14) all could be held together in the palm of your hand. Similarly, the spark that turned Bavarian duchess Sophia Charlotte into a human torch (May 4), and the pen-stroke that proved fatal for Lichtenstein nobleman Christoph von Hohenlohe (August 6) were barely visible to the naked eye.

Something bigger was needed to see off other members of the nobility. For the unfortunate George, Duke of Clarence (February 18), it was a large barrel of wine, while for Maori chief Te Heuheu II (May 7), it was a huge landslide.

## ❧ 8) Death can be self-imposed

One cannot deny there is something rather beautiful in how Gertrude Bell slipped away (June 12), how Roman emperor Otho got his affairs in order before falling on his sword (April 16), and how Cleopatra wielded her asp (August 12), but for every dignified suicide in this book, there is another utterly devoid of beauty or composure. The bodies of Princess Leila of Iran (June 10) and 'Queen' Marilyn Monroe (June 12), sprawled on beds surrounded by pill bottles, and that of Lord Sutch, hanging from the stairs awaiting his girlfriend's return home (June 16), remind us that suicides can be shattering, selfish, and steeped in tragedy.

## ❧ 9) Death can be imposed by others

Assassins, with a variety of agendas, lurk around every page of this book. Some are disgruntled staff, such as the murderers of George, Duke of Buckingham, on August 23, while others are revolutionaries, like the monk who knifed King Henry III of France on August 2. Some, like Prince Dipendra of Nepal, who gunned down his father on June 1, are relatives with dynastic aspirations, while others, for instance the killer of King George I of Greece on March 18, are just weirdos. Collectively, they are a harsh reminder that political power is a precious and fragile commodity and some people will do anything to get it, or prevent others from enjoying it.

And as one would expect from a book on the deaths of people of such power, executions abound. Beheadings by axe, including the hugely messy affair of poor Countess Margaret of Salisbury on May 27, are the most common, while decapitations by sword, such as the supremely dignified end of the Ceylonese Dissawa Keppetipola on November 26, come a close second. Elsewhere, the swish of the guillotine blade – a fate not just reserved exclusively for French nobility, as the Scottish Earl of Morton found to his cost on June 2 – and the creak of the hangman's rope, including the 'silken' demise of Earl Ferrers on May 5, are interlaced with more exotic executions like firing squad (the Emperor Maximilian on June 29), garrotte (the Emperor Atahualpa on August 29), and the extraordinary 'Extraordinary Question' (imposed upon the Marquise de Brinvilliers on July 17).

## ❀ 10) Death can be a mystery

The precise circumstances in which Sir Edmundbury Godfrey (October 12) or the enigmatic Kaspar Hauser (December 17) met their ends will probably never be known. Similarly, how exactly Philip, Duke of Orleans, almost made it to fifty despite his astonishingly debauched lifestyle (December 2) will perplex historians for many years to come.

## ❀ 11) Death can be downright silly

Duelling, let's be honest, is a really silly way to die, especially if carried out in a balloon (June 22). To die because of one's hairstyle (October 15) seems pretty silly too, but dying because someone addresses you incorrectly on an envelope (October 24) surely takes the biscuit of silliness. The demise of Maria Alexandrovna through snobbery may evince more mirth than sympathy, but you cannot but feel sorry for aristocratic composers Scriabin (April 27) and de Lully (March 22), whose deaths from engaging too vigorously in normal day-to-day pursuits underscore the sheer absurdity of Fate. And how ridiculous for the Earl of Bute's seemingly harmless passion for flowers (March 10) to prove his undoing?

Hardly comparable with the eleven edifying woodcuts of *Ars moriendi*, these conclusions are, of course, little more than truisms, but they do support the poet Horace's contention that 'pale death kicks with impartial foot at the hovels of the poor and the palaces of kings.' Nobility may be born and may die with more fanfare, but death curries no favour with the aristocratic. Death doesn't give a hoot about status, station, or social rank. So many aspects of our lives, including the circumstances of our death, are little more than a lottery.

The bestselling *Ars moriendi* was a remarkably short book, and in order to keep this modern 'Book of the Dead' brief, I have focused exclusively on the deaths of 'nobility' – a term employed loosely, thus enabling me to bring in American movie kings and queens and even a couple of sportsmen with 'royal monikers'. Using the calendar format, I have also constrained myself in selecting people whose death has a specific date. No space is therefore available to write at length on minor nobleman and Greek playwright Sophocles, who died when he choked on a grape, or on King Attila the Hun, who keeled over following a nosebleed on his wedding night. No space to dwell on how Emperor Lucius Verus raped his mother-in-law, Faustina, and how she got her revenge by sprinkling poison on his oysters, and sadly no space even for Sir Thomas Urquhart, the seventeenth-century essayist who famously died – but no-one is sure exactly when – from an uncontrollable fit of laughter on hearing that the monarchy had been restored.

And laughter, or at least the occasional smile, is the fundamental goal of this book. Yes, *Royal Dates with Destiny* is a highly-researched work of history, and maybe someone will footnote it in their PhD thesis, but my main purpose is to share my delight in the funny, bizarre, and ultimately very human manner in which royals have started their journey across the River Styx. As evidenced by an offbeat list of 'Causes of Death' and an index that begins with 'abbot, lecherous' and ends with 'wrestling, with bears', this is not a doleful book about doom, but a cheerful book that looks squarely at something so many of us shy away from ... and cannot but see the funny side.

During the course of my research, I chanced upon the publications – and intriguing stories of the deaths – of two priests who, like me, also dabbled in matters historical. Both are long dead. The first is the eighteenth-century clergyman, James Granger. Granger was a biographer and book collector who saw nothing wrong in bulking up his *Biographical History of England from Egbert the Great to the Revolution* into a six-volume set by inserting pictures and biographies he had stolen from other books. His life and questionable editorial practices aside, what pleased me was the manner of his passing. By his own admission, Granger had the excellent fortune to retire early to 'independence, obscurity and content', and after several years of comfortable ecclesiastical anonymity he died – as so many priests dream of so doing – while administering Holy Communion.

The second is William Coxe, the early nineteenth-century royal physician and Archdeacon of Wiltshire, whose history of the House of Austria may lack sparkle but nevertheless produced the diamond of information on the molluscan demise of Empress Bianca Maria on December 31. Like Granger, however, it is Coxe's death – a death that so many of us, lay and ordained, would like to emulate – that makes him worthy of note. John Sharp, in a letter to the painter Constable, writes that he 'died of old age, unable to contend with two helps of salmon in lobster sauce, washed down with large draughts of Perry.' While I hope that the prose of *Royal Dates with Destiny* is less turgid than that of Coxe, and trust that I have not borrowed too much à la Granger, I do thank them for providing examples of how to die, be it in a state of grace or domestic contentment.

❧ *Few, I suspect, would deem it a compliment to be acknowledged in a book on death, but I do want to thank Doug Norris, James Jones and Matthew Godfrey for August 12, August 26 and October 12 respectively, and the staff of the British Library in London and St Deiniol's Library in North Wales where I undertook much of my research. During the writing of this book two of my closest friends died. My father Stephen (who would have approved of the typeface) and my fellow Brighton resident Michael Richey both lived full and noble lives and taught me much.*

*I am deeply grateful to Newton Perera for avoiding the potholes and to Harry Easton for his unconditional affection but most of all to Kai – as Sir Arthur Conan Doyle said to his wife eighty years ago this very day: "you are wonderful".*

Unawatuna, 7 July 2010

# JANUARY

## JANUARY 1

❀ **1204: Haakon III, king of Norway**
† *Cause of Death: Wicked Stepmother*

During the Christmas festivities of 1203 Haakon suddenly and unexpectedly fell ill and took to his bed. When he died a few days later, Norwegian courtiers took no time at all to claim that someone had poisoned him, and that "someone" was none other than Margareta Eriksdotter, the king's Swedish stepmother.

Margareta professed her innocence, and to prove it volunteered one of her servants to undergo a trial by ordeal on her behalf. The unfortunate stand-in was forced to walk nine paces holding a red-hot iron bar. If his mistress really was innocent, he would do so without injury. The hapless servant, however, was horribly burned ... and summarily executed. On hearing the news Margareta fled back to Sweden.

❀ **1515: Louis XII, king of France**
† *Cause of Death: Sex*

When his wife Anne of Brittany died on January 9, 1514, a distraught Louis donned the black of mourning and insisted that his court did the same. "Make the vault ... big enough for us both," he told his servants. "Before the year is over I'll be with her." His prophecy proved to be wrong ... but only by a whisker.

A few months later and the gouty old king was having the time of his life with his new bride, the buxom and beautiful Princess Mary Tudor, sister of Henry VIII. By all accounts, the couple took their mission to produce a male heir very seriously indeed. Louis, for instance, made it known that on their wedding night he had "crossed the river" three times.

At 51, however, Louis simply could not keep up with the pace of his eighteen-year-old wife. His doctors were alarmed by the change of both his diet (bland, boiled beef was replaced with far richer dishes) and lifestyle (the couple often danced into the small hours before racing to bed), and warned him to slow down. But Louis didn't slow down, and few were surprised when, on Christmas Eve 1514 – just months after his marriage – Louis suffered an extreme attack of gout and died eight days later.

Mary spent the next forty days in confinement to ascertain whether she was pregnant (she was not) and then sailed back to England, her body dripping with the jewels that Louis had lavished upon her. The body of Louis XII, meanwhile, joined that of Anne of Brittany in the Saint Denis Basilica.

# JANUARY 2

❀ 1512: Svante Sture, regent of Sweden
† *Cause of Death: Mineshaft*

Early in the sixteenth century, Sweden literally uncovered a new source of income – silver – and the nation's economic future took on a shinier hue. Despite this financial boon, the country's nobility wanted to depose Svante in favour of a nobleman who was better disposed to neighbouring Denmark. How lucky for them, then, that while visiting a mine to negotiate rights, Svante should die in a fall.

# JANUARY 3

❀ 1670: George Monck, duke of Albemarle
† *Cause of Death: Dropsy*

Many admired the way in which Monck, a soldier in the English Civil War for the forces of both Oliver Cromwell and later for Charles II, faced his final battle. When all conventional medicine had proved useless against his debilitating asthma, he courageously swallowed some pills prescribed to him by a former army colleague now turned quack doctor. To the amazement of one and all they appeared to work, and for a few months he was able to carry out his day-to-day duties in London. When winter returned, however, so did his illness. One of his supporters wrote that he died "like a Roman general and soldier, standing almost up in his chair ... all his officers about him." Not everyone considered Monck to be a paragon of virtue, however. The diarist Samuel Pepys thought him a "blockhead".

## ❄ 1948: William, Lord Haw Haw
† *Cause of Death: Rope*

Noble by nickname only, William Joyce, dubbed "Lord Haw Haw" by a frenzied British press, was hanged in London's Wandsworth Prison for being the voice of Nazi propaganda during the Second World War. During his trial it turned out that he couldn't be executed for treason since he was actually an American citizen. They hanged him anyway.

# JANUARY 4

## ❄ 1066: Edward the Confessor, king of the English
† *Cause of Death: Stroke*

Christmas 1065 was, for Edward, not a particularly festive occasion. According to the historian and monk Osbert of Clare, the king "was afflicted with an indisposition", and although he dutifully sat at dinner in his "festal robe" he "had no stomach for the delicacies which were served." As soon as possible, Edward (who in all likelihood had suffered a stroke) went to bed. But even in sleep he found no relief. He had a dream in which two monks warned him that many of his chief advisors were "servants of the devil", and that soon his kingdom would be taken over by the enemy "with fire and sword and the havoc of war". When he relayed this to his courtiers, some ran about in stupefied horror. Stigand, the Archbishop of Canterbury, on the other hand, laughed off the prophecy and told Harold Haroldson, soon to be Harold I, that this was nothing more than the prattling of an old man. Be that as it may, it wasn't just Edward who was soon dead. Within the year, Harold fell at Hastings (*see* October 14) and Stigand suffered a fatal cerebral haemorrhage.

# JANUARY 5

## ❄ 1387: Peter the Ceremonious, king of several places
† *Cause of Death: Old Age*

Peter had achieved much when, aged seventy, his number came up. Not least amongst his successes was the numerical accolade of being known as Peter I in Majorca, Sardinia and Romania, Peter II in Valencia, Peter III in Catalonia and Peter IV in Aragon.

## ❀ 1477: Charles the Bold, duke of Burgundy
† *Cause of Death: Halberd and Spear*

The ground was like frozen tundra, the hags had stripped the soldiers' bodies of all their clothes and then the wolves had done their worst. The task of identifying the body of the duke was not going to be easy. The search party headed out of the town of Nancy, onto the battlefield, and to a pool where a pageboy named Baptista Colonna was adamant he had seen Charles fall. Strewn like spillikins lay a dozen or so bodies – some mutilated beyond recognition, but others identifiable as the duke's most loyal retainers – suggesting a final stand had been made here. But where was the duke?

A few yards away lay a solitary, mangled body, one cheek chewed away by wolves, the other embedded in icy slime. Charles's physician knelt beside it and, from telltale scars from previous injuries, confirmed that this was indeed their man. The corpse was hacked out of the ground and thawed out in wine and warm water, revealing three fresh wounds – a blow from a halberd to the head and two spear thrusts to the groin and stomach. Charles had clearly died in bitterly fought hand-to-hand combat.

And what made all of this all the more stomach-churning was that it needn't have happened at all. Charles's advisers had unanimously urged him to lift his siege of Nancy and return in the spring.

## ❀ 1589: Catherine de Medici, queen of France
† *Cause of Death: Pneumonia*

According to contemporary Pierre de L'Estoile, "Her death made no more stir than the death of a goat."

## ❀ 1827: Frederick, duke of York
† *Cause of Death: Whist*

The duke had a dicky heart and suffered from dropsy. But for Frederick's physician these were minor ailments compared with his "fatal habit of sitting up at night … play[ing] cards so long as anyone would play with him." Such behaviour, stated Dr Parr, led to "a corrupt state of the blood", the inability to lie down and, eventually, death.

# JANUARY 6

## ❊ 1537: Alessandro de Medici, grand duke of Florence
† *Cause of Death: Naked Lust*

Alessandro was famed for "an indecent lust", and Caterina Ginori, the young wife of a local elderly nobleman, was famed for her modesty. The grand duke, therefore, must have been thrilled to bits when his distant cousin Lorenzaccio said he had arranged a tryst between the two of them. To the grand duke, the plan seemed foolproof. He would make love to Caterina in Lorenzaccio's house on the night of the Feast of Epiphany, when the streets would be full of revellers and his movements would go unnoticed. Itching to preserve his reputation as a ladies' man, he did not think to question his cousin's Republican motives.

On the appointed night, Alessandro excitedly took off his clothes and jumped into bed. The door creaked open. Someone came to his bedside. "Are you awake?" a voice whispered. Before he could answer, Lorenzaccio and a hired thug plunged their daggers into his throat and stomach.

# JANUARY 7

## ❊ 1536: Catherine of Aragon, queen of England
† *Cause of Death: A Certain Welsh Beer?*

Stripped of her titles, exiled from court and abandoned by her husband, Catherine of Aragon died a gloomy death in a gloomy manor house in the country. Eustache Chapuys, the Imperial ambassador to London, visited her there in early January and was upset to find her "so wasted that she could neither stand nor sit up in bed". Catherine, on the other hand, was overjoyed to see her trusted old friend and made a sufficient recovery to keep her food down, comb her hair and dictate a letter to Henry tenderly stating, "I pardon you everything, and I wish to devoutly pray God that he will pardon you also."

A relieved Chapuys headed back for London, but on arrival learned that, with him gone, Catherine had suffered a relapse and died. The ambassador was distraught, and when he learned that the informal autopsy revealed a heart with "a black growth, all hideous to behold", he immediately suspected poison. Catherine's doctor, moreover, compounded his fears by stating that her condition had deteriorated markedly after she had drunk "a certain Welsh beer". Within days, the gossip in courts throughout Europe was that Anne Boleyn had done away with her rival.

To the disgust of Chapuys, King Henry was far from unhappy. Indeed he was "like one transported with joy." In response to the death of his former wife, he dressed "from top to toe in yellow", held a ball at Greenwich and proclaimed to his guests, "God be praised, the old harridan is dead."

## ✽ 1989: Hirohito, emperor of Japan
† *Cause of Death: Duodenal Cancer*

When Hirohito was rushed to hospital, an atmosphere of self-restraint or "jishuku" blanketed the nation. Parties were cancelled, weddings postponed and laughter was considered ill-mannered. When he underwent surgery (the first Japanese emperor to do so), some six million people signed official get-well cards. When he died, Japan wept. But some have suggested that these were crocodile tears, shed to divert media attention away from a damaging political scandal that was rocking the government of the day. Japan, some said, cared little when their emperor died, and when television broadcast eulogies for the grand old man, most people watched videos instead.

# JANUARY 8

## ✽ 1880: Joshua Norton, emperor of the United States
† *Cause of Death: Apoplexy*

Vegetarian itinerant newsagent "Father Elphick", journalist "Philosopher Pickett", and "White-Hat McCarthy" whose lifelong ambition was to own a white hat made of beaver fur, are just three of the many eccentrics who inhabited the streets of San Francisco in the second half of the nineteenth century. Oddest of all these oddballs, however, was Joshua Norton, failed property developer and self-styled emperor of the United States. Instantly recognizable by his exotic headgear and navy blue coat, Norton printed his own money and issued a number of decrees, including the announcement of the construction of a bridge spanning the Bay of San Francisco — an idea considered ludicrous at the time.

Californians adored their resident emperor – whenever he arrived at the theatre, the entire audience would stand until he had taken his seat – and were deeply saddened when he collapsed and died on the corner of California Street and Grant Avenue, ending a glorious 23 year reign. Thousands mourned his passing, but none more so than his two faithful canine companions, Lazarus and Bummer.

# JANUARY 9

❀ 1878: Victor Emmanuel II, king of Italy
† *Cause of Death: Malaria*

In early January 1878, two men lay dying. One was Victor Emmanuel who had succumbed to a fever – quite possibly the malaria that was endemic to the swampy city of Rome – and the other was his rival, the pope. From his own deathbed to that of the king, Pius IX sent a message of forgiveness, but a dithering cardinal meant that the communiqué didn't arrive in time.

# JANUARY 10

❀ 1999: Frederick Hervey, marquis of Bristol
† *Cause of Death: Wantonness*

A wastrel par excellence, Hervey was addicted to four things:

1. Vodka. His binging started, we are told, when he was a pupil at Harrow.
2. Sex. He boasted that he had enjoyed the company of more than two thousand rent boys, whom he dubbed "twinkies".
3. Cocaine. While flying his helicopter, he would snort lines off his navigation chart.
4. The Jet Set. Fast cars, luxury yachts and wild parties at his country estate in Suffolk were the trappings of a life devoid of any real substance.

Following a couple of stretches in prison for drug offences, Frederick died, aged 44, having managed to squander the family's millions. The official line was that he died of "multiple organ failure brought about by chronic drug abuse", although many suspected that he had developed AIDS.

# JANUARY 11

### ❋ 1055: Constantine IX, Byzantine emperor
† *Cause of Death: Cold Dip*

Nothing amused Constantine more than seeing someone topple into his garden pond. It was so cleverly disguised to look like the surrounding ground that unsuspecting subjects would stroll about gathering pears or apples and then suddenly get a soaking. As well as a source of amusement, however, the water also proved to be the source of his undoing. One day he caught a chill after bathing in it, and died soon thereafter, hoist by his own comic petard.

# JANUARY 12

### ❋ 1519: Maximilian I, Holy Roman Emperor
† *Cause of Death: Lack of Sun*

Imperator Cæsar Diuus Maximilianus Pius Felix Augustus

Dr Tannstetter, Maximilian's physician, had a no-nonsense bedside manner. He told his imperial patient that given his various illnesses – from gallstones to gout – the end was definitely nigh. From that moment on Maximilian travelled with his coffin, which his entourage used as a combination of treasure chest and glorified stationery cupboard.

Tannstetter was an astrologer as well as a medic, and prophesied that the next eclipse of the sun would herald Maximilian's death. In this he was correct, but not, perhaps, as he expected. When the skies turned black one summer's day in 1518, the innkeepers of Innsbruck, who had learned of Tannstetter's unorthodox prognosis, immediately refused Maximilian any further credit. On hearing the news, Maximilian threw a massive temper tantrum and suffered a stroke, from which he never fully recovered.

# JANUARY 13

## ❊ 42 BC: Ptolemy XIII, king of Egypt
† *Cause of Death: The Nile*

Young Ptolemy XIII briefly shared the Egyptian throne with Cleopatra, who happened to be both his sister and wife. As siblings (and married couples) do, the two fought like cat and dog, but in their case the fighting involved very real armies. While they squared up to each other on the eastern fringes of the kingdom, Julius Caesar sneaked in and captured Alexandria.

The war that followed was a messy affair, a predominantly urban conflict, made complex by guerrilla tactics and curiously motivated treaties. At one point Caesar escaped almost certain death by swimming from a sinking warship to safety. For Ptolemy, the very opposite was the case. During some particularly keen fighting, he and dozens of his fellow men retreated to the Nile and swam to one of their warships to escape certain death. As they clambered aboard, the vessel keeled over and most of the soldiers – Ptolemy included – drowned.

# JANUARY 14

## ❊ 1892: Albert, duke of Clarence
† *Cause of Death: Influenza*

As a precaution against the flu that was coursing through Britain at the time, Albert and the rest of the royal family gulped down doses of quinine as if there was no tomorrow. Sadly for Albert, on this day in 1892 there was no tomorrow.

Seeking refuge in the royal estate at Sandringham, Albert, who was known as "Eddy" by his family, was too ill to come downstairs for his own 28th birthday party (and the after-dinner treats of a ventriloquist and a banjo player). At first, no one thought his condition was that grave. "Poor Eddy" Princess Alexandria wrote casually to Queen Victoria, "got influenza, cannot dine, so tiresome". Her mood changed, however, when she and everyone else twigged that no amount of quinine was going to help. "All we could hear were the sounds of terrible agony in his throat and chest, and our own sobs," she remembered.

❀ 1977: Robert Anthony Eden, earl of Avon
† *Cause of Death: Liver Cancer*

When doctors agreed there was nothing more they could do to help, the former British prime minister was flown back from Florida to end his days in his Wiltshire village home. As he lay dying, some of his much cherished Impressionist paintings were brought into his bedroom for a final viewing.

# JANUARY 15

❀ 69: Galba, Roman emperor
† *Cause of Death: Swords*

Like so many Roman emperors, Galba was murdered on the orders of a former supporter who now wanted the biggest role for himself. In this instance, it was a man called Otho, one-time governor of Lusitania. Otho's forces attacked as the feeble old man was being carried through Rome on a chair. Seeing the litter being tossed about like a cork in a barrel, the crowds dispersed – not in fear, but to get a good vantage point of yet another imperial assassination.

As the sword blows rained down upon him, Galba offered no defence, and all too quickly his corpse was flung onto the street, where a common soldier cut off his head. Galba was as bald as a coot, and so the soldier was unable to carry his trophy by the hair. He therefore shoved his thumb in the dead emperor's mouth and, using this crude but effective method, brought it back to Otho's followers, who stuck it on a lance and paraded it before the people.

❀ 1815: Emma, Lady Hamilton
† *Cause of Death: Drink*

Emma survived her husband for ten pathetic years. The same nation that exalted Horatio Nelson (*see* October 21) disowned his widow, and allowed her to sink into obscurity and penury. She ended her days in virtual exile in Calais where, according to Horatia, her teenage daughter, she had the "baneful habit ... of taking wine and spirits to a fearful degree". While the column honouring her husband is visible to one and all in Trafalgar Square, the precise location of her pauper's grave is unknown.

❀ 1996: Moshoeshoe II, king of Lesotho
† *Cause of Death: Car Crash*

In rural southern Africa, cattle are the principal measure of a person's wealth. Few, therefore, thought it odd when Moshoeshoe made a late night inspection of the royal herd. In the mountain kingdom of Lesotho the roads are notoriously unsafe. Few, similarly, suspected foul play when they heard his car had plunged into a ravine as it returned to the capital, Maseru. A royal car crash always brings out conspiracy theorists, however, and there are some who speak of a rifle shot being heard, a bullet hole in one of the car tires and the chauffeur being blind drunk.

## JANUARY 16

❀ 1400: John Holland, duke of Exeter
† *Cause of Death: Axe*

Of all those who watched the grisly execution of John Holland, few spectators would have done so with greater satisfaction than eighteen- year-old Thomas Fitzalan, earl of Arundel. Holland was beheaded for his part in what became known as the "Epiphany Rising", a conspiracy to kill King Henry IV and restore the imprisoned Richard II to the throne. Three years earlier, when Richard had been in power, Holland had arrested Thomas's father, and had him beheaded for treason. Now, much to the relish of the young Fitzalan, the tables had turned.

## JANUARY 17

❀ 1369: Peter I, king of Cyprus
† *Cause of Death: Being Caught with One's Trousers Down*

As a sign of his devotion to his wife, Queen Eleanor of Aragon, Peter always travelled with one of her nightgowns in his luggage. Despite this love token, he openly kept a couple of mistresses, and it was while he was in the very act of making love to the Lady Echive de Scandelion, that three barons stabbed him to death. A stench of hypocrisy hangs over his murder, however. The Cypriot noblemen, supposedly indignant at Peter's infidelity, happily turned a blind eye to Eleanor's well-known propensity to sleep around.

## JANUARY 18

❀ 1797: Sarah, countess of Exeter
† *Cause of Death: Class Consciousness?*

Sarah Hoggins, a peasant girl from Shropshire, married Henry Cecil, Marquis of Exeter, thinking her husband was a humble landscape painter and not a member of the aristocracy. In his poem *The Lord Burleigh*, Tennyson describes how Sarah only discovered her partner's true rank when they visited a large mansion and all the servants bowed towards him. From that moment on, her health deteriorated: "With the burden of an honour / Unto which she was not born" laments Tennyson, she "drooped and drooped before him" until "before her time she died." This appears to be poetic hogwash. While she was indeed from a family of lower social standing, "Sarah the Cottage Countess" was a rather robust, hearty type who did not waste away on learning of her good fortune, but from complications after the birth of her second child.

## JANUARY 19

❀ 639: Dagobert I, king of the Franks
† *Cause of Death: Sex*

Prematurely exhausted by his exertions with his twelve wives, Dagobert died at 34.

## ✿ 1547: Henry Howard, earl of Surrey
† *Cause of Death: Axe*

Henry was a poet and soldier. After his ignominious defeat by the French at St Etienne, where all his captains died and most of his men mutinied, it was clear he was a better writer than warrior. The military debacle sparked his spectacular fall from favour in the court of Henry VIII, ending with his death a year later. While in the Tower awaiting his execution, he wrote paraphrases of psalms 55, 73 and 88 – works in which the psalmist appropriately feels alone and misunderstood.

## ✿ 1927: Charlotte, princess of Belgium
† *Cause of Death: Madness*

It took Charlotte nearly fifty years to die. On her return to Europe in 1866, the one-time empress of Mexico was already mildly deranged. She was convinced, for example, that her life was in danger, and ate only oranges and nuts that she herself had peeled or cracked, and eggs from chickens that she had tied to the legs of her hotel table. Sure that her comb was poisoned, she left her hair unkempt. Most embarrassing of all was her visit to see Pope Pius IX when she would only drink the pope's cup of hot chocolate and demanded to stay the night at the Vatican. She slept, we are told, in the Papal Library.

Her family quickly had her secured in a castle in Belgium, where she spent half a century quite oblivious to the world around her. The death of her husband before a firing squad (*see* June 19), the horrors perpetrated by her brother Leopold in the Belgian Congo, indeed the entire First World War, completely passed her by. Something of her adopted homeland always stayed with her, however. One spring day each year she would step aboard a dinghy moored in the castle moat and inform her attendants, "Today, we leave for Mexico."

# JANUARY 20

## ✿ 1891: David Kalakaua, king of Hawaii
† *Cause of Death: The Good Life*

Needing a rest after fifty years of over-indulgence and general dissipation, David sailed aboard the US Cruiser *Charleston* to California. There he received a rapturous reception, and a string of invitations to social functions. Nine days later, however, and "The Merry Monarch" was found dead of kidney failure in his room at the Palace Hotel in San Francisco. The *Charleston* ferried his body back to Honolulu where his subjects had replaced "Welcome Home" streamers with mourning crepe. "Nalohia ka Makua" they cried, "Gone is the Father."

## ✽ 1936: George V, king of England
† *Cause of Death: Involuntary Euthanasia*

Shortly after midnight on January 21, 1936, a radio broadcast solemnly declared that "death came peacefully to the King at 11.55 p.m.". What the broadcast omitted to say, since the information only came to light fifty years later, was that death came to the king sooner than nature had intended.

There was no doubt that King George, whose heart had all but packed in, was at death's door. His doctor, Lord Dawson, however, "decided to determine the end" by injecting morphine and cocaine into the royal jugular. The reason for hastening the king's death was twofold. Firstly, Dawson wanted the king to die with dignity. Secondly, he wanted to ensure that the announcement of the king's death appeared in the "salubrious" morning papers such as *The Times* rather than the more sensationalist evening "rags".

# JANUARY 21

## ✽ 1793: Louis XVI, king of France
† *Cause of Death: Guillotine*

*At his last meal, noticing there is no knife on the table:*
"Do you think me so eager to die that I would commit suicide?"

*To the drummers beating out their slow rhythm at the base of the scaffold:*
"Oh do shut up!"
*[They are silent as he calmly walks towards the guillotine]*

*As his neck is being thrust onto the groove on the block:*
"I die perfectly innocent of the so-called crimes with which I was accused …
I hope the shedding of my blood will contribute to the happiness of Fr-----".

## JANUARY 22

✿ 1901: Victoria, queen of England
† *Cause of Death: Natural Causes*

Unlike her reign, Victoria was very short, and as she lay dying at Osborne House on the Isle of Wight, carpenters were fashioning her satin-lined coffin, barely five foot long. Victoria had always been something of a hypochondriac, complaining of a variety of problems from lumbago to ill-fitting false teeth, but by the autumn of 1900, she was really and truly unwell. Her maid of honour, Marie Malle, expressed concern that a royal diet of roast beef and chocolate ices was not the most appropriate for one in her condition.

From her bed, she spoke to her doctors. "Am I better at all?" she asked. "I have been very ill." Assured that she was a little better, she asked, "Then may I have Turi?" The small Pomeranian dog was placed on her bed, but it nervously hopped back to the floor. Perhaps Turi knew something. Shortly afterwards Victoria died in the arms of her grandson, Kaiser Wilhelm II.

The coffin was then put to use. As well as the queen, it was filled with an alabaster cast of Prince Albert's hand, one of his dressing gowns and a lock of the hair of John Brown, her servant (and possible lover) from the Highlands.

## JANUARY 23

✿ 1820: Edward, duke of Kent
† *Cause of Death: Wet Stockings*

In 1820 the younger brother of King George IV was massively in debt and, on the pretence of taking in a long holiday (but in reality to save money) he moved, together with his wife and their little "Vickelchen" (the future Queen Victoria), to the charming but modest Woolbrook Cottage in Sidmouth. They literally received an icy reception, as the region was in the grip of one of the worst winters on record. Ever the optimist, Edward wrote to a colleague that all was well, although he did admit that the West Country water was beginning "to play the very deuce with my bowels".

Determined to enjoy the bracing Devon air, the duke, together with his equerry Captain John Conroy, went on an invigorating hike along the shore. By the time they returned, both men were soaked through. Conroy sensibly went and changed his stockings, but Edward, who had always prided himself on his bovine constitution, hurried upstairs instead to coo over his baby daughter. That night the duke went to bed complaining of a tight chest, and within days developed a fever that, despite the best efforts of a slew of doctors, proved fatal.

Now in quite desperate financial straits, the duchess begged her brother-in-law for some relief. The king refused to give her a penny.

## ❀ 1570: James Stewart, earl of Moray
† *Cause of Death: Hackbut*

The would-be assassin, James Hamilton of Bothwellhaugh, had it all planned to the last detail:

*The Vantage Point* – the first floor of a house in the centre of Linlithgow lent to him by the Archbishop of St Andrews, who was in on the plot.

*The Avoidance of Detection* – Hamilton placed a feather mattress on the floor to silence his footsteps and draped the room in black linen to ensure his shadow could not be spotted.

*The Weapon of Choice* – the hackbut, a cross between a cannon and a shotgun. Hamilton was a puny man and unable to use a dagger with any force, so something a little bigger was required.

*The Getaway* – Hamilton extricated the lintel stone of the gate in the town wall so that he could escape at a gallop.

*A hackbut.*

And the plan worked beautifully. As the earl of Moray rode past, Hamilton fired his hackbut. According to near-contemporary George Buchanan, the lead bullet found its mark "a little below the navel" and Stewart was soon dead. The archbishop was later executed for his part in the conspiracy. Hamilton, meanwhile, escaped scot-free.

## JANUARY 24

❀ 41: Caligula, Roman emperor
† *Cause of Death: Daggers*

Flamingo blood, the by-product of an over-ebullient sacrifice, spattered the imperial toga. But on what was the last day of the Palatine Games and (unbeknownst to him) the last day of his life, Caligula happened to be in a good mood and cared not one jot. After the morning's entertainment, he got up and made his way down a narrow passage towards the palace for a spot of lunch and a bath.

Reports are confused as to what happened next. The historian Josephus states that Chaerea, an officer in the Praetorian Guard, stabbed the emperor in the shoulder, whereupon a swarm of fellow assassins joined in. Suetonius insists that Chaerea drove his sword through Caligula's jaw. Cassius Dio, meanwhile, claims that some of his assailants actually ate the emperor's flesh – a practical, vivid and gruesome demonstration that he was not a god. Whatever the nitty-gritty, it is undisputed that Caligula's blood mingled with that of the flamingo.

## JANUARY 25

❀ 1559: Christian I, king of Denmark, Norway and Sweden
† *Cause of Death: Natural Causes*

The Danes disliked their king because he placed the mother of his mistress in charge of the country's finances. The Norwegians couldn't stand a monarch who was obstinate, overbearing and offhand with their nobility. The Swedes, meanwhile, utterly despised the man responsible for the "Stockholm Bloodbath", when dozens of the nation's nobility were murdered and when the body of their much loved regent, Sten Sture, was dug up and publicly burned. It can be of little surprise that Christian ended up in prison. What might raise an eyebrow or two is that Christian was never convicted of any crime and languished in jail until his death a full 27 years later.

# JANUARY 26

✿ 1947: Gustaf Adolf, prince of Sweden
† *Cause of Death: Rudder Lock*

The pilot of the KLM Douglas DC-3 must have been aware of the two VIPs on the passenger manifest. Not only was the voluptuous American opera singer Grace Moore on board, but also Prince Gustaf Adolf, on his way home to Stockholm from a hunting trip in Holland. Perhaps he was nervous. Perhaps he was tired. Perhaps he was pressed for time. Whatever the reason, he failed to perform the routine pre-flight checklist, which would have alerted him to a rudder lock still in place. His oversight proved fatal, for the plane had barely taken off from Copenhagen airport when it stalled, flipped over, and plummeted back to earth. No one survived the subsequent explosion.

# JANUARY 27

✿ 1556: Humayun, Moghul emperor
† *Cause of Death: Falling down the Stairs*

One day, the emperor was sitting on the flat roof of his library chatting to his astrologers and some pilgrims who had recently returned from Mecca. Then, according to a contemporary called Abul Fazl, he walked to the rectangular opening in the roof and began to carefully pick his way down the steep stairway that led to the floor below. He had barely begun his descent, however, when a muezzin from a nearby mosque started to sing out the summons to prayer. Humayun, who was a devout Sunni, turned to bend his knee in reverence, but as he swivelled round, he slipped on the polished stone and caught his foot in the skirt of his robe. The imperial courtiers could only gasp as their master teetered and then spiralled downwards, smashing his right temple on one of the steps below.

# JANUARY 28

✿ 814: Charlemagne, Holy Roman Emperor
† *Cause of Death: Poor Medical Attention*

Charlemagne detested doctors. He considered their presence unhealthy, their medicines dangerous and their advice that he should stop eating roast meat as impertinent. Consequently, when he developed a high fever (and later pleurisy) after taking a hot bath, he prescribed for himself bed rest and a liquid-only diet. His personal remedy, however, proved to be of little help, as a week later he was dead. In accordance with his will, he was buried in an upright position. His body was embalmed, dressed in imperial purple, and then buried sitting on a throne with a crown on his head, a sceptre in his hand and an open Bible on his knees.

## ❋ 1547: Henry VIII, king of England
† *Cause of Death: Excess*

Henry liked to leave everything to the last minute. Much to the consternation of his court, he would never make a decision in the afternoon that couldn't wait until last thing at night, when everyone wanted to go to bed. And his penchant for procrastination remained with him right up his very last hours, making his death a rather untidy affair.

Ulcerous, malarial and almost spherical from years of excessive eating and drinking, Henry was warned by his Chief Gentleman, Sir Anthony Denny, to "prepare himself for his death". And then, according to John Foxe, Denny asked him if there was any "learned man" he would like to speak to. Entirely in character, Henry responded that he might possibly like to share some words with Archbishop Cranmer, but first he would take a nap, "and then as I feel myself, I will advise upon the matter". These turned out to be his last words.

As the bloated king heaved his last breaths, Cranmer came to his side, but there was to be no conversation. Henry had delayed too long. England mourned the death of their monarch with great public pomp. A massive hearse, so heavy that it crushed the road beneath it, ferried the corpse from Westminster to Windsor Chapel. Cranmer, meanwhile, in a symbol of private mourning, vowed never to shave again.

## ❋ 1725: Peter I, tsar of Russia
† *Cause of Death: Strangury and Stone?*

In all probability a number of factors contributed towards the death of the great emperor. They included:

*The Drink*: like so many Russians of the time, Peter was a huge drinker. He and other members of his "Jolly Company" would hold parties where everyone drank to debauched excess. These wild bacchanalian nights continued even into his fifties.

*The Fits*: Peter suffered from a lifelong malady that first exhibited itself when he was only 22. It was something like epilepsy, and brought about occasional fits, some so severe that he fell unconscious.

*The Sea*: sailing in the Gulf of Finland in November 1724, Peter saw a boat full of soldiers run aground. Fearing that it may capsize, he leaped into the freezing waters and helped to drag it off the shoal bank. Once on dry land he went to bed but rapidly developed a fever.

*Strangury and Stone*: against this complaint, defined as "a blockage in the urethra and bladder caused by muscle spasms or infection" the emperor took the waters of various spas, but with only limited relief.

More tantalizing than his precise cause of death, however, is the last message he left to the world. The day before he died, Peter called for a writing tablet and, before the pen slipped from his fingers, scrawled "Give all to ..."

# JANUARY 29

## ❋ 1730: Peter II, tsar of Russia
† *Cause of Death: Smallpox*

On what was supposed to be his wedding day, a few weeks after becoming engaged to the stunning teenager Catherine Dolgoruki, Peter lay dying of smallpox. In a desperate and futile attempt to preserve the male line of the Romanov dynasty, court officials forced the terrified Catherine between the sheets.

## ❋ 1820: George III, king of England
† *Cause of Death: Porphyria*

As his porphyria worsened, George's condition descended from dottiness to delirium. His eccentric behaviour – such as insisting he eat his favourite food of mutton standing up – deteriorated into something more distressing. He would pace from room to room in his purple dressing gown, repeatedly tying or untying knots in his handkerchief and conversing with people long dead.

He would stuff his handkerchief in his mouth, for fear of saying something blasphemous. His end mercifully came after a 58-hour frenzied marathon of sleeplessness and talking gibberish when, in a moment of perfect lucidity, he thanked a servant for wetting his lips with a sponge. "It does me good," the king said, and then died.

## JANUARY 30

✺ 1649: Charles I, king of England
† *Cause of Death: Axe*

Charles wasn't afraid to die, but was determined to do so on his own terms. To that end, he took his time in saying his final prayers, wore two shirts to prevent him from shivering and appearing scared, and arranged with the headsmen that the axe should fall only when he made the sign of stretching out his hands.

After a short and pretty incoherent speech to those who had come to witness the beheading, he knelt and laid his head on the block. One of the executioners bent down to tuck some loose hair under his white cap, and for a moment the king was caught off his guard.

"Stay for the sign!" he barked.

"I will, an' it please Your Majesty," came the reply.

The king composed himself, took a deep breath and then – only when he was well and truly ready – stretched out his hands. The executioner needed just one blow to fulfil his duty.

✺ 1889: Rudolf, crown prince of Austria
† *Cause of Death: Six Bullets?*

The bodies of Rudolf and his mistress, Baroness Mary Vetsera, were found at Mayerling, a hunting lodge in Lower Austria. How and why they died remains a mystery. The official line is that it was a double suicide – during an argument Rudolf battered Mary to death and then shot himself. How then, asked the sceptics, did the prince manage to shoot six bullets when the first would have instantly caused his death? Political conspiracy theories abound. Some think Rudolf was murdered by Austrian secret police because of his Hungarian sympathies and Mary was unfortunately "collateral damage". Others, as they are wont to do, blame the French.

# JANUARY 31

## 1788: Charles Edward Stuart, the Young Pretender
† *Cause of Death: Drink*

The Young Pretender died a broken old sot. Eking out a sorry existence in Rome, his aberrant behaviour – from lashing out indiscriminately with his stick to yelling obscenities in the theatre and casino – drove his wife Louise to distraction, then to a convent, and finally into the arms of another man.

Alcohol was his undoing. The once Bonnie Prince Charlie cut a miserable figure, drinking morning, noon and night "like one absent of mind", and alarming one of his servants who noted that "no street-porter could equal him". Charles eventually died, in the arms of his daughter Charlotte, on January 31, 1788. Or did he? A persistent rumour has it that Charles actually died on January 30, but that his retainers withheld the information, as they thought that the death of their beloved "Charles III" on the same day as Charles I was unseemly.

# FEBRUARY

## FEBRUARY 1

### ❀ 1908: Charles I, king of Portugal
† *Cause of Death: Charcoal Burners*

Would-be assassins Alfredo Costa and Manuel Buica trudged through Lisbon's city centre muttering under their breath. Somehow their intended target – Portugal's premier, Joao Franco – had given them the slip, and now they had to return to HQ with their pistols still loaded and their mission unaccomplished.

A cheering sight suddenly evaporated their gloom, for who should come clattering across the square in an open carriage but King Carlos and the rest of the royal family! Hardly believing their luck the two hit men leaped into action. Franco, a despot who threw anyone who disagreed with him in jail and ruled the country by fiat, may have been Enemy Number One, but Carlos was Enemy Number Two. Yes, the plump and affable king was generally liked, but he was monarch of a country steeped in economic misery and corruption – and he had to be eradicated. And so, as the carriage rolled in front of them, the men fired, and the shots found their target. The royal bodyguard immediately rained bullets on Manuel and Alfredo, and they too collapsed dead.

Blame for the regicide was understandably laid at the door of the Republicans, but they quickly made it known that the gunmen were not on their payroll but instead members of a secret revolutionary patriotic society known as the "Carbonária" or "Charcoal Burners". That said, the Republican movement benefited massively from Carlos's death, and wasted no time in raising money for the welfare of Alfredo and Manuel's families.

# FEBRUARY 2

✤ 1995: Alexis Brimeyer, European "prince"
† *Cause of Death: AIDS*

Alexis Brimeyer claimed to be the great grandson of the Tsar Nicholas I of Russia, and a member of several other European royal families. He wasn't. He styled himself "Prince Alexis d'Anjou Romanov-Dolgorouki, Duke of Durazzo" and spent his entire life trying to convince anyone who would listen that his body coursed with blue blood. There wasn't a drop.

In reality he was nothing more than a Congolese-born fruitcake, the delusional son of a Belgian housewife and Luxembourgian storekeeper with too much time on his hands. Even after Brimeyer succumbed to the AIDS virus while in Madrid, a small band of misguided supporters continued to press his spurious claim to the Serbian throne, but anyone with a modicum of common sense recognised that he, and his claim, were utterly bogus.

# FEBRUARY 3

✤ 1014: Swein Forkbeard, king of Denmark, Norway and England
† *Cause of Death: Holy Javelin?*

Just a few weeks after his coronation, Swein and his forked beard swaggered into East Anglia with booty on the brain. He rode up to the abbey in Bury St Edmunds and commanded the monks to hand over half their treasure, or be tortured horribly. At this point, the chronicler John of Worcester states that St Edmund himself, already dead for well over a century, appeared on the scene and, furious at Swein's impudence, ran him through with a spear. Swein apparently toppled from his horse and "tormented with great pain until twilight ... ended his life with a wretched death". Less sensationalist accounts, such as that of the usually reliable Snorri Sturlsson, record that Swein actually died in his bed.

✤ 1537: Thomas, earl of Kildare
† *Cause of Death: Rope and Axe*

State papers inform us that Thomas Fitzgerald was "hongyd and heddyd" [hanged and beheaded] for his part in a rebellion against King Henry VIII. Death may have come as something of a release, given the misery he appears to have experienced while awaiting execution. Forced to borrow "old hosyn and shoys and old shyrtes" from fellow inmates, he had little to do but carefully engrave his name on the wall of the Beauchamp Tower. One can visit his cell today, and see that he had only completed "THOMAS FITZGERA" before he was hauled off to the scaffold at Tyburn.

## FEBRUARY 4

❈ 211: Septimius Severus, Roman Emperor
† *Cause of Death: Gout*

Third-century Roman imperial propaganda would have us believe that Severus and his two sons Caracalla and Geta collaborated seamlessly in their management of both civil and military operations in Britain. Not so. The two teenage boys hated each other's guts and were constantly at loggerheads, while Severus was incapacitated by gout. The emperor finally died of the condition while visiting the city of York, but before he did so, he gave his warring sons three pieces of advice: get along with each other, get along with your soldiers, and don't get along with anyone else. His words of wisdom fell on deaf ears. Caracalla had his younger brother assassinated, and was gruesomely murdered himself by some disgruntled soldiers (*see* April 8).

## FEBRUARY 5

❈ 1520: Sten Sture the Younger, regent of Sweden
† *Cause of Death: Cannonball*

Cannonballs bounce. If you don't believe me, ask Sten Sture the Younger. Well, actually, you can't because he's dead, killed when a cannonball ricocheted off the ice of a frozen lake during the Battle of Bogesund and slammed into his horse. The horse died instantly of its wounds. Sten Sture died of his a couple of weeks later, as he sped his way back to Stockholm in the hope of proper medical attention.

## ✿ 1721: James Stanhope, earl Stanhope
† *Cause of Death: Philippic*

Philip, the youthful, hell-raising Duke of Wharton, stood up in the House of Lords and accused Stanhope of fomenting the dissensions between King George I and the Prince of Wales. Wharton compared the earl with a Roman consul called Sejanus whose "first step" was "to wean the emperor's affections from his son; the next to carry the emperor abroad; and so Rome was ruined." A furious Stanhope leaped to his feet and retorted that Romans were a wise people who "showed themselves to be so in nothing more than by debarring young noblemen from speaking in the Senate till they understood good manners and propriety of language." James then singled out another Roman luminary, Lucius Junius Brutus, "who had a son so profligate … that he had him whipped to death." So furious was Stanhope while making this brilliant reply that he burst a blood vessel, and died the next day.

## FEBRUARY 6

## ✿ 1378: Jeanne, queen consort of France
† *Cause of Death: Cold Bath*

The idea that Jean of Bourbon's fever, contracted while giving birth, would be reduced by immersion in a cold bath was, at best, misguided.

## ✿ 1668: Charles II, king of England
† *Cause of Death: Doctors*

What with the clocks in the room chiming every fifteen minutes (and infuriatingly out of sync) and the snoring of the twelve dogs on or near the bed, Thomas Bruce, the king's "gentleman of the bedchamber", had spent a restless night. So, it turned out, had Charles, who had been kept awake by a throbbing pain in one of his heels.

Once out of bed, the king called for a doctor to come and examine his foot and, somewhat stiffly, sat down to receive his morning shave. But then, according to Bruce, Charles suddenly let out a piercing scream and slumped to the floor "on a violent fit of apoplexy". Doctors piled into the room, hurriedly put the monarch back into bed – and proceeded to kill him.

They blistered his head with red-hot irons, gave him enemas of rock salt and syrup of buckthorn, and let so much of his blood as to render his kidneys useless. They forced him to drink a julep of black cherry water and did something decidedly peculiar with a stone removed from the stomach of a goat. Difficult as it may seem today, no one was remotely aware that it was his physicians, with their barbaric emetics, purgatives and knives who, ironically, were hastening rather than delaying the king's death.

Astonishingly, Charles remained almost serene throughout the ordeal, even apologizing for taking "such an unconscionable time a-dying". After he did finally slip into a coma and die, his doctors solemnly filed out of the room until the only person left was Thomas Bruce, charged to watch over his master one last time.

## ✤ 1952: George VI, king of England
† *Cause of Death: Blood Clot*

Excerpts from the imagined 1952 diary of King George:

January 30: Went to the West End to see *South Pacific* at the Drury Lane Theatre with the family.

January 31: Said farewell to young Elizabeth and her husband at London Airport as they embarked upon an exciting trip to East Africa and the Antipodes.

February 5: Excellent shooting here at Sandringham in Norfolk. Bagged nine hares myself today, three with my last three shots. And so to bed.

During the night, a blood clot, small but lethal, did its worst.

# FEBRUARY 7

## ✤ 1592: James, earl of Moray
† *Cause of Death: Gordon*

James Stewart, "The Bonny Earl", wasn't so bonny when George Gordon, earl of Huntly, burned his mother's house down. This was because he was inside it at the time. A companion – perhaps the Sheriff of Moray – ran out through the flames and created a diversion while the horribly charred Stewart desperately scrambled to the rocks on the nearby beach to hide. Farcically, the smoking plumes of his helmet gave his position away and Huntly, whose orders had been to arrest rather than murder him, approached to polish him off.

With his "dirk" or little hunting knife, Huntly sliced open his enemy's cheek. Stewart, so badly burnt that he couldn't hold a weapon, responded the only way he could – with words. Aware of his reputation as one of the most handsome men in the country, James glared at his murderer and mocked: "You have spoiled a better face than your own."

## FEBRUARY 8

✻ 1884: Cetshwayo, Zulu chief
† *Cause of Death: Snuff?*

Zulu witch doctors with murder on their minds would sprinkle pulverized poison into their victim's snuff. Cetshwayo, like all chiefs, enjoyed his snuff a lot, and while mystery surrounds his sudden demise, there is no doubt that on the day of his death he took a pinch of snuff, sniffed it, and then a few hours later, snuffed it.

Surgeon Scott, the British medical officer summoned to the scene, suggested that a post-mortem should be carried out to ascertain the true cause of his death, to which one of the witch doctors replied "if you cut our chief, we will cut you." The chief's body remained intact.

## FEBRUARY 9

✻ 1977: Alia al Hussein, queen of Jordan
† *Cause of Death: Helicopter Crash*

While a student in New York, Alia developed a taste for fast cars, blue jeans and the company of the rich and famous. King Hussein, who fitted the final category very well, liked her good looks and her sophisticated charm mixed with American pizzazz, and he quickly dumped his second wife, Princess Muna, to marry her.

A mere five years later, however, she was killed in a helicopter crash while returning to Amman after visiting Tafileh Hospital in South Jordan. Hussein was inconsolable, until he quickly fell in love again, this time with another ravishing American Lisa Halaby, later Queen Noor. In the company of rock legend John Lennon, the politician Charles de Gaulle, and the actor Ronald Reagan, Queen Alia has an airport (in her case that of Amman) named in her honour.

## ❀ 2002: Margaret, princess of England
† *Cause of Death: Chesterfields and Grouse*

Margaret drank too much. Her favourite tipple was Famous Grouse whisky when in Europe, and gin when at her holiday home on the Caribbean island of Mustique. She also smoked too much. At her peak she used her signature tortoiseshell cigarette holder to puff on 60 Chesterfields a day. As a result, her last few years were a miserable lurching from one stroke to another, a decidedly unglamorous end for the glamorous party princess of the fifties and sixties. Bloated and nearly blind, she died in her sleep in the London hospital named after her great grandfather, Edward VII.

# FEBRUARY 10

## ❀ 1242: Shijo, emperor of Japan
† *Cause of Death: Polish*

The child emperor Shijo was a mischievous little imp. One of his favourite pranks was to have the palace floors so highly polished that his ladies-in-waiting would lose their balance and tumble to the ground. One day he slipped and took a nosedive himself – and bashed his little brain in.

## ❀ 1567: Henry, Lord Darnley
† *Cause of Death: Sleeves*

It was all a bit like the first pages of an Agatha Christie whodunnit. Early one morning detectives arrived at the Darnley's house on the Royal Mile in Edinburgh to find him, together with his valet, dead on the lawn. Behind him lay the smouldering remains of his home, charred to a crisp following a huge explosion in the middle of the night.

Count Moretta, the Savoyard ambassador to Scotland, didn't require the acumen of Hercule Poirot to deduce from Darnley's unburned body that he had not died in the fire. Telltale marks around his neck proved that he had been strangled "with the sleeves of his own shirt". But who exactly was behind this dastardly deed has been a much trickier mystery to solve. Many members of the Scottish nobility found Darnley loathsome, so perhaps it was some of them. Or maybe – just maybe – the real killer was none other than his wife, Mary Queen of Scots, who found him cold as a kipper and preferred the warm embraces of Lord Bothwell.

# FEBRUARY 11

✤ 1940: John, baron of Tweedsmuir
† *Cause of Death: Stroke*

If you must have a stroke, it is probably best if you do so while not handling razor sharp objects. John, Baron Tweedsmuir – better known as John Buchan, author of such adventure classics as *Prester John* and *The Thirty-Nine Steps* – died of a stroke while shaving.

# FEBRUARY 12

✤ 1554: Jane, queen of England
† *Cause of Death: Axe*

"Guildford! Guildford!" Lady Jane Grey mournfully repeated as she looked out of her cell window on the day earmarked for her execution. She was not pining for the county town of Surrey, but reacting instead to the sight of the recently decapitated body of her husband, Lord Guildford, (with his head in a bag beside it) being trundled back inside the Tower of London for burial.

As she climbed the steps of a different scaffold a few hours later, the teenage queen exhibited remarkable composure, with one onlooker writing later how she was dry-eyed and "nothing abashed". All semblance of calm, though, disintegrated when Jane tied a handkerchief about her eyes, and then couldn't find the block. "What shall I do?" she wailed with arms outstretched, "Where is it?" Frozen with horrified embarrassment, nobody on the scaffold moved, and it was up to an enterprising spectator to jump from below onto the platform and guide his queen into position.

✤ 1771: Adolf Frederick, king of Sweden
† *Cause of Death: That Fourteenth Semla*

Ask any Swedish schoolboy how King Adolf Frederick died and he'll tell you gleefully that he ate himself to death. The king, we are told, keeled over after gorging on a meal of lobster, herring, caviar and cabbage, all washed down with champagne and followed by no less than fourteen servings of his favourite pudding of "semla", a kind of bun served in a bowl of warm milk.

## FEBRUARY 13

❀ 1542: Catherine, queen of England
† *Cause of Death: Axe*

Catherine Howard's dalliances with courtier Thomas Culpeper brought about her downfall, but the idea that Henry VIII's fifth wife was composed enough on the scaffold to state: "I die a Queen, but would rather die the wife of Culpeper" is hogwash. According to the French ambassador Charles de Marillac, she was "so weak that she could hardly speak." Unlike Lady Jane Grey (*see* February 12) Catherine had no difficulty in locating the executioner's block. This is because the night before her beheading she had the block brought to her cell "that she might know how to place herself".

❀ 1542: Jane, Viscountess Rochford
† *Cause of Death: The Same Axe*

The luxury of preparing for one's execution was not afforded to Catherine's lady-in-waiting. Jane Boleyn's neck was thrust down on a block still warm and wet with her mistress's blood.

## FEBRUARY 14

❀ 1400: Richard II, king of England
† *Cause of Death: Toadstool*

Shakespeare's depiction of Richard dying in battle is just plain wrong. The chronicler Raphael Holinshed's assertion that the king was starved (or starved himself) to death after just ten days' imprisonment in Pontefract Castle also seems wide of the mark. More plausible is the suggestion that that he was poisoned.

The poison of choice, thinks medical historian Clifford Brewer, would have been amanita philodes, the "death cap" toadstool, which is easy to chop finely and sprinkle into food and does its worst in approximately ten days. In an attempt to scotch rumours that he had suffered a violent death on the orders of King Henry IV, Richard's unmarked body was paraded on a bier through the streets of London. Holinshed may have got the wrong end of the stick but not everyone was fooled.

# FEBRUARY 15

## ❀ 1965: Nat "King" Cole
† *Cause of Death: KOOLS*

Nathaniel Adams Coles, elevated to royal status for wearing a gold leaf crown in some of his early performances, maintained that smoking up to three packs of KOOL cigarettes a day gave his voice that unforgettable velvety timbre. The menthols may have helped, but they also produced a nasty, inoperable tumour on his left lung.

# FEBRUARY 16

## ❀ 1391: John V, Byzantine emperor
† *Cause of Death: Humiliation*

The Golden Gate of Constantinople was John's pride and joy. Reusing marble from crumbling buildings throughout the city, his craftsmen painstakingly renovated and then polished the archway until it was a magnificent, shining architectural symbol of his power and might. But then Bejazet, the Ottoman Sultan at the time, demanded that he tear it down. All too aware of Bejazet's military superiority, and fearful that the sultan would follow through on his promise to do unspeakable things to his family, John did as he was told, razed the building to the ground ... and died of shame.

## ❀ 1919: Sir Mark Sykes, baronet
† *Cause of Death: Spanish Flu*

Of all the millions who succumbed to the Spanish Flu epidemic of 1919, what distinguishes Sir Mark is not his aristocratic line but what accompanied him to the grave. His coffin was lined with lead and, as such, has apparently preserved the viral particles intact. And what killed him may save millions of others. Scientists have been granted permission to exhume his body, isolate these particles and use any data they can glean from them to fight the next terrifying epidemic.

# FEBRUARY 17

❀ 1934: Albert I, king of Belgium
† *Cause of Death: Scramble*

Albert was an accomplished mountaineer, and when royal duties prevented him from visiting the Alps, he would practise his technique on small, local rock faces. While travelling on the road from Namur to Liege, he spotted an escarpment – nothing more than a quick, run-of-the-mill scramble for such an experienced climber – and with a couple of hours before his next engagement, he decided to keep his hand in. Telling his trusted old retainer, Van Dyck, that he would be back soon, he began his solo ascent.

An hour passed. No king. Two hours passed and a search party was hurriedly organised. All too soon a member of the Belgian Alpine Club found him at the base of the cliff, his arms outstretched, his head caved in, and his body "soaked in blood, like one of the dead in the Great War".

# FEBRUARY 18

❀ 1294: Kublai, khan of the Mongols
† *Cause of Death: Pancakes and Milk*

Distraught at the death of his favourite wife, Chabi, Kublai Khan put himself on a calorie-uncontrolled diet. A daily intake of dozens of pancakes stuffed with boiled mutton, offal and seasoned vegetables – a sort of medieval Mongolian Cornish Pasty – washed down with flagon or two of fermented mare's milk proved his undoing.

❀ 1478: George, duke of Clarence
† *Cause of Death: Malmsey*

George is perhaps best known for the manner of his death. Found guilty of treason against his brother Edward IV, the duke ended up a prisoner in the Tower of London where, according to contemporary and near-contemporary reports, he underwent an unusual execution. An Italian visitor to England, one Dominic Mancini, wrote that rather than being hanged or beheaded, George was killed "by being plunged in a jar of sweet wine". The jar in question was a "butt" or barrel, and the sweet wine was "malmsey", now known as "Madeira".

## FEBRUARY 19

✿ 197: Clodius Albinus, Roman emperor
† *Cause of Death: Dagger*

On the death of Emperor Pertinax, Albinus, then governor of Britain, declared himself Caesar. Annoyingly, a nobleman called Septimius Severus (*see* February 4) also wanted the job, and so the two imperial contenders mustered their armies and battled it out in France's Saône valley. Severus won the day (just) and Albinus, holed up in a house on the banks of the Rhône, did the noble thing and cut his throat. A gleeful Severus got on his horse and formally trampled over Albinus's body and then had his head chopped off and sent to Rome. Britain, like Albinus's corpse, was also divided in two after his death. Ebor (York) and Londinium (London) became the capitals of the northern and southern provinces.

## FEBRUARY 20

✿ Edward II, king of England
† *Cause of Death: Red Hot Poker*

The infamous modus operandi of Edward's execution was actually a back-up plan. His jailers initially hoped that they could bump him off by filling his cell in Berkeley Castle with the stench of decaying human corpses, and only when this failed did they turn to the "red hot poker" method. The mechanics of Edward's murder have been variously ascribed as a commentary on his homosexuality and/or a desire that there were no visible signs of injury on his body. Chroniclers John Capgrave and Raphael Holinshed record that his assassins forced a heavy door (or a couple of feather beds) on his back, thrust a horn funnel into his rectum and then rammed a red hot iron poker through it. The poker was then rolled to and fro in order to burn him to death from the inside out.

Papal notary Manuel de Fischi sounds a lone alternative note in claiming that Edward actually managed to flee from the castle, and travelled extensively through Europe before settling down in a hermitage.

## FEBRUARY 21

### ❀ 1437: James I, king of Scotland
† *Cause of Death: Tennis Balls*

Chatting one evening with his wife in her chambers in a friary in Perth, James's first inkling that something wasn't right was when he sent his page, Walter, to fetch some more wine, and the boy didn't return. The second hint that things were amiss was the decidedly un-monastic clanking of armour outside the room. Thinking, correctly, that this was no pastoral visit, the king quickly used some fire tongs to rip up some floorboards and squeezed himself into the sewer below, knowing it had to lead to an outside wall.

A mob, led by one Robert Graham of Kinpunt, burst into the room above. After thumping the queen to the floor, Graham dropped into the stinking pipe and followed James through the ordure. The king soon came to the mouth of the drain, only to remember in horror that he had ordered it walled up because wayward tennis balls from a nearby court kept on ending up covered in sewage. Wearing only a dressing gown and with just a pair of tongs for a weapon, James turned to faced his opponent. It was no contest.

## FEBRUARY 22

### ❀ 1071: Arnulf III, count of Flanders
† *Cause of Death: Uncle*

February 22, 1071 — for most people the date of the hitherto unknown Battle of Kassel. On one side were ranged the forces of Robert the Frisian, a highly experienced and utterly ruthless warrior. On the other side were assembled the troops of his sixteen-year-old nephew Arnulf the Unfortunate, a young man completely untried, untested and unready for military action. Before Arnulf knew what was happening Robert attacked, and in the fray the hapless teenager came a cropper.

# FEBRUARY 23

❋ 1546: Francis of Bourbon, count d'Enghien
† *Cause of Death: Horseplay*

On a cold winter's day, some of King Francis I's younger courtiers were larking about in the snow that lay deep and crisp and even at his royal chateau at Roche-Guyon. The snowball fight got somewhat out of hand when some prankster picked up a chest full of bed linen and threw it out a window. It landed smack on Bourbon's head.

# FEBRUARY 24

❋ 1563: Francis of Guise, French nobleman
† *Cause of Death: Handgun*

The siege of Orleans was such a long drawn-out affair that Francis, commander of France's Catholic forces, arranged for his family to be billeted in a nearby village. One evening, he sent a message to his wife to say that a broken bridge on his usual commute home meant that he would be a bit late for supper. Very late indeed, as it turned out, because as he rode past a copse of walnut trees on his diversion, a bullet thumped into him. "I am killed!" cried the duke, correctly if laconically. (He could also have correctly added "And here's one for the record books. I am the first person to be assassinated by a handgun.")

❋ 1810: Henry Cavendish, English nobleman
† *Cause of Death: Inflammation of the Colon*

One of the greatest scientists of all time, Cavendish wore a violet-coloured suit, ate a diet consisting almost exclusively of mutton, and spoke as often as a Trappist monk. He was also terrified of women, and avoided their company whenever possible. But this brilliant scientist wasn't afraid of his own death. On the contrary, he demanded to be left alone so he could accurately record the final advances of his disease.

Aware that his end was nigh, Cavendish called his valet. "Mind what I say," he told him, "I am going to die. When I am dead, but not until then, go to Lord George Cavendish and tell him of the event." His cousin George must have been sad at the news when it came, but chuffed to bits to learn that Henry had left him his fortune of well over a million pounds.

# FEBRUARY 25

❋ **1713: Frederick I, king of Prussia**
† *Cause of Death: Underwear*

Two women unwittingly collaborated to bring about Frederick's death. One was his lunatic wife, Sophia Louise of Mecklenburg, and the other was the Hohenzollern family ghost called "The White Lady", who appeared on the scene every time someone was about to die. One day the queen, in a moment of particular loopiness, burst into her husband's bedroom sporting nothing but her underwear, and Frederick, never having seen his wife in such skimpy attire, assumed she was the prophetess of doom. "Die Weise Frau!" he cried in horror, and promptly fell over and died.

# FEBRUARY 26

❋ **1154: Roger II, king of Sicily**
† *Cause of Death: "Immense Efforts"*

Archbishop Romuald of Salerno reported that Roger died "of a fever". The less kindly diagnosis of the chronicler "Hugo Falcandus" was that the king, still in his fifties, died an old man, "worn down by his immense efforts and more devoted to sexual activity than the body's good health requires."

❋ **1525: Cuauhtemoc, Aztec emperor**
† *Cause of Death: Rope*

When the Aztec capital of Tenochtitlan fell to the Spanish, conquistador Hernan Cortes promised Emperor Cuauhtemoc that he would come to no harm. "A Spaniard knows how to respect valour even in an enemy," he declared. But then, when he found out that Cuauhtemoc might know the whereabouts of hidden treasure, he had him tortured by smothering his feet in oil and roasting them over a fire. Later, while commandeered to join Cortes on a march to Honduras, Cuauhtemoc was accused – many say on trumped up charges – of treason, and summarily hanged from the branches of a ceiba tree. The ignominy of the emperor's treatment and death still rankles among many Mexicans today.

❀ **1577: Erik XIV Wasa, king of Sweden**
† *Cause of Death: Pea Soup*

When lucid and calm, Erik came across as a charming and dutiful monarch, but when suffering one of his bouts of frenzied lunacy he was a danger to himself and to those around him. As the king aged and sank ever deeper into his personal slough of schizophrenic despond, the job of royal courtier became an increasingly high-risk occupation. Two guards, for example, were sentenced to death merely for "annoying the king", while some smartly uniformed servants were executed for clear "intent on seducing the ladies of court". Finally imprisoned on the orders of his half-brother John, Erik died in the dungeon of Örbyhus Castle, after eating his favourite dish of pea soup, liberally laced with arsenic.

## FEBRUARY 27

❀ **1699: Charles, duke of Bolton**
† *Cause of Death: Nightlife*

Charles Paulet was nocturnal. At sunset he would get out of bed, have breakfast and go hunting with his hounds by torchlight. Later he would engage in Bacchanalian orgies in a purpose-built banqueting hall in the woods of his estate. He died in his 70s, worn out by his nightly exertions.

## FEBRUARY 28

❀ **1485: Nicholas, count of Abensberg**
† *Cause of Death: Varlet*

Arrest a nobleman while he's out hunting, fine. Arrest him at court, not a problem. Arrest him while he's taking a bath, well, it's simply not the done thing.

Fourteen years after being arrested in his bath by Nicholas – fourteen long years of being a laughing stock in taverns throughout the land – Christopher, duke of Bavaria, got his own back. A posse of his men ambushed the count on his way home one day and forced him to dismount. Realising he was outnumbered, Nicholas raised his arms in surrender, but Christopher, utterly indifferent to proper procedure, had one of his varlets stab him where he stood.

# FEBRUARY 29

## ❈ 1868: Ludwig I, king of Bavaria
† *Cause of Death: Lola Montez*

Her name was Lola. She was a showgirl. She wore flowers in her hair and rocked the theatrical world with her erotic "Spider Dance" in which she would shake rubber tarantulas from the folds of her chiffon dress and stamp on them.

*Lola Montez.*

His name was Ludwig. He wore a diamond, and became infatuated with the Irish-born dancer when she stormed into his private study and demanded that the manager of the Munich Theatre be fired for rejecting her arachnid act as clumsy and unsophisticated.

Ludwig was impressed not only with Lola's bravado, but also with her bosom – Eduard Fuchs, one of Lola's biographers, noted that Lola's substantial breasts "made madmen everywhere" – and he inquired if her lovely figure was nature's work alone. In reply, the dancer, still in costume, grabbed a pair of scissors lying on his desk and sliced open her skin-tight bodice down to the waist. Ludwig was awe-struck, the theatre manager was sacked, and Lola became Austria's unofficial queen.

She was an unmitigated disaster. Conservative Austria simply could not stomach her extravagance, political naivety and shockingly liberal views, and the government hastily offered her a massive sum of money to leave the country and never return. Lola huffily refused and commanded Ludwig to close down Munich's university to show who was boss. The aging king meekly complied, but the public rose up in fury. Students took to the streets, revolution filled the air and Ludwig was given an ultimatum – either Lola went, or he must abdicate. "I will never abandon Lola," the king retorted and stomped off into self-imposed exile on the Riviera. To the surprise of no one except Ludwig himself, Lola soon abandoned him and sought fortune and fame (unsuccessfully) in America, and although Bavaria's former king lived in comfortable retirement for a further twenty years, all the life force really left him when Lola left his side.

# MARCH

## MARCH 1

❀ 1244: Griffith, Welsh nobleman
† *Cause of Death: Knot*

Brave, ingenious but rather too chubby for his own good, Griffith spent much of his life behind bars. As a boy he was used as a hostage of King John of England, and later his own brother David held him prisoner before handing him over to Henry III, who incarcerated him in the Tower of London.

For stir-crazy Griffith, this third stretch was one too many. On the morning of St David's Day, he manufactured a rope out of bed sheets and attempted to shimmy down the outside wall of the White Tower to freedom. His heavy build, however, coupled with one poorly tied knot conspired to undo him, and he plunged the ninety feet to his death.

## MARCH 2

❀ 1619: Anne, queen consort to James I of England
† *Cause of Death: Dropsy*

The death of her son Prince Henry from typhoid at the age of eighteen hit Anne of Denmark hard, and she never really recovered from the loss. In 1619, royal doctor Sir Theodore de Mayerne prescribed the sawing of wood to improve her blood flow. It didn't work. In fact it only made her worse, and she died, blind, exhausted and with unusually rough hands for a queen, a few months later.

## MARCH 3

❉ 1837: Edward, viscount Kingsborough
† *Cause of Death: Publishing Venture*

Kingsborough spent some £32,000 – a huge sum back then – on publishing a multi-volume work entitled "Antiquities of Mexico, Comprising Facsimiles of Ancient Mexican Paintings and Hieroglyphics". It was a critical success but a commercial flop, and the bills mounted up. Unable to pay his paper-merchant, printer or illustrator, Edward was arrested for debt and thrown into Dublin's notoriously filthy Sheriff's Prison. Within a few months he had died of typhus. Had he survived another year, he would have inherited the title of earl from his father, together with the tidy annual income of £40,000.

## MARCH 4

❉ 1484: Casimir, prince of Poland and grand duke of Lithuania
† *Cause of Death: Religious Devotion*

Earthly pleasures held nothing for Casimir, who willingly substituted the lavish opulence of his palace for a life of prayer and self-mortification. Not a man for half measures, the king took his ascetic regime very seriously indeed, wearing a hair shirt, sleeping on bare earth and often fasting for days. What may have been good for the soul, however, was dreadful for the flesh. In his perpetually weak physical state, Casimir was an easy target for any bout of tuberculosis that happened to be whistling through court, and he died very quickly and very young.

## MARCH 5

❉ 1995: "Sir Henry Rawlinson", English nobleman
† *Cause of Death: Dodgy Electrician*

An English nobleman by the name of Sir Henry Rawlinson died of old age on March 5 1895. He was a highly respected diplomat, Member of Parliament and specialist on cuneiform inscriptions.

By extraordinary coincidence, the British musician and comedian Vivian Stanshall, who was famous for playing a fictitious English nobleman by the name of "Sir Henry Rawlinson" on British radio, died exactly a hundred years later – to the day. Stanshall, who before his Rawlinson years was a member of the madcap "Bonzo Dog Doo Dah Band", died in a fire in his flat in north London. Given his addiction to booze and cigarettes and his habit of falling asleep and setting his beard alight, it was generally expected that the coroner would report that he had accidentally brought about his own death. There was some surprise, therefore, when the blame was laid on faulty wiring in his bedroom.

## MARCH 6

✾ 1964: Paul, king of Greece
† *Cause of Death: Thrombosis of the Lungs*

Queen Frederika of Greece writes that her husband's dying words were "I still see the Light. It is much larger now, and the peace is getting stronger. Now we go." She also states that at the very moment he gave up the ghost, a small oil lamp burning in front of an icon across the room suddenly went out. "Was it a sign," Frederika asks, "that we should always live within the Light?" Some might agree. Others might say Her Majesty was talking complete drivel.

## MARCH 7

✾ 161: Antoninus Pius, Roman Emperor
† *Cause of Death: Swiss Cheese*

Perhaps it was a fondue. All the imperial biography says is that one evening at dinner Antoninus overindulged in some "Alpine Cheese", and that the next day he developed a fever and died.

## MARCH 8

✾ 1702: William III, king of England
† *Cause of Death: Mole*

In 1696, the Jacobite conspirator Sir John Fenwick was condemned to death for treason, and had all his possessions, including his favourite horse, Sorrel, confiscated by the crown. Five years later William was riding Sorrel at Hampton Court, when it stumbled over a molehill and shipped its rider. William fell

awkwardly, shattered his
collarbone and, despite liberal
doses of cordial, died from his
injuries. For many years after
the event, Jacobites secretly
drank to the mole, "the
gentleman in black velvet", that
had unknowingly collaborated
with a horse to bring about the
king's literal downfall.

*A mole.*

## MARCH 9

✤ 1888: William, emperor of Germany
† *Cause of Death: Old Age*

At the age of 24, William fell in love with his cousin Princess Elisa Radziwill,
a young beauty of fine and noble stock, but apparently not noble enough for
the Prussian royal family. William was forced to renounce her and find a more
"appropriate" bride – someone from a reigning House. Cruelly spurned by
dynastic politics, Elisa faded away and died, but William never forgot her. On his
deathbed nearly seventy years later, he asked for a miniature of Elisa to be brought
to him, and breathed his last with his first love by his side.

## MARCH 10

✤ 1792: John Stuart, earl of Bute
† *Cause of Death: Picking Flowers*

Politically, John was something of a cold fish,
carrying out his duties as Prime Minister
with a serious and unimaginative austerity. He
approached his passion for natural history with
equal dour single-mindedness, and it was in the
course of botanical research that he sustained
the injuries that brought about his end.

Walking near Highcliffe, his retirement villa
on the Hampshire coast, John spotted a

particularly fascinating specimen clinging tenaciously to the cliff edge. As he stretched out to pluck it, the ground beneath him gave way and he fell some thirty feet, injuring his leg badly with, it turned out, fatal consequences. Some cold-hearted political foes remarked that just as he had overreached himself in trying to grab the flower, so had he overextended himself in his public life.

## MARCH 11

❀ 1870: Moshoeshoe I, Sotho chief
† *Cause of Death: Sex*

Concerned elders told their chief that if he really knew what was good for him, he would stop having so much sex. Moshoeshoe, aged 84, agreed that he was worn out, but from the cares of public administration, not his private life. The chief was nevertheless aware that he would soon be joining his ancestors, and so one day, in front of his officials, he took an egg and threw it in the air. If it remained intact when it hit the ground, he declared, his government would stay intact after his death. If it broke, there would be bedlam. The egg dropped, cracked … but stayed in one piece. They say that as Moshoeshoe breathed his last, the pots in every house in Lesotho rattled, but did not fall.

## MARCH 12

❀ 1699: Peter Schumacher, Count Griffenfeld
† *Cause of Death: Pardon*

Arrogant, certainly, but hardly a traitor, Peter was the political mastermind behind Denmark's foreign policy in the seventeenth century. He was a strategic and diplomatic genius, and almost succeeded in forging an alliance between Denmark, France and Sweden that would have seen a dramatic increase in Danish power on the international scene. But it was not to be. Peter had his enemies – enemies who conspired to have him arrested on fraudulent charges of bribery and lèse-majesté.

Although he spent the weeks before his trial incarcerated in a pitch-black dungeon without books or writing materials (let alone legal assistance), he defended himself with great ardour and skill. But the decision of the court was never in doubt, and soon Peter found himself with his neck on an executioner's block. Just before the axe swung down, however, his sentence was commuted to life imprisonment. A distraught Peter moaned that the pardon was ironically a worse punishment than decapitation, and spent the next twenty years in comfortless misery, hoping that every day would be his last.

## MARCH 13

❋ **1881: Alexander II, tsar of Russia**
† *Cause of Death: Curiosity*

Curiosity killed the tsar. Alexander was going for a Sunday drive through the streets of St Petersburg when a terrorist threw a bomb, wrapped in a handkerchief, at his carriage. The explosion killed a Cossack, but the tsar was unhurt. Alexander then climbed down to take a good look at his would-be murderer, only for a second assassin to lob a second bomb, this time right at his feet. It blew his legs off.

## MARCH 14

❋ **1757: John Byng, British nobleman**
† *Cause of Death: Incompetence*

The British government sent Admiral Byng in a woefully under-equipped ship to relieve the garrison of Fort St Philip on the island of Minorca. Forced to employ outdated tactics, he was unsuccessful, and for his "error of judgment" the Admiralty had him shot.

On the day assigned for his execution, Byng calmly walked across the sawdust-strewn quarterdeck of HMS *Monarch*, and knelt on a cushion. Declining

*Admiral Bing drops his handkerchief..*

the assistance of a colleague, he blindfolded himself and then bowed his head for a minute in prayer. Finally he held out his arm and dropped a handkerchief. On this a pre-arranged signal a platoon of nine marines fired, and Byng bought the farm.

In 2007, some of Byng's descendants petitioned the British government for a posthumous pardon. The Ministry of Defence refused.

# MARCH 15

## ❀ 44 BC: Julius Caesar, Roman dictator
† *Cause of Death: 23 Blows*

Lying in bed on the morning of the Ides of March, Julius Caesar must have pondered — momentarily at least — whether this was not a good day to turn over, snuggle down and go back to sleep. A mental tally, for and against going to work, would have read something like this:

*Reasons to stay at home.*

Yesterday his prized horses had spurned their food and burst into tears, and a cute little wren with a sprig of laurel in its beak had fluttered into Pompey's house, only to be set upon by a flock of birds and torn into shreds. Both he and his wife had experienced troubling dreams. Caesar had dreamed that he was soaring above the clouds and holding hands with Jupiter. His wife, Calpurnia, had dreamed that the foundation of their house had crumbled and, ominously, that Caesar had collapsed onto her bosom having been stabbed. And then there was Spurinna, the old soothsayer who had warned him that he was in grave danger — danger which would not pass until the Ides had passed.

*Reasons to go to work.*

Duty.

Caesar was late for the senate meeting. Calpurnia had tried to stop him leaving the house, and he had stopped to have a brief conversation with Spurinna whose presence gave him one final opportunity to listen to his words of portent, turn on his heel and head back home. But the dictator did not listen, and instead chided the seer, noting that the Ides of March were here but he was fine and well. "Indeed", Spurinna replied, "but they have not yet gone."

Soon after he had sat down, twenty-three dagger blows rained down upon his body – at least one from his closest ally Brutus – and he collapsed dead on the steps below the throne. "The pedestal was drenched with blood," writes Plutarch.

## ❀ 493: Odoacer, king of Italy
† *Cause of Death: Gift of God*

The Ides of March is clearly a day for betrayal by one's closest colleagues. Odoacer was invited to dine with Theodoric – whose name literally means "Gift of God" – to seal a treaty agreeing that they should be co-rulers of Italy. The party was going swimmingly. People were mingling, the canapés were delicious, and Theodoric even stood up and gave a toast. But then the trouble started. Theodoric's thugs suddenly wrestled Odoacer to the ground and disarmed him. Realising that his number was up, he cried, "Where is God?" but the "Gift of God" was in no mood for theological debate and picked up his broadsword and pretty much sliced him in two.

# MARCH 16

## ❀ 1322: Humphrey, earl of Hereford
† *Cause of Death: Pike*

During a skirmish between rebellious barons and forces loyal to Edward II, Humphrey was leading his troops across a bridge, when an enemy soldier crouching beneath it thrust his pike upwards and skewered him. The pikeman then twisted his blade and Humphrey – now a human kebab – screamed so horribly that his men turned tail and fled.

# MARCH 17

## ❀ 659: Gertrude, Austrasian noblewoman
† *Cause of Death: Lack of Breakfast*

When her wealthy parents died, the extremely devout Gertrude built churches, hospices and monasteries on the land she inherited, including a double monastery at Nivelles in Belgium where she herself became abbess. By her early thirties, her ascetic regime, including days without food or sleep, forced her to resign her office. Weak and clearly not long for this life, she sent one of her monks to her friend St Ultan at Fosse to ask whether God had revealed to him the hour of her death. Ultan replied that actually yes, he did have the information, and that she would in fact die the very next day during Mass. The prophecy was fulfilled, and Gertrude of Nivelles was immediately venerated as a saint. She is the patron saint of people suffering from a fear of mice.

# MARCH 18

## ❀ 1314: Jacques de Molay, French nobleman
† *Cause of Death: Flames*

King Philip the Fair of France detested the Knights Templar. He was deeply jealous of the military order's power, hated its wealth and despised its influence. And so, on Friday the 13th of October 1307 (a truly unlucky day for the order) he had its Grand Master, Jacques de Molay, arrested on trumped-up charges of heresy and homosexuality.

After seven years of torture, de Molay was taken to an island in the middle of the River Seine and burned at the stake. Templar histories record that his executioners intensified his agony by slow-roasting him over a smokeless fire. As his flesh blackened, de Molay cursed both Philip and Pope Clement V, declaring that they would both join him in death within the year. His prophecy came true. The pontiff died just over a month later, of suspected cancer of the bowel, and Philip came to a grisly end while on a hunting trip that winter (*see* November 29).

## ❀ 1913: George I, king of Greece
† *Cause of Death: Bullet*

King George liked to take a walk in his grounds after a spot of lunch. One day, during a visit to the city of Salonika, a deranged Greek named Alexander Schinas interrupted his afternoon stroll by shooting him in the head. The king died instantly. His murderer died soon thereafter, "falling" out of a second-storey window during questioning.

## ✺ 1965: Farouk I, king of Egypt
† *Cause of Death: Lobster*

With a voluptuous Italian blonde at his side, the exiled monarch drove to one of his regular haunts for a midnight supper. There he ate a meal fit for a king; a dozen raw oysters with Tabasco sauce, lobster, a whole roast leg of lamb with string beans, roast potatoes and chips, a massive chestnut trifle, a couple of oranges and a Coke. He then lit a large Havana, inhaled ... and dropped dead. Given that he was enormously fat, his death was not entirely a surprise, but the lack of an autopsy has fuelled theories that he was murdered by the Egyptian secret service. The mistress of the head of the Egyptian CIA at the time has written that Farouk's assassination – a poison called alacontin was slipped into his lobster thermidor – was a "gift" for President Nasser.

# MARCH 19

## ✺ 1286: Alexander III, king of Scotland
† *Cause of Death: Uxorial Duty*

It was a dark and stormy night. Worried courtiers at Edinburgh Castle counselled their king to stay the night and not head out to his palace at Kinghorn until the morning, but Alexander was having none of it. The following day, he reminded them, was his queen Yolande's nineteenth birthday, and he had promised he would be there to see her open her presents.

After a hasty dinner of eels, the king set out with three colleagues to the Firth of Forth. At Queensferry, according to the chronicler Lanercost, the alarmed ferryman urged them not to cross in such atrocious conditions. But cross they did, and Alexander, who knew the territory like the back of his hand, rode off ahead of his party into the murk and gloom. When his three companions finally struggled into Kinghorn, they expected to find their king tucked up in bed with his young bride, but he was nowhere to be found. At first light a search party soon discovered Alexander and his horse sprawled dead on a nearby beach.

Romantics suggest that the king galloped over the cliff and broke his neck, but this is preposterous, as no one could have ridden at such speed in such appalling weather. An anonymous Benedictine monk offers an alternative, prosaic version of events. Alexander's horse, he states, "stumbled, and when pricked by a spur ... tried to rise and fell again more heavily, and crushed the king under him."

# MARCH 20

## ❋ 1413: Henry IV, king of England
† *Cause of Death: Rye Bread?*

With soap and clean water in short supply,
the people of early fifteenth-century
Europe, including royalty, were a smelly,
filthy lot. Nasty, disfiguring skin diseases
were as common back then as acne is
on the faces of teenagers today. Henry
developed a particularly repulsive and
incapacitating collection of boils, rashes
and pustules, but his precise condition, and
cause of death, continues to bamboozle
modern medical historians as it did
Henry's own doctors. Theories include:

1. Eating rye-bread infected with ergot.
2. St Anthony's Fire.
3. Divine retribution for ordering the beheading of an archbishop.
4. Leprosy, perhaps a punishment from God for unseating Richard II from the throne (*see* February 14).
5. Syphilis.
6. Just a really bad case of eczema.

Prophets foretold that the king would die in Jerusalem. They were close. Henry collapsed while praying in the Jerusalem Chamber of Westminster Abbey.

## ❋ 1751: Frederick Louis, Prince of Wales
† *Cause of Death: Cricket Ball*

King George II cared little for his subjects and even less for his son Frederick. The prince, on the other hand, tried to assimilate himself into English culture by having cricket equipment shipped over to Hanover, so he could understand the finer points of the game. He became an enthusiastic, if second-rate player and when he moved to London, he played in several matches. During one game, a ball hit him on the head (a bouncer, perhaps, bowled by a courtier in the employ of his father?) and he died from the blow. George was delighted at his son's death at only forty-four. Many English, however, were stumped as to why one so clubbable should have so short an innings.

## MARCH 21

❁ 1617: Pocahontas, Native American princess
† *Cause of Death: Passive Smoking*

In 1614 the daughter of the ruler of the Algonquin Indians of Virginia married English tobacco farmer John Rolfe, and changed her name from Pocahontas to Rebecca. Two years later Mr and Mrs Rolfe, together with their son Thomas, sailed to England where the princess was used as a marketing device, pacifying would-be investors in the Virginia Colony, assuring them that America's Indian "savages" could be tamed. Pocahontas found British aristocratic society agreeable (although King James I impressed her little) but the smoke of London (and possibly that from her husband's pipe) left her struggling for breath, and barely a year after landing in England, she died from an unspecified lung disease.

## MARCH 22

❁ 1687: Jean-Baptiste of Lully, secretary to Louis XIV of France
† *Cause of Death: Stick*

Rather than using a short, harmless baton, musical conductors in the seventeenth century used to keep time by banging a long cane against the floor. One day Jean-Baptiste was conducting a Te Deum that he had composed for the king, when he momentarily got carried away and struck his foot rather than the ground. The resulting abscess turned gangrenous, and Lully limped away from court to die an untimely death.

# MARCH 23

❀ 1801: Paul I, tsar of Russia
† *Cause of Death: Scarf*

Paul woke with a start. It was the middle of the night and the soldiers thumping on his bedroom door were clearly not paying a social call. He sprang out of bed and ran to and fro desperately looking around for a hiding place. There was no secret passage, no time to shimmy down the drainpipe. He had to conceal himself in his room. The question was where? The conspirators bashed down the bedroom door and found Paul's cot empty but still warm, indicating he couldn't be far. The imperial bedchamber was cavernous, full of furniture and very dark, but their prey, they knew, still had to be in the room. The question was where?

Paul's murder was then lunar-assisted. Emerging from behind a cloud, the moon shone through a large window and onto the imperial feet comically sticking out from beneath a nearby screen. He was wrestled to the ground (some accounts say that one of the assassins gave him a massive blow on the head with a golden snuff-box) and strangled with a guardsman's sash.

# MARCH 24

❀ 1603: Elizabeth I, queen of England
† *Cause of Death: Old Age*

From the turn of the seventeenth century onwards, Elizabeth cut a pathetic, lonely figure. According to her senior courtier and godson Sir John Harington, she was "much wasted" by depression, and turned her nose up at any rich dishes that were offered, preferring instead a simple diet of "manchet" (fine white bread) and "succory pottage" (chicory soup). Harington confided to his colleague Sir Philip Sidney that he was also alarmed that she didn't change her clothing as much as she should, and that she swore repeatedly at her devoted ladies-in-waiting.

By the winter of 1603 a "strange silence" lay upon the whole of England. "Not a bell rang out, not a bugle sounded," recalled a priest in the Tower of London. In her chamber, Elizabeth sat on a pile of cushions on the floor with her finger in her mouth, staring at the floor and refusing to lie down in the (correct) belief that if she did, she would never get up again. After four days of this trance-like state, she was so faint that she offered no resistance as she was carried to bed. Archbishop Whitgift knelt at her side and prayed. After half an hour, he stood up and backed away, but the queen made a gesture with her hand that was interpreted as a command that he should continue praying. Whitgift duly knelt back down. Thirty minutes later and the prelate again started to get up, but again Elizabeth made a gesture for him to stay put. Back down went Whitgift, this time uttering loud exclamations, begging God for mercy on her soul.

England received news of her death in eerie silence. Following a reign of nearly 45 years, most of her subjects had known no other monarch than their "Good Queen Bess".

## ✿ 1953: Mary of Teck, dowager queen mother
† *Cause of Death: "Gastric Problems"*

Buckingham Palace would have us believe that Mary, the mother of Edward VIII and George VI, died of "gastric problems" and not lung cancer. Edward was less precious in describing a woman who refused to accept Wallace Simpson as her daughter-in-law. "I'm afraid," he remarked, "the fluids in her veins have always been as icy cold as they now are in death." Edward wasn't that impressed with the living members of the royal family either. "What a smug stinking lot my relations are," he said. "[Y]ou've never seen such a seedy worn-out bunch of old hags."

# MARCH 25

## ✿ 1975: Faisal, king of Saudi Arabia
† *Cause of Death: Killjoy*

The presence of a Kuwaiti delegation visiting his palace in Riyadh only mildly tarnished the king's celebrations of the 1,405th birthday of the Prophet Muhammad. The presence of his nephew, Prince Faisal bin Musaed, proved more of an inconvenience.

On seeing his nephew in the Kuwaiti reception line, the king lowered his head so that the prince might, as custom demanded, kiss the tip of the imperial nose. Rather than kiss it, however, Prince Faisal pulled a revolver from beneath his cloak and shot it – and most of his face – off.

# MARCH 26

## ✽ 1936: Adolf II, prince of Schaumburg-Lippe
† *Cause of Death: Sightseeing*

En route between Mexico City and Guatemala, the pilot of an asthmatic chartered plane made a detour to show the beauty of his country to his celebrity passengers, Prince Adolf and his wife Ellen. As he banked to show the royal couple the twin peaks of Popocatépetl and Ixtaccíhuatl, his rust bucket of a crate coughed, spluttered and then silently nosedived between the two dormant volcanoes.

# MARCH 27

## ✽ 1482: Mary of Burgundy, duchess of Burgundy
† *Cause of Death: Falcon*

One spring day Mary and her husband, the Austrian emperor Maximilian I, went hunting with their birds of prey. Mary's falcon swooped and spooked her horse. The horse shied and ditched the duchess. The duchess sustained a severe bruise on her leg (which, spurred by "motives of delicacy", she kept secret) and died a few days later.

# MARCH 28

## ❀ 4 BC: Herod, king of Judea, Galilee and Peraea
† *Cause of Death: Bowel Cancer?*

The last days of Herod the Great were ghastly. With unprofessional relish the Jewish historian Josephus records that the king must have felt he was burning to death from the inside out, as he endured "moist suppurations of the feet and an invasion of the genitals by worms".

Not for the first time, well-meaning but misguided physicians tried their best but made things worse. They carried him to a spa on the north-eastern shore of the Dead Sea and gently lowered his dropsical, syphilitic, gangrenous body into a bath of warm oil, whereupon he lost consciousness with the pain.

Back in Jericho, Herod one evening asked for an apple and a paring knife, since it was his habit to peel his own fruit. Knife in hand, and thinking no one could see him, he raised the blunt blade to end it there and then, but much to his disgust a cousin was on hand to intervene and allow a few more days of excruciating agony.

# MARCH 29

## ❀ 1792: Gustav III, king of Sweden
† *Cause of Death: Big Shiny Badge*

Part of the fun of a masked ball is that revellers can trip the light fantastic incognito. If Gustav was hoping to conceal his true identity when he attended the ball at Stockholm's Royal Opera House, he should have looked in the mirror before he stepped onto the dance floor. His killers had little difficulty in identifying their target since he was wearing the large star of the Order of the Seraphim, the Swedish royal order of chivalry, on his cape. As it happened, the murder was something of a botch job. The assassin shot him just above the left hip and Gustav remained alive for nearly two weeks. His last words were, "I feel a bit sleepy. A little rest might do me some good."

# MARCH 30

❋ 2002: Elizabeth, queen consort of George VI of England
† *Cause of Death: Old Age*

Asked to explain her remarkable longevity, the Queen Mother would habitually reply: "if you ignore an illness, it will go away". Following a lifespan of more than a century, however, both she and her doctors were forced to acknowledge the terminal double whammy of a virus and chronic anaemia. A fawning biography states that as she lay dying in her darkened room in Windsor, a chaplain, aware of her deep love for Scotland, read her an "ancient highland poem" entitled "I am going now into the sleep". The chaplain seems to have been unaware that "I am going now into the sleep" are actually words by St Aidan, an Irish monk famous for founding the monastery on the island of Lindisfarne ... in England.

# MARCH 31

❋ 1621: Philip III, king of Spain
† *Cause of Death: Bug*

Some Spanish wags thought it hilarious to circulate a rumour that Philip died after standing too close to a "brasero" or pan of hot charcoal. This was neither true nor, to be honest, particularly funny. The probable, if less colourful truth proffered by historian J. H. Elliott, is that he caught a nasty bug during a state trip to Portugal. Once he was back in Madrid, his health markedly improved, thanks, it was said, to the intercession of St Isidore, whose remains were brought into his bedroom. But after a few months, the prayers of Isidore – ironically the patron saint of peasants – could no longer keep a king from his eternal reward.

# APRIL

## APRIL 1

❀ 1205: Amalric II, king of Jerusalem
† *Cause of Death: Mullet*

What is it about kings and fish? Henry I of England couldn't get his fill of lampreys (*see* December 1), Sarsa Dengel of Ethiopia was fatally attracted to them (*see* October 4) and on this day, Amalric keeled over after eating too much of his favourite seafood. In all other respects he seems to have been a sensible chap, but we are told that he died after consuming "a surfeit of white mullet". The fool.

## APRIL 2

❀ 1118: Baldwin, king of Jerusalem
† *Cause of Death: Fish*

And it's not as if kings of Jerusalem and fish hadn't tangled before. The twelfth-century chronicler Fulcher of Chartres describes how Baldwin and some of his knights took a break during their incursion into Egypt to spend a quiet afternoon fishing on the banks the Nile. The fish tasted delicious, but after a couple of platefuls Baldwin began to feel a bit queasy. Seventeenth-century chronicler Thomas Fuller succinctly completes the sorry story. "Baldwin", he says "caught many fish, and his death in eating them."

❀ 1930: Zewditu, empress of Ethiopia
† *Cause of Death: Holy Water*

It was the Christian season of Lent, and even though she was in bed with what seemed to be a bad dose of flu (she was in fact a severe diabetic), the devout

Zewditu was adamant that she would eat nothing until three in the afternoon, when Mass was over. Although she refused to break her fast, the Empress did allow her doctors to try the unorthodox remedy of bathing her up to her neck in holy water. And so it was that a group of her servants lugged pitchers of holy water from a local church and sloshed it into a large bathtub. As soon as her feverish body was lowered into the frigid water, however, she fainted from shock, and died later that day.

## APRIL 3

❀ 1203: Arthur I, duke of Brittany
† *Cause of Death: John?*

Upon the nasty death of Richard I (*see* April 6) Arthur became the rightful heir to the English throne, but his uncle (later King) John took no notice of the niceties of rights of succession and clapped him in irons. Whether John was then guilty of the young man's murder depends on which monk you find most trustworthy.

Ralph, the abbot of Coggeshall, tells how some soldiers, sent to Arthur's cell in the Castle of Falaise to kill him, were so moved by his tears that they "stayed their bloody hands". Later, when Arthur had been moved to a prison in Rouen, he wasn't so lucky. The abbot continues that there "the helpless orphan was startled from his sleep" and taken to the edge of the Seine where John or John's esquire, Peter de Mulac, stabbed him and slung his corpse into the river. Another Cistercian document, the *Margam Annals*, is in no doubt that John was personally responsible for Arthur's death. After a boozy supper, it claims, John "drunk and possessed of the devil ... slew him with his own hand and, tying a heavy stone to the body, cast it into the Seine."

## APRIL 4

❀ 1588: Frederick II, king of Denmark
† *Cause of Death: Wine*

Wine consumption in the court of King Frederick was breathtaking, with the average daily intake amongst the aristocracy totalling some twelve pints a day – perhaps a couple of gallons on festive occasions. And at the vanguard of this binge-drinking culture was Frederick himself, who simply basked in his reputation as party animal and right royal boozer. At Frederick's funeral, the priest sighed that had the forty-three-year-old king "drunk a little less, he might have lived many a day yet."

## APRIL 5

❀ **1923: George Herbert, Lord Carnarvon**
† *Cause of Death: Curse of the Mummy?*

Velma, Lord Carnarvon's personal psychic, gazed into her crystal ball and didn't like what she saw. Carnarvon was soon to return to Egypt to open the recently discovered tomb of Tutankhamen, and Velma saw her client standing in the Valley of the Kings flailing about in a storm of weird mystical flashes. "Don't go," she begged, but Carnarvon, who loved a challenge only a little more than he loved the occult, set off for Cairo ... and was soon dead from an infected mosquito bite.

Rumours soon circulated about a magical clay brick with the inscription "Death will slay with his wings whoever disturbs the peace of the pharaoh" that had been found at the tomb's entrance. Marie Corelli, an American writer who specialised in the Gothic horror novels, said she had the tablet in her possession (although no one ever saw it), and media hype about "The Curse of the Mummy" was given universal currency when the fervent spiritualist (and creator of Sherlock Holmes) Arthur Conan Doyle supported her claims.

It was, of course, absolute balderdash. There was no tablet, Corelli was a kook and Carnarvon fell prey not to a mummy but a midge.

## APRIL 6

❀ **1199: Richard I, king of England**
† *Cause of Death: Ant*

When Richard and his men prepared to lay siege to the castle of Chalus, they found that it was defended by just two knights, and comically under-equipped knights at that. One of them, variously called Bertrand, Peter or John, wore a "suit" of armour cobbled together from scraps of metal, and carried a shield fashioned from a frying pan.

Seeing the king casually inspecting the castle walls below him, a hopeful Bertrand/Peter/John fired a bolt from his crossbow in his general direction and, more by luck than judgement, struck him in his left shoulder. In itself it wasn't a mortal injury, but Roger of Hovedon writes how, thanks to a "butcher" of a doctor – who managed to "mangle the king's arm" before removing the bolt – gangrene set in, and it was soon clear that "the lion by the ant was slain". Richard summoned the "ant" to his deathbed and found that his assassin was little more than a boy. "Youth," he croaked, "I forgive you," and after ordering that the lad should be released unhurt with 100 shillings, sank back and died.

The young man failed to profit from the king's kindness. He was dragged away and flayed alive.

# APRIL 7

❁ 1498: Charles VIII, king of France
† *Cause of Death: Lintel*

*Game*

One afternoon Charles and his wife decided to watch a game of tennis on a makeshift court marked out in the dry, wide moat between the old and new parts of their castle. Somewhat curiously, the couple decided that the best place from which to watch the game was a "gallery" that until recently had been used to house the royal hunting birds.

*Set*

The only access to this glorified dovecote was up a narrow stairway and through a low door. Even though he stooped (and even though he was far from tall) Charles managed to bash his head on the lintel, but making light of his mishap, he settled down to watch the match.

*and Match*

During a break in the proceedings Charles popped off to powder the royal nose. On his return from the latrine, he fainted and fell to the ground, and was carried back to the gallery, where he spent the last nine hours of his life in delirium among the falcon guano.

# APRIL 8

## ✿ 217: Caracalla, Roman emperor
† *Cause of Death: Being Caught with One's Trousers Down*

Julius Martialis, an officer in the imperial bodyguard, caught Caracalla in a vulnerable position. While travelling to Carrhae in modern-day Turkey, the emperor dismounted to answer a call of nature and, out of respect and politeness, all his men looked the other way. All, that is, except for Martialis, who held some sort of grudge (Cassius Dio thinks he was angry at not being made a centurion) and killed him with a single sword thrust in his most private of moments.

# APRIL 9

## ✿ 1626: Sir Francis Bacon, Lord St Alban
† *Cause of Death: Chicken*

In his delightfully frank work, *Brief Lives*, the seventeenth-century antiquary John Aubrey entertains his readers with the story of how one of England's greatest philosophers and essayists met his end … thanks to a chicken. Bacon was travelling with a colleague one snowy day in north London, Aubrey writes, when he wondered aloud "whether flesh might not be preserved in snow, as in salt." Deciding that there was no time like the present, the two men jumped out of their coach, bought a hen from a local woman and paid her to gut it. They then began to stuff the carcass with snow. This action, however, gave Bacon such a chill "that he immediately fell … extremely ill." He was rushed to the warmth of the nearby house of the earl of Arundel, but idiotically was put in a bed which hadn't been slept in for a year. The damp sheets brought on pneumonia and he died two days later. His widow, Aubrey gleefully tells us, quickly married a gentleman usher named Sir John Underhill "whom she made deaf and blind with too much Venus."

# APRIL 10

## ❂ 1599: Gabrielle d'Estrées, marquise of Monceaux
† *Cause of Death: Lemon*

Gabrielle is famous for being the subject of a risqué painting by an unknown artist in which she sits naked in a bath holding the coronation ring of King Henry IV of France, while her sister, sitting nude beside her, pinches her right nipple. When Henry gave her his precious ring and asked her to marry him, the heavily pregnant Gabrielle was cock-a-hoop. "Nothing," she whooped, "but God or the king's death could spoil things for me now." Three days before the service, she journeyed from Fontainebleau to Paris ahead of Henry, and had supper with Zamet, the king's Italian banker. As a special treat, Zamet had his chefs cook a dish using a lemon, at that time a rare and exotic fruit. A few hours after the meal, when Gabrielle fell ill and died, her gormless doctors, utterly unschooled in gynaecology, concluded that the lemon was "corrupt".

*The best-known painting of the marquise of Monceaux.*

# APRIL 11

## ❂ 1034: Romanos III, Byzantine emperor
† *Cause of Death: Michael*

Romanos bucked the Byzantine imperial trend by being surprisingly tolerant, going so far as to look the other way while Zoe, his wife, amused herself regularly and often with a lusty peasant boy called Michael the Paphlagonian. Zoe, by contrast, was the typical cow of an empress. She considered her husband to be over the hill, persuaded her toy boy to strangle him in the bath, and, as a reward, married him the very same day.

## APRIL 12

❀ 1856: Ngakuku Panakareao Nopera, Maori chief
† *Cause of Death: Double-Crossing*

According to one Colonel Despard, this chief of the Rarawa and Aupouri tribes was "shrewd, sensible, thoughtful and deliberate in his judgement". He must have temporarily lost his senses, then, when he rode his horse through a swollen stream, twice, and died of cold.

## APRIL 13

❀ 1868: Tewodros II, king of Ethiopia
† *Cause of Death: The British*

When Queen Victoria sent him a fancy revolver, Tewodros was doubly pleased, since he loved nothing more than guns and anything to do with the British Empire. His passion for weaponry was very much in evidence when he compelled Christian missionaries whom he had imprisoned to forge a huge cannon called Sebastopol, and then had it dragged hundreds of miles to his stronghold in Magdala. In his continued obsession for modern weaponry he then jailed several European diplomats and said he would only release them when Britain sent him a large supply of armaments. The British refused.

Instead, Britain sent an expeditionary force of 32,000 men under Sir Robert Napier to lay siege to Magdala, which they did with great efficiency thanks to their new Snyder long-range rifles. In reply, Tewodros fired his highly-prized homemade howitzer, but to his horror it simply blew up. The rest of his artillery was similarly useless, falling short of the British lines. Desperate, Tewodros then freed his European prisoners and sent them down to Napier, asking that they now go away. The British, again, refused.

As enemy soldiers converged on his palace and began looting the town's treasures, Tewodros took out the much cherished pistol that Queen Victoria had given him, and shot himself through the mouth.

# APRIL 14

## ❋ 1578: James Hepburn, earl of Bothwell
† *Cause of Death: Danish Hospitality*

Whereas Mary Queen of Scots was eloquent, graceful and well mannered, Bothwell her third husband was an uncouth, rowdy loudmouth. His exile and imprisonment in Denmark must have pleased those Protestant nobles who saw him as little more than a jumped-up womaniser, but even they must have gasped at the truly frightful conditions of his incarceration. In pitch-black squalid solitary confinement, the once vigorous earl was permanently chained to a pillar half his height. Bent over double in his own excrement for ten long years, he died overgrown with hair, black with filth and utterly mad.

# APRIL 15

## ❋ 1053: Godwin, earl of Wessex
† *Cause of Death: Morsel*

Godwin was having supper with King Edward the Confessor, when it was mooted that he might have had something to do with the untimely death of Alfred, the king's brother. Picking up a crust of bread, Godwin said, "May this morsel choke me, if even in thought I have ever been false to you." He popped the bread into his mouth, rapidly turned green and sank against his footstool dead as a dodo.

# APRIL 16

## ❋ 69: Otho, Roman emperor
† *Cause of Death: Dagger*

Ancient Rome loved nothing more than a good suicide and, as you read their histories, you can almost see Suetonius, Tacitus, Plutarch et al. nodding with approval at the manner in which Otho went to meet his forefathers.

When he heard that Vitellius, his challenger, had won a crucial battle, Otho knew the die had been cast. He examined the points of two daggers, chose one and tucked it under his pillow. He then called his servants and handed them a little money and went to bed, where he slept so soundly that his chamberlain at the door could hear him snoring. Early the next morning, he told his chamberlain to go and show himself to the soldiers guarding the front door, explaining that he was worried they might kill him for helping his master to die.

Otho then jammed the hilt of the dagger into the ground and fell upon it with such force that he expired with one groan ... and the chroniclers of Rome let out a collective sigh of satisfaction.

## APRIL 17

❀ 1355: Marino Falieri, Italian nobleman
† *Cause of Death: "Stenography"*

In his capacity as doge, or chief magistrate, of the Republic of Venice, Marino habitually held extravagant parties. At one such banquet, a nobleman called Michael Steno behaved indiscreetly in front of a number of the female guests, and was told to leave. In a fit of pique, Steno went up to the doge's throne and wrote on it some salacious remarks about Marino's wife, the dogaressa. For his impudence, the senior council of Venice had him imprisoned for a month. Marino was flabbergasted by the leniency of the sentence and hatched a plot to overthrow the council and declare himself "prince" if not "king" of Venice. His autocratic designs were foiled, however, and he was arrested, dragged across the "Bridge of Sighs" and thrown into the palace dungeons. Some days later he was dragged back across the bridge to the palace courtyard – the very place where doges took the oath – and beheaded.

## APRIL 18

❀ 1552: John Leland, English nobleman
† *Cause of Death: Catalogue*

Impressed with his passion for lists, King Henry VIII made Leland his "royal antiquary" – a title never before or since conferred – and sent him to record, in all its minutiae, the true lie of the land. To carry out his mandate, Leland spent six years criss-crossing the country painstakingly noting "every bay, river, lake, mountain, valley, moor, heath, wood, city, castle, manor-house, monastery and college". It sent him nuts.

Having compiled this mini Domesday Book of England's bays, rivers, lakes mountains, valleys, moors, heaths, woods, cities, castles, manor-houses, monasteries and colleges, Leland "fell beside his wits", was certified insane, and remained completely gaga until the day he became a statistic himself.

# APRIL 19

## ❁ 1689: Christina, queen of Sweden
† *Cause of Death: An Abbot's Amorous Advances*

Angelica Quadrelli was "a Virgin, incomparable both for Beauty and Wit" and as such something of a headache for Pope Innocent XI. Innocent – "a very severe and angry Pope" – considered the charming, leggy blonde to be an unnecessary distraction to the men of Rome, and dispatched her to a convent. Luckily for Angelica, Queen Christina, who was living in Rome in self-imposed exile at the time, intervened and sheltered her in the sanctuary of her palace, where she was safe from papal control. Unluckily for Angelica, the palace did not protect her from the demands of another senior cleric.

A lecherous abbot called Vanini somehow managed to contrive a private audience with Angelica, and during their meeting, threw himself upon her and had his way with her before escaping down an alleyway. A distraught Angelica fled to her room, locked the door and refused to come out, and an incandescent Christina, when she learned of the reasons for her seclusion, hired a hit man to polish the abbot off. The assassin, however, was bought off by the Vatican, and apologised to the queen that his mission was simply impossible.

Christina could not accept that her money could not buy her revenge and "fell into a fury", trying in vain to strangle Merula with her bare hands. When she finally realized there was nothing she could do to relieve her beloved protégée's distress, she fell into a fever and died.

## ❁ 1824: George, Lord Byron
† *Cause of Death: Lyon and Moretto?*

From early childhood, the poet surrounded himself with animals, some more exotic than others. It is said that while a student at Cambridge he kept a tame bear in his rooms. When he moved to Italy, his menagerie moved with him, and a string of visitors list encountering, among others, monkeys, geese, an eagle, a crow, a falcon, a badger, several peacocks and an Egyptian fish-eating crane.

Byron's favourite pet by far, however, was Lyon, a Newfoundland "that doted on me at ten years old and very nearly ate me at twenty!" Although the dog was mad, bad and dangerous to know – "he bit away the backside of my breeches!" – Byron adored him. Lyon, however, together with a bulldog called Moretto, may have inadvertently caused the death of his master. The current medical consensus is that, rather than malaria, Byron died from Mediterranean tick fever, an infection spread by dog ticks.

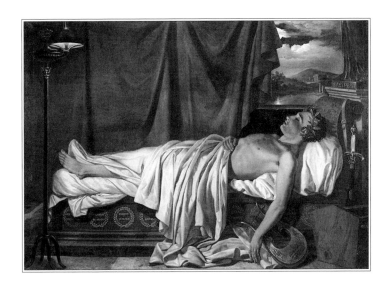

*Lord Byron on his deathbed.*

# APRIL 20

### ❀ 1521: Zhengde, emperor of China
† *Cause of Death: Liquid Lunch*

Leaving the government of the country to others so he could spend his days in his palace pampering exotic animals and being pampered by exotic women, the slack-jawed Zhendge was a sorry excuse for a ruler. His death – he drank himself into a stupor while on a pleasure cruise on the Qianjiang River, fell overboard and swallowed a fatal amount of fetid water – was a fitting end for an emperor supremely unfit for purpose.

# APRIL 21

## ✾ 1509: Henry VII, king of England
† *Cause of Death: Quinsy*

April was the cruellest month for Henry. In the successive springs of 1507-09, his illness – described by his doctors as a "quinsy" (a sort of acute tonsillitis), but in all likelihood a variant of tuberculosis – returned with a vengeance, with the sharp pains in his chest making him bad-tempered and moody. His misery was compounded by encroaching blindness, and in vain desperation he bathed his eyes with a gloop made from roses, fennel water and celandine, a kind of poppy with a poisonous orange sap. He died worn out by the demands of kingship, but not before extracting a promise from Harry, his teenage son, to marry Catherine of Aragon.

# APRIL 22

## ✾ 1806: Pierre-Charles-Jean-Baptiste-Silvestre de Villeneuve, French nobleman
† *Cause of Death: Lack of Victory*

Under an agreed exchange of prisoners, the French admiral who lost the battle of Trafalgar to Nelson was repatriated to France and told to wait in the city of Rennes for further orders. Presuming he was going to be arraigned before a council of war, Villeneuve sat at his desk in the Hôtel de la Patrie, wrote a short suicide note thanking his lucky stars he "did not have any children to be disgraced with the burden of my name", and then jammed a long "pin" through his heart. Other accounts saying that he was found with six self-inflicted stab wounds to the chest are just silly.

## APRIL 23

✤ 1014: Brian Boru, high king of Ireland
† *Cause of Death: Blue Naked People*

Brian Boru's young attendant nervously helped his elderly master pitch his tent just a mile or so away from where the troops of Prince Murchad were ranged against those of the king of Leinster. The aged king knew that the men of Leinster had some crack Danish troops with them and, to ensure victory for his son, felt it incumbent to pray for victory as close to the action as possible. As battle was joined, he fell to his knees.

   "Sire," the page whimpered, "the noise of battle is getting louder!" Brian Boru paid no attention and continued to pray. "Sire," the boy begged, "move before it is too late!" When the king did not move a muscle, the terrified attendant peeked through the tent flap. "Sire!" he yelled, "Blue naked people are advancing on us!" As Brian Boru, momentarily nonplussed, turned round, three Danish soldiers in their tight, metallic blue tunics burst in and, after a brief argument whether he was a king or a priest (they decided on the former), stabbed him to death.

## APRIL 24

✤ 1986: Wallis, duchess of Windsor
† *Cause of Death: Lack of Love*

Wallis Simpson died a full half century after King Edward VIII abdicated to marry her. Over those fifty years, the couple spent a stint in the Bahamas before drifting rather aimlessly between the salons of America's eastern seaboard and the south of France. Without doubt it was a lavish lifestyle for the duchess, but it was also a terrifically lonely one, made all the more when the duke died from cancer in 1972. True friends were few and far between. America, the country of her birth, largely dismissed her. Great Britain, whose queen she never became, was polite but indifferent.

   She ended up an enfeebled, dried-up walnut of a recluse in Paris, cared for by a tiny retinue of nursing staff and a gorgon of a lawyer. Before she lost the power of speech, she summed up her life with an uncharacteristic attempt at humour. "You can't abdicate and eat it," she observed.

## APRIL 25

❀ 1644: Chongzhen, emperor of China
† *Cause of Death: Shame*

The city guidebooks might not tell you this, but the famous "Guilty Chinese Scholartree" in Beijing's Jingshan Park is in fact a replica; the original, uprooted during the Cultural Revolution, is dead – as is Chongzhen who hanged himself from its branches.

Before abandoning his palace to the pillage of the popular army, Chongzhen ordered his entire household (with the exception of his sons) to commit suicide. Many did as they were told, but one daughter, Princess Chang, refused, and for her disobedience had her right arm chopped off at the shoulder. While prevented, therefore, from applauding her father's suicide, she was able to wave farewell to both her father and the Ming dynasty that perished with him.

## APRIL 26

❀ 1892: Sir Provo Wallis, Canadian nobleman
† *Cause of Death: Old Age*

In 1870 the British Admiralty introduced a new retirement scheme that retained on the "active list" any old and doddery officers who had commanded a ship during the Napoleonic wars. They hadn't bargained for Sir Provo. The Canadian admiral, who began service in the Royal Navy when in his teens in 1804, collected his pay for a further 22 years.

# APRIL 27

❀ **1794: James Bruce, Scottish nobleman**
† *Cause of Death: Gallantry*

Bruce had been the first European to visit Abyssinia for well over a century, and his stories of derring-do delighted the general reader, but were dismissed by scholars and fellow explorers alike as a confusion of dates and facts, marred by a tendency to embellish in order to spice up the narrative. Deeply hurt by these criticisms, Bruce retired to his estate in Scotland where he regaled local gentry with his African exploits.

One evening he was chatting to a young lady in his drawing room when he noticed through the window that the woman's elderly mother was walking to her carriage unattended. Bruce hurtled down the grand staircase to be of assistance and "in this effort," laments his biographer Sir Francis Head, "the foot which had safely carried him through all his dangers happened to fail him." The great explorer slipped, flew into the air, did a triple forward somersault, crashed down and split his skull open (or something like that) and never regained consciousness.

❀ **1915: Alexander Scriabin, Russian nobleman**
† *Cause of Death: Boil*

The aristocratic Russian composer was notorious for his incomprehensible harmonies, his synaesthesia (he saw music as colours – C was red, C sharp was violet, D was yellow etc) and for his big mouth. "I am God!" he would proclaim to all and sundry. "I am freedom! I am the peak! I am life!" This self-exalted claptrap ended – as did Scriabin's life – when on this day he combed his long, curly moustache a bit too exuberantly and burst an abscess that had grown on his upper lip, and succumbed to blood poisoning.

# APRIL 28

❀ **1772: Johann Friedrich, count von Struensee**
† *Cause of Death: Lèse Majesté*

Struensee's rise to power in the court of Christian VII of Denmark was nothing short of meteoric, an achievement all the more remarkable given that the German doctor could hardly speak one word of Danish. From humble royal physician he rapidly became the most powerful man in all the land, making laws, making enemies among the nobility, and making himself a count along the way. With considerable ease, he had somehow managed to seduce the mentally unhinged king into allowing him to take control of the country. With similar ease, it appears, he has also seduced Christian's wife, Queen Caroline Matilda.

Eventually the Danish elite tired of this arrogant, foreign upstart and had him arrested on the completely valid charge of usurping royal authority. Because his right hand had done things only the king's right hand should have done, they chopped it off. And because he had illegally been the nation's head, they chopped his head off too.

# APRIL 29

❋ 1776: Edward Wortley Montagu, English nobleman
† *Cause of Death: Ortolan*

ROASTED ORTOLAN (SERVES 1)

*Ingredients*

1 ortolan (a tiny, cute yellow song-bird)

*Method*

Force feed on millet, then drown in Armagnac.
Pluck, chop the feet off and roast in a ramekin for eight minutes.
Serve.

*Method of eating (very important)*

The diner drapes a napkin on their head (some claim this is to preserve the precious aromas, while others say it is to hide the monstrously messy process from polite society and God) and puts the entire bird into their mouth. The sizzling fat is allowed to drizzle down the gullet, before the gourmet crunches down on the bones, releasing the twin subtle flavours of game and hazelnuts.

Now banned in France, this delicacy was apparently the last meal of François Mitterrand, the former French president, when he was terminally ill with cancer. It was also the last meal of the eccentric British traveller, author and parliamentarian, Edward Montagu.

Edward spent his retirement "in the Turkish manner" in a palazzo in Venice. Wearing his customary turban, long flowing robes and an amulet in the shape of a pair of goat's testicles, he would recline at his table and regale his visitors with his adventures, garnered from a lifetime of far-flung travel and sexual escapade. As he was munching on an ortolan one night, a miniscule but needle-like wing bone lodged in his throat and ushered him on to his next big adventure.

*The ortolan.*

## APRIL 30

✻ 1865: Robert Fitzroy, English nobleman
† *Cause of Death: Razor*

"Portland, Plymouth, Biscay, Trafalgar ..."

Nestled in the BBC's shipping forecast we find the sea area of "Fitzroy", named after Vice-Admiral Robert Fitzroy, the founder of the Meteorological Office, although he is perhaps better known as the captain of HMS *Beagle*, which took a young naturalist by the name of Charles Darwin to the South Seas. Fitzroy asked Darwin to accompany him so he might have an equal to talk to. He wanted to

avoid falling into a mood of depression and killing himself, as had been the fate of his uncle, Viscount Castlereagh (*see* August 12), the Beagle's previous captain.

Fitzroy settled in England following an unhappy spell as Governor of New Zealand, and started his work as the world's first professional meteorologist. His claim that one could forecast the weather a whole day ahead was met by many with barely concealed derision, and one Sunday morning he padded through to his dressing room, took out his razor and slit his throat.

"... Sole, Lundy, Fastnet, Irish Sea ..."

# MAY

## MAY 1

❀ 1633: Venetia Stanley, English noblewoman
† *Cause of Death: Viper Wine?*

"Take of the best fat vipers, cut off their heads, take off their skins, and unbowel them. Then put them into the best canary sack, four or six according to their bigness into a gallon [and l]et them stand two or three months."

The alchemist John French guaranteed that drinking this alcoholic snake soup would work wonders. Not only would it "cure the leprosy and such like corruptions of the blood," he promised, but also (and most crucially for its commercial success) it would "provoke venery". In other words, it was the Elizabethan equivalent of Viagra. The nation's viper population consequently shrunk as, in the words of English dramatist Philip Massinger, "grey-bearded gallants" drank the stuff by the jugful in a bid "to feele new lust, and youthful flames again".

It seems that Venetia, a celebrated beauty, gulped down some of her husband's supply in the hope of increasing her already good looks. When she died soon afterwards, a coterie of malcontents accused her diplomat husband, Sir Kenelm Digby, of poisoning her. Viper wine, however, even consumed by the bucket load, would have had little toxicity, and in all likelihood she died of a cerebral haemorrhage.

## MAY 2

❀ 1200: William, lord of Abergavenny
† *Cause of Death: Rope*

Llewellyn the Great, ruler of most of Wales, found William in his (Llewellyn's) bed with his (Llewellyn's) wife, and had him hanged.

## MAY 3

✿ **1589: Anna, Contessa Trotti**
† *Cause of Death: Cuckoldry?*

Nimble-fingered dexterity on the lute and a sensational singing voice made the young countess a rising star on the Italian Renaissance "madrigal circuit". Anna looked a shoe-in for the big time, but then the rumour mill started to spin. Anna was accused – unjustly by most accounts – of sleeping with a cavalry officer, and her elderly, envious husband decided to do something about it.

One evening, Count Trotti burst into her room as she lay in bed with a fever.

"Get up!" he demanded.

"I can't, I'm too ill," Anna whispered weakly.

"Then commend yourself to God" spat the count. Without further ado, he yanked her out of bed and flung her to the floor where (assisted by, of all people, Anna's brother Girolamo) he sliced her to ribbons with a razor and a hatchet.

## MAY 4

✿ **1897: Sophie Charlotte, duchess of Bavaria**
† *Cause of Death: Spark*

Sophie was running a stall at a charity bazaar in Paris when a spark from a nearby gas lamp set her clothes on fire. Helping hands soon doused the duchess, but not before the whole building around them had caught light. As everyone else rushed for the exits, a heroic Sophie remained inside, shepherding the girls who had been working with her through the flames to safety. The girls all made it, but not the duchess. Her body was so charred that it could only be identified by dental records.

## MAY 5

✿ **1760: Laurence Shirley, earl Ferrers**
† *Cause of Death: Silk?*

At his trial for the shooting of his steward, Ferrers conducted his own defence … unconvincingly. His argument, that he was insane at the time, didn't impress the judges one jot, and when they sentenced him to death, he surprised them by immediately admitting that they were right, he was wrong, and he deserved what was coming to him.

On the gallows at Tyburn, Ferrers gave five guineas to the man he thought was his hangman. The recipient turned out to be his assistant, and for a couple of minutes the two executioners wrestled each other over the money. Composure was finally restored, and Ferrers, dressed in his white and silver satin wedding suit, was hanged – some say using a silk cord in consideration of his aristocratic status. The incompetent hangman, one Thomas Turlis, didn't deserve the five guineas. He had measured the drop incorrectly, and his junior had to pull hard on the earl's feet to put him out of his misery.

### ✵ 1821: Napoleon I, emperor of France
† *Cause of Death: Stomach Cancer*

Imprisoned on the island of St Helena, Napoleon became strangely obsessed with liquids. He repeatedly spoke of the nutritious quality of lemonade and questioned Grand Marshal Henri Bertrand *ad nauseam* about drinks made with cherries, pears, almonds and even walnuts. Just before he died he suffered a convulsion in which he somehow managed to leap out of bed and pin a very surprised General Montholon to the carpet. His post mortem, conducted on a billiard table, proved that he died of stomach cancer, although voices are heard to this day claiming underhand alternatives.

## MAY 6

### ✵ 1910: Edward VII, king of England
† *Cause of Death: Heart Attack*

Punters who put a few bob on "Witch of the Air" were as pleased as punch when it won the 4.15 at Kempton Park. The horse's owner, though dying, is reported to have been pleased too. "I am very glad," smiled King Edward, on hearing the news. The heavily obese king, who had already suffered a series of heart attacks in Buckingham Palace that afternoon, collapsed once more while admiring some caged canaries. His supposed final words of "I shall go on ... I shall go on" were patently more appropriate to his horse than himself.

# MAY 7

### ✿ 1846: Te Heuheu II, Maori chief
† *Cause of Death: Erosion of a Nation*

British colonists were not just impressed by the dignity and regality with which Te Heuheu received them. They were also impressed by his bulk. New Zealand's chief justice, Sir William Martin, described him as "a grand old heathen chief, a man of huge size and weight; a regular aristocrat". His death sadly lacked the dignity that had been the hallmark of his life. A landslide in his home village unceremoniously enveloped him, his wives, his eldest son and fifty-four others, in mud.

# MAY 8

### ✿ 1819: Kamehameha I. king of Hawaii
† *Cause of Death: Natural Causes*

"Aloha Kamehameha!" Hawaiians rejoiced at the arrival of a leader who not only brought unity among their islands and but also offered legislative and economic reform without making them forfeit the traditions they so revered. In their joy, the islanders even agreed to his suggestion that it was time to put a stop to their custom of offering a human sacrifice whenever one of their leaders was on his deathbed. Accordingly, when Kamehameha lay gravely ill – the local priests had tried (and failed) to cure the king through prayer, and a "haole" (non-native)

Spanish doctor called Marin had determined that there was nothing his medicine could do either – the gods were left unappeased.

As soon as Kamehameha had breathed his last, however, ancient Hawaiian practices came once more to the fore. Priests desiccated the corpse and burned the royal flesh upon a temple fire. They then wrapped the bones in large leaves, tenderly placed them in a basket woven from fibrous "ie ie" vines, and buried them a secret location. Concealing the royal remains meant they retained their "mana" or power, and this was deemed the only fitting way for a nation to say farewell to their first – and some would argue greatest – king. "Aloha Kamehameha!"

# MAY 9

❀ 1766: Thomas, comte de Lally
† *Cause of Death: Recklessness*

De Lally was one of the most courageous and most despised of generals. With a string of military achievements to his name he was put in charge of an expedition to India against the English, but given his arrogance, vindictiveness, and utter contempt for the indigenous population, he garnered no support and the campaign was a total flop. Back in Europe he learned that he had been charged with treason and, against the advice of the very few who deigned to give him the time of day, returned to Paris to face charges. It was a brave action – and a foolhardy one. After two years of incarceration, de Lally was found guilty and sentenced to death.

Prefiguring the Revolutionary craze for daylight executions, rooms with a view of the gallows were rented out at exorbitant prices, while some non-paying spectators removed tiles from roofs to give themselves a precarious, bird's-eye view. Bound and gagged, de Lally was paraded through the crowds on a common criminal's cart before being dragged to the block. There, the executioner gave his apprentice son the privilege of the first blow. Unfortunately for the lad (and more so for de Lally) his aim was a few inches "high", and the father had to step in and finish the job with a second swipe.

# MAY 10

❀ 1774: Louis XV, king of France
† *Cause of Death: Smallpox*

"I have governed and administered badly, because I have little talent and I have been badly advised." Louis' summary of his career may have been an attempt to win sympathy, but the French couldn't have agreed more. The duke of Liancourt, the Grand Master of the Wardrobe, was there when doctors diagnosed smallpox, and recalls that everyone, with the exception of his daughters, seemed rather relieved at the impending death of one so deeply unpopular. The king, wrote the duke, was "so debased and so despised ... that nothing that could be done for him could possibly interest the public".

# MAY 11

## ✱ 1778: William Pitt, earl of Chatham
† *Cause of Death: American Independence*

There was something rather epic about Pitt the Elder's final speech in the House of Lords and its aftermath. The statesman was dying, and he knew it, but he demanded that he speak in the House one more time to register his "unspeakable concern" at the popular idea that Britain should seek peace with a bellicose France and cede her American colonies to the Americans. Though elderly and tortured with gout, he made the excruciatingly painful journey from his home in Kent to Westminster where he took his seat in a chamber hushed with awe and reverence.

When bid to do so, he struggled to his feet. "I am old and infirm," he said. "I have one foot, more than one foot, in the grave, perhaps never to speak again in this House ... [but] shall we tarnish the lustre of this nation by the ignominious surrender of its rights and fairest possessions?" With the closing words, "My Lords, any state is better than despair; if we must fall, let us fall like men," he sat down, then rose again and then fell.

Back home, he died listening to his son William reading from *The Iliad* of Homer. It was a fitting passage: the description of the death of the courageous Trojan nobleman Hector.

# MAY 12

## ✱ 1863: Radama II, king of Madagascar
† *Cause of Death: Bloodless Coup*

Several cultures, including the Merina society of Madagascar, considered the spilling of royal blood to be taboo. In the case of Radama, the decision to polish him off not by the sword or axe, but by having henchmen kick him senseless and then strangle with a silken sash, was made by the island's prime minister Rainivoninahitriniony, who just couldn't bear to see his nation go to waste.

Radama's reign had actually started rather promisingly – a healthy improvement in foreign relations led to the reopening of trade routes – but then the king rapidly lost the plot. Ignoring parliament entirely, he repaired to his palace and, together with his childhood friends (nicknamed "the red-eyes") embarked upon a conflagration of violence and debauchery. The final straw was the royal decree that from now on all disputes were to be settled by combat, preferably duelling. The PM was having none of it and sent in the boys.

# MAY 13

❀ 2008: Saad Al-Abdullah Al-Salim Al-Sabah, emir of Kuwait
† *Cause of Death: Stroke*

England has its "Nine Days' Queen" (*see* February 12) and Kuwait its "Nine Days' Emir". Suffering from colonic bleeding and cancer, the wheelchair-bound sheikh assumed the throne of the Gulf State in early 2006, but quickly agreed to abdicate in favour of the country's Prime Minister. A couple of years later he had a stroke while having his tea.

# MAY 14

❀ 1610: Henry IV, king of France
† *Cause of Death: Traffic Jam*

Those around the king should have seen it coming. Back on May 14, 1554, King Henry II had ordered all booths and stalls along the rue de la Ferronierie near Les Halles in Paris to be pulled down because they clogged up traffic. No one paid any attention, and here they were, fifty six years later (to the day), stuck in a jam.

Most of the footmen took a short cut through some back alleys to await the carriage at the end of the road. Of the remaining two attendants, one went ahead to try and clear the way. As the other bent over to tie up his garter, the assassin, a large red-bearded loon called Ravaillac seized his moment and struck. He leaped onto one of the carriage wheels, leaned over and stabbed the king three times in quick succession.

Henry didn't see it coming. He had left his glasses at home, so all he saw was a big red blur.

❀ 1781: Gannibal, African prince
† *Cause of Death: Old Age*

Peter the Great liked to collect freaks of nature, among them an eight-legged lamb, a three-legged baby and two puppies supposedly born to a sixty-year-old virgin. In 1704 he added to this menagerie a whimpering slave boy who claimed to be an Abyssinian prince. What made Gannibal such a find was not his possible nobility, but his colour. He was black, and therefore a rare and unusual exhibit, whose skin pigmentation made him not just exotic but excitingly scary.

We don't know what hopes the tsar had for his "noble moor", but we do know that he surpassed all expectations, becoming a suave diplomat, a courageous soldier and even a rather good spy. Gannibal's great grandson, the poet Pushkin, writes, somewhat enigmatically, how his ancestor quietly slipped away "like a *philosophe*" on his estate outside St Petersburg. Russia hardly noticed the passing of a national treasure: at 85 (he had outlived Peter by more than half a century and had served under a further seven tsars and tsarinas) Gannibal was little more than a historical curiosity from a former age.

## MAY 15

### ❀ 1591: Dmitry, tsarevich of Russia
### † *Cause of Death: Game of Darts?*

The official enquiry into Dmitry's death concluded that he had accidentally stabbed himself in the neck during an epileptic fit. This did not go down well with the young boy's mother, Maria Nagaya, who made it known that she was sure that he had been assassinated on the orders of Boris Godunov.

"No," said the authorities, "it was an accident."

"But it can't have been," Maria replied. "You see, during an epileptic fit, your hands naturally become unclenched. You cannot hold anything."

"Aah…" said the authorities. "What we meant to say was that actually he stabbed himself while playing a game of darts – a game in which you held the blade towards yourself before throwing it to a target."

Maria's response is unprintable. Her understandable fury sparked a riot in which fifteen Godunov supporters were killed, and the authorities, having silenced Dmitry, now turned to his mum, exiling her to a convent far, far away.

# MAY 16

## ❀ 1657: Andrew Bobola, Polish nobleman
† *Cause of Death: Cossack*

Members of the Polish "Solidarity" movement of the 1980s sold little paper labels depicting the face of Andrew Bobola to raise money for the trade union's campaign against Communist martial law. They chose Bobola because everyone knew his story of glory through affliction.

Andrew was a Jesuit missionary, martyred by Cossacks on the payroll of the Russian Orthodox Church, and his death has been dubbed "the most cruel ever recorded". On capturing the man they called the "robber of souls", the Cossacks:

- ❀ Stripped him, tied him to a tree and whipped his back to shreds.
- ❀ Punched him in the face knocking out several teeth.
- ❀ Thrust onto his head a crown of young oak branches, slightly wetted so that when they dried they contracted and pressed deeper into his flesh.
- ❀ Bound and dragged him behind two horses to their chief.

A brief conversation then occurred between the chief and the priest. The chief didn't like what he heard so he:

- ❀ Cut off one of Andrew's feet and three of his fingers.

One of the soldiers saw him looking up to heaven, and thinking he was seeking divine intervention:

- ❀ Gouged out one of his eyes with his sabre.

There's more. Grabbing his "good" leg, they hauled Andrew to the local butcher's and stretched him on the block. There they:

- ❀ Charred his body with flaming torches.
- ❀ Forced splinters of wood under his fingernails.
- ❀ Told him his tonsure wasn't big enough and cut off his scalp.
- ❀ Ripped out his tongue.
- ❀ Cut off his lips and nose, and threw his body upon a dunghill.

A crust of comfort, perhaps, for those in the bread queues of Gdansk.

# MAY 17

## ❋ 1606: Dmitry, tsar of Russia
† *Cause of Death: Orthodox Blessing*

Another Dmitry (*see* May 15), another nasty death. It was custom for a woman of another denomination to convert to the Russian Orthodox Church when she married the tsar. But this did not happen in the case of Dmitry's Catholic wife Marina, and the reason became abundantly clear within a few weeks of the wedding. From his eccentric behaviour – he ate veal, refused to take a bath and enjoyed wrestling with bears – an enraged Russia soon cottoned on to the truth that Dmitry was not, as he claimed, the son of Ivan the Terrible, but in reality a slightly deranged Polish monk called Gregory who, by a combination of luck and bravado, had engineered himself onto the Russian throne, with the goal of converting Russia to Roman Catholicism.

A posse of enraged boyars stormed the Kremlin, seeking his life. In a bid to escape, Dmitry leaped some one hundred feet from his wife's bedroom window, amazingly only breaking a leg. The mob soon caught up with him, and dragged him back inside where he underwent a series of humiliations mirroring the Passion of Christ. He was jostled and slapped and spat upon. His imperial robes were torn off him and replaced with a dirty shirt. Mocking cries of "Behold the tsar of all Russia!" were soon replaced with demands to "Crucify him!" Two men, lesser boyars, then pushed their way to the front. One of them said, "I'll give this Polish heretic an Orthodox Blessing!" and shot him point blank in the head. The corpse of "False Dmitry" was then burned, and his ashes stuffed into a cannon and blown to the winds.

# MAY 18

## ❋ 526: Pope John I, Italian nobleman
† *Cause of Death: Gift of God*

A "Gift of God" by name, though not by nature, King Theodoric the Great, Pope John's earthly master, had little interest in the Ten Commandments, least of all the sixth. He murdered his rival King Odoacer (*see* March 15), put his father-in-law to the sword, and even sent the philosopher Boethius to an early grave.

As the elderly pontiff made the long, tortuous journey back from Constantinople to Ravenna, having done as he was told and made peace with the emperor Justin, he must have hoped that the bloodthirsty Ostrogoth would be pleased with his efforts. No such luck. Assuming that he had colluded with Justin and was planning some sort of coup, Theodoric slung God's representative on earth in jail and let him rot.

# MAY 19

## ❉ 1536: Anne Boleyn, queen of England
† *Cause of Death: Sword of Calais*

Many of the executions mentioned in this book (*see*, for example, Laurence Shirley and Margaret Pole on May 5 and 27 respectively) were clumsy, unpalatable, amateur affairs. Anne's, by contrast, was a supremely professional display by a master of his craft.

Witnesses to the beheading were amazed at the speed of the queen's dispatch. One moment she was kneeling down and whispering, "To Jesus Christ, I commend my soul", and the next ("before you could say a paternoster" according to one French bystander) her headless corpse was being carted off to the nearby chapel. How was it done so quickly?

The secret behind this fast – almost magically fast – deed was the headsman's brilliant tactic of concealing the famous "Sword of Calais" beside him under some straw. As a terrified Anne put her head near the block, he wheeled round to an assistant standing on the scaffold steps and called out, "Bring me the sword". Anne instinctively turned her head towards the steps, baring her neck at just the right angle, and in a flash the executioner whipped out the sword and carried out his duty. Ta da!

# MAY 20

## ❉ 1622: Osman II, sultan of the Ottoman Empire
† *Cause of Death: Nutcracker*

Osman blamed his failed invasion of Poland on the cowardice of his elite guard, the Janissaries. Once back in Istanbul, he curbed their powers by closing down the coffee shops (where they liked to linger and hatch plots) and banned cigarettes and alcohol (which they liked to consume a lot). The Janissaries were not pleased.

They were upset even further when their teenage sultan announced he was journeying to Mecca, but seen packing jewels and other treasures – not exactly travel essentials for a pilgrimage. They duly sent the Grand Vizier to polish him off by the unusual method of "compression of testicles", a form of execution apparently reserved exclusively for Ottoman sultans.

## MAY 21

### ✱ 1471: Henry VI, king of England
† *Cause of Death: Edward?*

Yorkist spin doctors would have us believe that Henry VI, imprisoned in the Tower of London, died "of pure displeasure and melancholy". This is codswallop – he died violently, as evidenced by the bloodstained hair on his skull. The question nevertheless remains: at whose hands? Many, including William Shakespeare and Thomas More, support the claim of historian Polydore Vergil that Richard, duke of Gloucester "killyd him with a sword". A recent suggestion, however, argues that yes, Richard was certainly present in the Tower at the time of Henry's death, but was there in his capacity as royal constable, delivering a royal warrant. Some nameless heavy did the dirty work, but the man squarely behind the king's death was another king, Edward IV, who would have ordered the regicide as a matter of political expedience.

## MAY 22

### ✱ 337: Constantine, Roman emperor
† *Cause of Death: Old Age*

Bishops considered the common practice of delaying one's baptism until one's death bed rather unseemly, as this, in theory, meant one could commit all manner of sins – then be forgiven – and appear pure as the driven snow on Judgement Day. Constantine, who converted to Christianity in 312 and who had quite a few major sins to his name (including killing members of his own family), delayed his baptism, not because he wanted to carry on sinning, but because he feared God. He was terrified that his soul would be in peril unless he stayed unbaptised until the last moment. He had it all planned. When it was clear that he was soon going to celebrate his "heavenly birthday", he would journey to Palestine and receive the sacrament in the waters of the River Jordan, just like Jesus a few hundred years beforehand. But it didn't quite go as the emperor hoped.

Eusebius writes how Constantine was near Nicomedia when he "experienced some slight bodily indisposition … soon followed by positive disease", and realizing that travel was out of the question, hurriedly arranged for an elaborate ceremony to take place at a local village church, at which he permanently replaced his imperial purple with the pure white of innocence.

Oblivious to the irony, Rome marked the passing of their great leader by elevating him to the status of a pagan god.

## MAY 23

❀ 1798: John Scott, earl of Clonmell
† *Cause of Death: Gluttony*

In a bid to lose weight, the Falstaffian Scott vowed to "refrain from snuff, sleep, swearing, gross eating, sloth, malt liquors, indulgence – and never to take anything after tea but water or wine". Despite his efforts, he grew so massive that when he died, the undertakers couldn't manoeuvre his body down the stairs and had to winch it, like a grand piano, out the bedroom window.

## MAY 24

❀ 1627: Luis de Gongora y Argote, Spanish nobleman
† *Cause of Death: Poet*

Gongora was a priest, poker player and poet who engaged in a long-running feud with fellow wordsmith Francisco de Quevedo. Gongora accused Quevedo of high-flown prose and impenetrable wordplay. Quevedo, in return, poked fun at his rival's big nose, calling it "a bowsprit of a mighty ship" and "a monstrous chilblain, purpley and fried". It all came to a head when Quevedo bought the house Gongora was living in solely in order to turf him out of it. Homeless, broken and broke, Gongora shuffled off to his native Cordoba, and soon thereafter this mortal coil.

## MAY 25

❀ 1915: Adeline, countess of Cardigan
† *Cause of Death: Old Age*

Like a character out of a P. G. Wodehouse novel, Countess Adeline Brudenel was the epitome of English eccentric aristocracy. Sporting a splendid blond curly wig with a red geranium fixed behind one ear, she shocked the locals in her Northamptonshire village by spending money extravagantly, smoking in public and a wearing a kilt which showed her bare knees.

As she aged, she became odder and odder, not least in her choice of clothing. Her top three outfits appear to have been:

1.  Her late husband's red military trousers and cuirass, over which she would throw a leopard skin and declare she was off bicycling.
2.  A flamenco dress in which she would dance and play the castanets, apparently with considerable skill.
3.  A habit. Adeline would pretend to be the "Grey Nun", a ghost who supposedly haunted her estate. Guests who saw the "apparition" were expected to faint or at least scream.

Fixated with death, she kept her coffin in the hall and from time to time would order Knighton, her butler, to lift her into it, so she could ensure it was comfy.

Wodehouse's characters were eccentric but never base, yet Adeline had her darker side. The high-class courtesan known as "Skittles" referred to her as the "head of our profession", and in a mean-spirited collection of memoirs, Adeline claimed that she had turned down Benjamin Disraeli's offer of marriage (when in fact he had refused her) because he had bad breath.

## MAY 26

### ✤ 946: Edmund, king of England
† *Cause of Death: Gatecrasher*

Ask most Christians in England today which feast falls on May 26 and they wouldn't have the foggiest. Had you asked the same question back in the tenth century, everybody would have told you that it was St Augustine's Day, a holiday to celebrate the life, work and witness of the first Archbishop of Canterbury. Edmund was throwing a party at his Gloucestershire villa in honour of the saint, when he spotted a gatecrasher – a man called Leofa whom he had banished from his kingdom six years earlier for robbery. The indignant king leaped from the table, grabbed the thief by the hair and wrestled him to the floor. Unfortunately for Edmund, Leofa happened to be carrying a dagger and, in the ensuing tussle, plunged it into his stomach. Edmund died almost instantly. Leofa quickly joined him in death as the remaining revellers tore him limb from limb.

## MAY 27

❀ 1541: Margaret Pole, countess of Salisbury
† *Cause of Death: Axe*

It just wasn't Margaret's day. Not only was she to be beheaded (on completely spurious charges) for treason, but also the regular executioner at Smithfield was away, and so she had to die at the hands of a substitute. As luck would have it, the replacement headsman was, in the words of Chapuys, the imperial ambassador, a "blundering garçonneau" – a young incompetent who could barely hold up the heavy axe, let alone wield it with accuracy.

The elderly Margaret (possibly having seen the awkward, inexperienced stand-in) refused to go quietly. Heavies had to hold her head down on the block and spring back just as the axe found its mark. Unfortunately for Margaret, the axe did not find its mark and struck her shoulder instead. What happened next depends on one's appetite for the macabre. Racy versions of the execution record how Margaret ran in panic around the gallows, while the equally panicking headsman ran behind her, lopping off bits of her with every swing. Calmer chroniclers such as Chapuys describe the execution as an embarrassment – a messy botch-job in which the amateur axe man "hacked her head and shoulders to pieces before she was pronounced dead".

## MAY 28

❀ 1972: Edward VIII, king of England
† *Cause of Death: Throat Cancer*

Edward and his wife Wallis loved pugs. They had four of them and fed them steak out of lead crystal bowls and perfumed their coats with "Miss Dior", the duchess's favourite scent. One of the pugs proved a portent. The royal doctor noticed that one of the dogs, who had spent the past few weeks snuggled against its master, had hopped off the bed onto the floor and was curled up some distance away. A few hours later the former king, who had been a heavy smoker since childhood, croaked.

## MAY 29

❀ 1873: Friedrich, prince of Hesse
† *Cause of Death: Defenestration*

It was a mother's worst nightmare. Princess Alice was sitting at one end of her L-shaped bedroom when she heard a commotion round the corner. She ran to find that during a game with his brother Ernest, two-year-old "Frittie" had scrambled onto a chair and toppled out of the unlatched window. Although his fall was broken by a balcony a few feet below, the haemophiliac toddler suffered bleeding of the brain and died that afternoon.

## MAY 30

❀ 1574: Charles IX, king of France
† *Cause of Death: Guilt*

Tormented by the carnage of the St Bartholomew's Day Massacre (*see* August 24) – carnage that had been carried out on his orders – Charles spurned all food and took to his bed. There he wasted away from a combination of fever and remorse, coughing up blood and spending what little energy he had to bemoan his fate. "O what streams of blood!" he wailed, remembering the thousands butchered. "God forgive me!"

❀ 1947: George Ritter von Trapp, Austrian nobleman
† *Cause of Death: Submarine?*

George, the head of the Austrian singing family immortalized in the movie "The Sound of Music" said "So long, farewell, auf Wiedersehen, adieu" to this world in America, some nine years after he and his talented family fled Nazi oppression. His wife Maria suggests that the cause of his lung cancer was the diesel fumes he would have breathed while captaining a U-boat in the First World War. She does admit, however, that he also smoked like nobody's business.

# MAY 31

❋ 1731: Philip, duke of Wharton
† *Cause of Death: Excess*

When Philip was good, he was very, very good. From an articulate, charming and well-mannered child prodigy, he matured into a magnificent orator, impressing his colleagues in the House of Lords with his rhetoric. Few soldiers, meanwhile, showed greater skill or courage on the battlefield.

But when he was bad, he was horrid. At just fifteen, Philip turned his back on his family and eloped with Martha Holmes, a young woman considerably beneath his station (unable to have the marriage annulled, his parents did the honourable thing and died of heartache within the year). When Martha herself died in childbirth, Philip hastily found another wife, but his contempt for his new bride was obvious even on his wedding day, when he leeringly exposed himself to her and the guests at the reception.

Philip gambled heavily: he once lost £13,000 at a meeting of the Newmarket Races – this at a time when the average salary was about £150 a year. He was a master rabble-rouser: he founded the notorious Hell-Fire Club, dedicated to binge drinking and blasphemy. And he just loved to annoy: he would wake people in the middle of the night to ask if he could borrow a pin.

Many were saddened to learn that, at only 32, after two decades of hedonistic overindulgence, Philip had fallen off his horse while in Spain, and died in a nearby Cistercian monastery. Many were saddened that he died surrounded by brothers, but no family or friends. Many were saddened, but few were surprised.

# JUNE

## JUNE 1

**❀ 1434: Ladislaus II, king of Poland**
† *Cause of Death: Nightingale*

Keats would have liked Ladislaus, a man who loved nothing better than to go down to the woods and spend the day listening to the melodious song of the "light-wingèd Dryad of the trees". But one day the king miscalculated just how chilly it was, and went birding in nothing warmer than a light sheepskin jerkin. He caught a cold and rapidly died "as though of hemlock he had drunk".

*The nightingale.*

**❀ 1879: Napoleon Eugene, Prince Imperial**
† *Cause of Death: Assegai*

The British Army was nervous at having a foreign prince in their ranks, and only allowed "Lieutenant Napoleon" to participate in the Zulu War on the condition that he stayed well away from the fighting. But little in war goes as planned. A posse of African warriors chanced upon his patrol and, unaware of their enemy's royal identity, forced him from his horse and tore him to shreds with their spears.

**❀ 2001: Birendra, king of Nepal**
† *Cause of Death: Son*

To this day, Kathmandu remains flummoxed as to why Dipendra, the amiable, Eton-educated heir to the Nepalese throne, gunned down his father and eight other members of the royal family. Some are convinced that the prince went berserk when his mother told him that he couldn't marry the girl of his dreams. Others, more prosaically, say he was drunk as a skunk.

## JUNE 2

**❀ 1581: James Douglas, earl of Morton**
† *Cause of Death: A Scottish Maiden*

Impressed with its simple efficiency, Douglas introduced the "maiden", a sort of primitive guillotine, into the Scottish justice system, only to be incriminated in the assassination of Lord Darnley (*see* February 10), and subjected personally to its blade.

*A Scottish Maiden, used to execute James Douglas.*

## JUNE 3

**❀ 1989: Ruhollah Musawi Khomeini, Iranian sayyid**
† *Cause of Death: Heart Attack*

The dour-faced ayatollah famously once declared that there was "no humour in Islam", and one doubts whether he would have considered the frenzy of his two funerals remotely funny.

*Funeral One*

It was mayhem. More than a million supporters packed the streets of Tehran to say farewell to the sayyid – a term given to male descendants of the prophet Muhammad and best translated as "Sir" or "Lord" – and city officials simply couldn't cope. Naively expecting a modicum of decorum, the funeral directors placed the body in a wooden coffin and flew it by helicopter to the cemetery 25 miles from the city centre. A sea of wailing, grief-stricken mourners greeted them. Some pounded their heads and chests. Others flagellated their backs with chains. Others, still, sacrificed sheep. Desperate for one final look of their leader, they swarmed like leaf-cutter ants around the flimsy casket and, in their bid to touch the dead man's shroud and kiss his face, managed to rip open the coffin. The corpse slid out and fell to the ground, and guards had to fire shots in the air and set water hoses on the crowd to give themselves room to haul it back into the helicopter and fly it away.

*Funeral Two*

Six hours later and this time they had encased the body in a metal casket. Nevertheless it still it took an age to carry the imam the final ten yards to his final resting place. Finally, once they had cleared the grave of fanatics who wished to be buried alive with their leader, they rolled the body in and covered it with massive blocks of concrete to prevent exhumation.

It had been a difficult day, not least for the city's hospitals. Nearly eleven thousand people had to be treated for injuries.

# JUNE 4

## ❋ 1849: Marguerite, countess of Blessington
† *Cause of Death: Heart Attack*

Marguerite had a big heart. The novelist was the most generous hostess and her house in central London attracted the learned society of the day as a flame does moths. Marguerite had a really big heart. When her lavish lifestyle left her in financial extremis, she stoically sold the house and its contents and, with her creditors paid in full, sailed away to a life of penury in France. Marguerite had a really, really big heart. At her post mortem, doctors found it to be three times the normal size.

## JUNE 5

❋ 1916: Herbert, Lord Kitchener
† *Cause of Death: Mine*

For fifteen awful minutes Kitchener stood on the starboard side of the quarterdeck of HMS *Hampshire*, knowing full well he was going to die. On his way from North Scotland to the city of Archangel to try to bolster the Russian war effort, he had been reading in his cabin when the cruiser hit a mine laid by a German U-Boat just a few days before. The seas were ferocious, the vessel was tossing like a cork in a barrel and it was bitterly cold. There was no hope.

Suddenly, as if yanked by an invisible hand, the stern of the ship lifted up. The *Hampshire* completed something close to a forward somersault and sank forty fathoms to the sea floor. The British simply couldn't believe that their military hero and War Minister was dead. Rather pathetically, Kitchener's sister Millie fuelled stories that he had to be alive since she had been unable to contact him in the spirit world.

## JUNE 6

❋ 1217: Henry I, king of Castile
† *Cause of Death: Tile*

On such incidents do dynastic fortunes swing. A capricious gust of wind whistling through the town of Palencia dislodged a roof tile. The shingle, in turn, slid off the roof and crashed onto the young king's head. Henry didn't know what hit him.

## JUNE 7

❋ 1329: Robert the Bruce, king of the Scots
† *Cause of Death: Morphew?*

Robert was convinced that the scurvy-like blisters that covered his body were divine punishment for his murder of John Comyn (*see* February 10), and he wasn't alone. Both Froissart and the Lanercost Chronicler thought so too, and the poet Edwin Muir even tried to put it into rhyme when he wrote that his decidedly unchristian behaviour in church caused his skin to turn "white as may / With wars and leprosy". Robert's condition certainly wasn't leprosy, but probably a severe form of psoriasis that medieval doctors termed "morphew", an even harder word for which to find a decent rhyme. In all likelihood, Robert died following a stroke.

## JUNE 8

❀ 1042: Harthacanute, king of Denmark and England
† *Cause of Death: Gluttony*

One moment Harthacanute was enjoying a couple of drinks with his colleagues, the next, according to the *Anglo-Saxon Chronicle*, he "fell to the earth with an awful convulsion". Henry of Huntingdon laments he was snatched away "in the flower of his youth", but his hobby of binge eating — he wolfed down four massive meals a day — surely helped him towards an early grave.

❀ 1795: Louis XVII, king of France
† *Cause of Death: Tuberculosis*

A prisoner from the age of seven, Louis died, aged ten, covered with sores, riddled with TB and wearing the same shirt since the previous year. His jailer, a cobbler called Simon, had forced him to drink alcohol, curse his parents, sing "La Marseillaise", and beaten him black and blue for good measure. Vive la Republique!

## JUNE 9

❀ 1701: Philip, duke of Orleans
† *Cause of Death: Argument*

King Louis XIV had been waiting, and as soon as his brother Philip came through the front door he began his tirade. What was he going to do to stop the disgusting behaviour of his dissolute and adulterous son? In reply, Philip told Louis that this was a bit rich coming from a man who allowed his mistresses to travel in the same carriage as his wife. The row continued through supper — during which the duke petulantly stabbed at his meat — and into the night, during which a footman felt compelled to warn the brothers that their raised voices could be heard throughout the court. Back home, Philip was pouring himself a stiff drink when his knees buckled and he collapsed into his son's arms.

On hearing the news of his brother's death, Louis replied that he was truly sorry to hear it … and ordered for the card tables to be set out as usual.

## JUNE 10

❀ 323 BC: Alexander, king of Macedon
† *Cause of Death: Strychnine?*

There are lots of theories about how Alexander the Great died at just 32. Here are the top three:

1. He was poisoned by his cup-bearer with some strychnine smuggled into Babylon in the hoof of a mule.
2. He succumbed to malaria, or an overdose of the hellebore given to cure it.
3. He drank himself to death.

Legend, meanwhile, obstinately insists that his body was preserved in a big box of honey and buried in a glass coffin.

❀ 1190: Frederick, Holy Roman Emperor
† *Cause of Death: Drowning*

Even though the Saleph River was only three feet deep, Frederick managed to drown in it. A popular explanation doing the rounds is that the emperor had a heart attack as he leaped into the freezing waters and that his armour, though not especially heavy, dragged him under.

❀ 1970: Leila, princess of Iran
† *Cause of Death: Drug Overdose*

With a physique that made Twiggy look positively plump, the princess collapsed in her £500-a-night London hotel suite surrounded by bottles of barbiturates and the so-called "date rape" drug Rohypnol. An inquest heard how the emaciated one-time model for the Italian designer Valentino had been taking over twenty times the recommended dose of several drugs in a losing battle against bulimia and depression, suggesting that perhaps you <u>can</u> be too rich and too thin.

# JUNE 11

❋ 1488: James III, king of Scotland
† *Cause of Death: Cleric?*

There is no contemporary evidence to support the sixteenth-century claim that James died not at the Battle of Sauchieburn but instead at the hands of a man impersonating a priest – but the story's worth the telling all the same. Robert Lindsay of Piscottie and several others would have you believe that James fled the field on his grey charger, but fell off it as he tried to leap across the burn at Bannock. He was carried to a nearby mill where he asked for a priest in order to make his confession. One just happened to be passing by – some say he was a servant of James's enemy Lord Gray in disguise – and after a few words of cordial introduction, stabbed the king in the heart.

❋ 1847: Sir John Franklin, explorer
† *Cause of Death: Map*

Sir John died of heart failure while his ship, the *Erebus*, lay marooned in the icepack around King William Island in the Canadian Arctic. Unwittingly, he was in sight of the Northwest Passage which he had first set out to find more than thirty years beforehand.

It now transpires that, compared with most of his crew, he had been lucky. Inuit oral accounts and the discovery of various artefacts from the expedition suggest that 25 of his colleagues starved to death some months later, and the remaining 105 died in their abortive attempt to walk the six hundred miles to The Hudson Bay Company post at Fort Resolution. In their plight, it appears that some had even resorted to cannibalism.

Franklin may have become ice-bound in the mistaken belief that King William Island was in fact a peninsula, as it was incorrectly printed in Sir John Ross's 1829 map of the region. Ironically, the only ice-free channel around the island was to the south and east.

# JUNE 12

## ❀ 1983: Norma, queen of MGM
† *Cause of Death: Alzheimer's Disease*

Signed by Metro-Goldwyn-Meyer in the early 1920s, Norma Shearer was one of the few Hollywood actresses to successfully cross the gulf between silent movies and "talkies". She won an Academy Award for her role in "The Divorcee" and, hailed as the "Queen of MGM" and elsewhere "Queen Norma", went on to enjoy a string of box office hits. Not quite following her dictum of "Never let them see you in public after you've turned thirty-five", she retired when she was forty and married a ski instructor twelve years her junior. The couple remained together until her death, by which time her memory had gone and she reportedly called Martin, her husband of more than forty years, "Irving".

# JUNE 13

## ❀ 1886: Ludwig II, king of Bavaria
† *Cause of Death: One Question too Many?*

Everyone at the small castle on Lake Stanberg, where the slightly unhinged king was being kept prisoner, was sick and tired of his interminable questions. The only respite they had from his bombardment of queries was when he was eating – and that, mercifully, was a lot of the time. Ludwig had a voracious appetite. At 4.30 p.m. on the day of his death, he consumed an enormous meal, washed down with a glass of beer, five glasses of wine and two glasses of arrack. He then asked his colleague Professor Gudden to accompany him on a walk so he could ask him some more questions. Gudden reluctantly agreed and two men left the fortress, never to return. Their lifeless bodies were found later that night floating in the lake, and questions still remain to this day about how they got there.

## JUNE 14

❀ 1662: Sir Henry Vane, English nobleman
† *Cause of Death: Axe*

The Parliamentarian and former governor of the Massachusetts Bay Colony was used to having his own way, and even as he stood on the scaffold at Tower Hill – sentenced to death for high treason – he was determined to die on his own terms. Samuel Pepys writes in his famous diary how Vane embarked on a lengthy speech, and how the flustered sheriff hurriedly rustled up some trumpeters to drown out his words. As he finally knelt down to face his end, Vane asked the executioner to make sure that the axe didn't touch a blister on his neck, because that would really, really hurt.

## JUNE 15

❀ 1467: Philip, duke of Burgundy
† *Cause of Death: Omelette?*

Poly Bulland, one of Philip the Good's servants, details the sudden death of his master. Since it was a Friday – a day on which his religious convictions forbade the consumption of anything that had been killed – the duke had a light supper of an omelette and a couple of gulps of almond milk before heading to bed. By two in the morning he and his supper had parted company. By three in the morning, Philip and this world had followed suit.

## JUNE 16

❀ 1999: David, Lord Sutch, earl of Harrow
† *Cause of Death: Lack of Publicity*

Putting two fingers up at British institutional politics, "Screaming" Lord Sutch injected colour and humour into many a drab political election. As head of the Monster Raving Loony Party, he campaigned in – and lost – dozens of elections. This may be in part because his policies included giving pets the right to vote, demoting John Major to Private, and setting accountants in concrete to be used as traffic bollards.

Sutch may have lost every election in which he stood, but he won the hearts of a nation that revels in the maverick – someone willing to dress outlandishly (his trademark outfit included a leopard skin jacket and a top hat), speak outlandishly (he famously posed the question of why there was only one monopolies commission) and make everyone else look rather foolish in the process.

As is so often the case with merry eccentrics, there lay behind the comic façade a desperately sad man. Sutch was a depressive and was distraught at the death of his mother and later her dog, both whom he adored. His greatest sadness, however, as his close friend and former madam Cynthia Payne explained, was that, by his late fifties, he wasn't making headlines any more. And so it was that Sutch's partner, Yvonne, opened their front door one day to find him standing on the stairs. He was wearing ordinary clothes – a grey jacket and a yellow silk flower pinned to his lapel – and she thought that he wanted her to take a photograph. She duly did, and then realized what he had done. Around his neck was a child's multi-coloured skipping rope.

# JUNE 17

## ✿ 1797: Agha Mukhammad Khan, shah of Persia
† *Cause of Death: Just Dessert*

One night Agha Muhammad summoned his three kitchen servants and told them he fancied a spot of melon for supper, and they duly brought him the fruit cut into slices. Unable to finish the entire thing, he told them to put it to one side until the next day, and warned them that if even one slice was missing, they would all die. During the night a peckish and extremely forgetful slave ate a piece, and since the shah was not one to go back on his promises, the three condemned men stole into his tent and stabbed him in the chest.

# JUNE 18

## ✿ 1815: Sir Thomas Picton, English nobleman
† *Cause of Death: Inappropriate Military Uniform*

Hats off to Picton who, for no other reason than that he could, wore a nightcap at the Battle at Bussaco. Respect, too, to a man who came out of retirement after the

Peninsular War, even though his nerves were shot to pieces, to fight for Wellington at the Battle of Waterloo. He did so sporting a top hat. During the fray, a musket ball whizzed through the band of his titfer, and gave him the dubious honour of being the most senior – and most ludicrously dressed – British soldier to die that day.

# JUNE 19

## ✾ 1867: Maximilian, emperor of Mexico
† *Cause of Death: Firing Squad*

Mexico's Republican forces led by Benito Juárez ousted Maximilian from power with little difficulty, and sentenced him to be executed as a deterrent to any other imperial upstart. Back in Europe, many people, including Princess Charlotte (*see* January 19) just couldn't entertain the idea that they would actually shoot a member of the Austrian royal family. But shoot him they did.

An escort of four thousand men brought Maximilian, together with two of his generals, to a low adobe wall on the outskirts of the city of Queretaro. The ex-emperor was loquacious to the end, commenting on the sunny day – "I have always wanted to die on a day like this" – and asking his firing squad to "aim well, muchahos". Then, with one foot slightly in front of the other, he raised his eyes to the heavens and calmly pointed to his heart. The musketeers were so close that they could not miss. They were so close, in fact, that his uniform caught fire.

*The execution of
Maximilian I.*

## JUNE 20

❋ 1837: William IV, king of England
† *Cause of Death: Pneumonia and Cirrhosis of the Liver*

News of the king's impending death was met with a range of emotions. From Westminster it was cynicism when, on June 15, Lord Melbourne informed his Cabinet that the queen wished all churches in the land to pray for her husband's health. "It is doubtful whether the king will survive long," the Prime Minister sighed, "but the order may as well be given." At Kensington Palace it was mild resentment, as a young Princess Victoria was told that her singing classes had been postponed until her uncle had passed away. At Windsor, meanwhile, the wheelchair-bound, asthmatic king prepared for his death by having his son Augustus read him prayers.

William was very keen to mark the anniversary of the Battle of Waterloo on June 18 and asked his doctor to "tinker" with him so he might last until the end the day. Last the day he did, and in fact managed another twenty-six hours before England's churchgoers turned to a different page in their Prayer Books and their new queen could book her next music lesson.

## JUNE 21

❋ 1377: Edward III, king of England
† *Cause of Death: Wanton Baggage*

The anonymous *Chronicon Anglia* suggests that Edward fell ill as soon as he began a liaison with "that wanton baggage Alice Perrers". The historian states that before the king met the courtesan he was full of beans, but soon afterwards he was slothful and suffering from a condition more usually found in "young men" (i.e. a venereal disease). Thomas Walsingham echoes this disparaging view of Alice, and records that even before rigor mortis had set in, Alice had removed the rings from Edward's fingers.

This is all very unkind on Alice. Her children with Edward were all fine specimens, making venereal disease highly unlikely. In all probability Edward died as result of one of the many blows he received to the head during his jousting days.

## ✤ 1727: George I, king of England
† *Cause of Death: Fruit and a Woman Scorned*

Was George's death attributable to a combination of soft fruit and hard truths?
While he was travelling on the Continent, the king was handed a letter from his
late wife, Sophia Dorothea, written on her deathbed some seven months earlier.
It was no billet-doux. Instead, the queen, who had been imprisoned for thirty
long years following a rather injudicious affair with a colonel in the dragoon
guards, accused him of cruelty and malice, and called him to join her before God
before a year was up. George, a sordid, emotionless man, appeared unfazed by
this summons from the grave, but the fruit that he ate later that day (some say
he consumed a large plate of strawberries and oranges, others a "vast quantity" of
melons) had a more profound effect.

Following a fitful night at his hotel in Delden, George drank a quick cup of
hot chocolate and sped off towards his beloved childhood home at Osnabrück,
but half an hour into the journey he had to answer a call of nature. As he stepped
back into the carriage, an attendant noticed that he was sweating profusely and
that his right hand was twitching. The royal surgeon, travelling in the carriage
immediately behind, recognised the telltale signs of a stroke and had the king
laid out on the grass verge and bled. He was bled later as well, but nothing could
prevent him from crossing over to "another country" where, some would contend,
Sophia Dorothea was eagerly waiting for him.

# JUNE 22

## ✤ 1808: Monsieur de Pique, French nobleman
† *Cause of Death: Blunderbuss*

De Pique and a fellow minor nobleman called de Grandpré had a quarrel over a
young dancer from the Imperial Opera, and agreed to fight a duel to settle their
dispute. Unusually, they decided to fight it while airborne.

In two identical balloons, the combatants, together with their seconds, rose
about half a mile above the Tuileries in Paris and, on a pre-arranged signal, took
out their blunderbusses (pistols would have pointless) and fired. The distance
between the two was only eighty yards or so, but somehow De Pique missed.
De Grandpré, on the other hand, found his mark and, as he gently floated off
in the north-westerly breeze, watched his rival's punctured balloon plunge to
the ground.

# JUNE 23

## ❀ 79: Vespasian, Roman Emperor
† *Cause of Death: Excessive Bathing*

Josephus writes how the sixty-nine-year-old Vespasian "died what appears to have been a natural death, from a stomach chill due to excessive bathing in the cold waters at Aquae Cutiliae near his birthplace" and that Titus, his son, "succeeded him without incident". No prizes for guessing how and where Titus died (*see* September 13).

# JUNE 24

## ❀ 1970: Man Singh II, maharaja of Jaipur
† *Cause of Death: Polo*

With a truly impressive handicap of 9, where 10 is "perfect", the maharaja was perhaps the greatest polo player of his time. His dream, he said, was to die "in a polo field, in the midst of a chukka, with my friends around me, my pony under me, my polo stick in my hand, and my boots on". And amazingly, this is exactly what came to pass on a rainy day at the Cirencester Park Polo Club. His body was flown to his beloved Jaipur where more than half a million people attended his funeral to say farewell to their much loved – and last – prince.

# JUNE 25

## ❀ 1218: Simon IV de Montfort, earl of Leicester
† *Cause of Death: Mangonel*

The mangonel was a sort of catapult – smaller and less accurate than its successor, the trebuchet – and was used in medieval sieges (usually by the attacking force) to sling large blocks of stone at immobile targets such as walls and bridges. Simon de Montfort was laying siege to Toulouse when a mangonel, operated (we are reliably informed) by some "girls and women" of the city, launched a boulder over its ramparts and hit Simon smack on the head.

## ❋ 1673: Charles, count d'Artagnan
† *Cause of Death: Musketeer*

Although D'Artagnan and his colleagues were called "musketeers", they are best known – thanks, in part, to the fiction of Alexander Dumas – as swashbuckling swordsmen. There is something rather fitting in the fact that during the Siege of Maastricht, as Charles, épée in hand, was acrobatically leaping across a narrow gorge, a musket ball should rip open his throat and stop him dead in his tracks.

## JUNE 26

## ❋ 1718: Alexis, tsarevich of Russia
† *Cause of Death: Knout*

Three forms of torture were prevalent in eighteenth-century Russia. Mild crimes resulted in being beaten with a small rod called a batog, while the most serious crimes could end up with the perpetrator being roasted on a spit. In between the two was the knout, a thick, hard whip about three and a half feet long which, when used with full vigour, would tear chunks of flesh from a criminal's back.

Prince Alexis, son of Peter the Great, was subjected to forty lashes of the knout for supposedly planning a coup against his father. Alexis confessed that he had spoken ill of his father but had been drunk at the time. This was enough for an ecclesiastical court to give Peter the Biblical authority – "Everyone that curseth his father or his mother shall surely be put to death" (Leviticus 20:9) – to kill his son. High-spirited accounts have Alexis being beheaded (one report has Peter himself wielding the axe) but the simplest explanation is the most likely, writes historian Robert Massie. "Forty strokes of the knout were sufficient to kill a robust, healthy man; Alexis was not robust."

## ❋ 1830: George IV, king of England
† *Cause of Death: Gastric Haemorrhage consequent upon Portal Hypertension, Cirrhosis of the Liver, Myocardial Degeneration with Old Pericarditis, Aortic Valvular Disease, Left Ventricular Hypertrophy, Chronic Bronchitis and Fundic Diverticulum of the Bladder with Calculus Formation.*

Don't be fooled by Dr Clifford Brewer's polysyllabic summary of George IV's pathology, which might suggest to some that the king fought courageously

against capricious diseases beyond his control. He didn't. The supersized monarch's entire life was one massive alcoholic, gastronomic and hedonistic binge, and he died, of his own making, a big fat bucket of lard.

## JUNE 27

❀ 1989: Sir Alfred Jules Ayer, British philosopher
† *Cause of Death: Chest Infection*

In 1965 Ayer was summoned to the deathbed of the novelist Somerset Maugham, who desperately sought reassurance that there was no afterlife. The famous philosopher and atheist duly put his mind at rest. A quarter of a century later, shortly before his own death from a chest infection, Ayer happened to choke on a piece of smoked salmon, and his heart stopped for some five minutes, during which he claimed to have had a near death experience. Dejectedly he confided to his doctor, "I saw a Divine Being. I'm afraid I'm going to have to revise all my books and opinions."

## JUNE 28

❀ 1349: Murad I, Ottoman sultan
† *Cause of Death: Milosh Obilic*

Two stories circulate as to the circumstances in which Serbian Milosh killed the sultan at the Battle of Kosovo. The first is that Milosh connived his way into the Turkish camp pretending to be a deserter and somehow slipped into the sultan's tent and stabbed him with a poisoned dagger. The second is that Murad, following his comprehensive victory, was triumphantly surveying the corpse-littered field, when Milosh, wounded but still very much alive, leaped up from among the dead and bumped him off. Either way, Milosh made mincemeat of Murad.

## JUNE 29

❀ 1520: Montezuma II, emperor of the Aztecs
† *Cause of Death: Stone*

For reasons that aren't particularly clear – perhaps he thought they were gods and thus invincible – Montezuma quietly surrendered to Cortés and his conquistadors and allowed himself to be imprisoned in his own palace. Most of his subjects, following his younger brother Cuitláhuac, refused to submit so placidly, and hurled themselves at the ramparts of their once great city of Cactus Rock. With far superior weaponry, the Spanish suggested to the man known as "The Great Talker" that he might want to speak to his people to prevent unnecessary bloodshed, and after initially grumbling that his men now considered him a "nobody", the emperor agreed. With great deliberation, he put on his ceremonial dress, painted his face in green, orange and white stripes, and went out and stood before his people.

On hearing their master's voice, some of the warriors laid down their arms and started to cry. Others, however, showed their fury at the man they now considered a traitor by throwing spears and rocks in his direction. One stone struck him hard on the head and he tottered backwards and into the arms of his captives, who carefully helped him back to his quarters. Deciding there was nothing to live for any more, Montezuma refused any medical attention and died three days later from the physical and emotional blow.

## JUNE 30

❀ 1670: Henrietta Anne, duchess of Orleans
† *Cause of Death: Peritonitis*

Paris: June 27, 1670
To: Thomas, Lord Clifford

> "This is the ferste letter I have ever write in inglis, you will eselay see it bi the stile and the ortografe … I expose myself to be thought a foulle in looking to make you know how much I am your frind."

Henrietta Anne's first letter in English was to be her last. Three days later, this younger sister of Charles II died following the perforation of a duodenal ulcer. Some suspected poison, but this is highly improbable. "Minette" as Charles called her, was simply a tender flower, plucked while in first bloom.

# JULY

## JULY 1

### ❁ 1681: Oliver Plunkett, Irish nobleman
† *Cause of Death: Rope and Butcher's Knife*

Plunkett was genuinely disappointed when his execution was postponed by a week, from June 24 to July 1. The main reason was that he thought it most suitable to die on the feast day of St John the Baptist (and like him be beheaded). As it was he was to be hanged, drawn and quartered on July 1, the feast day of St Simeon the Crazy, an eccentric Syrian hermit best known for his work with prostitutes. At least, Plunkett mused, it would still be a Friday.

The Roman Catholic Archbishop of Armagh met his end fearlessly, forgiving all those who participated in his unwarranted arrest for treason, his sham trial and his gruesome execution. Like that of St John the Baptist, the severed head of St Oliver (he was canonized in 1975) is a much revered relic. Rescued from a bonfire at Tyburn with only minor scorch marks, it is on display in St Peter's Church in Drogheda.

## JULY 2

### ❁ 2007: Gottfried, count of Bismarck-Schönhausen
† *Cause of Death: Excess*

Gottfried was a hell-raising, coke-snorting, pleasure-seeking, booze-swilling, cross-dressing playboy who had the unfortunate habit of throwing parties at which people ended up very much the worse for wear. A champagne-sated shindig at Oxford University (where he somehow managed to earn a third-class degree) turned sour when the young heiress Olivia Channon was found dead from an overdose. And another party, ten years later, finished abruptly when a man fell from the roof garden of the count's multi-million pound flat in Chelsea. The tabloids claimed that he had died during a drug-fuelled orgy – a claim that Gottfried denied until his dying day.

That day occurred within the year, by which time Gottfried's day job was, somewhat incongruously, promoting holiday packages to Uzbekistan.

# JULY 3

## ✿ 1582: James Crichton, Scottish nobleman
† *Cause of Death: Rapier*

James was the consummate polymath, brilliant at everything at which he tried his hand, be it riding, philosophy, mathematics or music. And he was rich and good-looking to boot. As such, he was given the soubriquet of "The Admirable Crichton" and, even at twenty-two, was considered the gold standard by which other men could gauge their abilities. Admiration was not the only emotion he engendered, however. Seething with splenetic envy, Vincenzo Gonzaga, the son of the Duke of Mantua, decided to bring this overachiever down a couple of notches.

James was strolling through Mantua's city streets one summer's night, when two men in disguise appeared out of nowhere and yelled at him to draw his sword. Thomas Wright, holidaying in the city, writes that one of the pair to pick the fight was Gonzaga, eager "to trie the Scots valour". Crichton's mastery at fencing was (of course) without equal. He quickly despatched Gonzaga's companion and then turned his attention to the other masked bandit, but stopped in his tracks when a terrified Vincenzo revealed his true identity. Wright tells us that Crichton then "fell downe upon his knees, demanding pardon at his hands, and gave the prince his naked rapier; who no sooner had received it, but with the same sword ran him thorow to death."

# JULY 4

## ✿ 1187: Raynald of Chatillon, Lord of Oultrejordain
† *Cause of Death: Bad Manners*

Raynald and King Guy of Jerusalem were sitting in a tent in the middle of the desert, dying for a drink. They were there as prisoners of Saladin, following the disastrous Battle of Hattin, and neither Crusader expected to live much longer. The sultan came in and catalogued how they had both violated agreements and broken promises. Death seemed imminent.

Proud of his reputation for chivalry, Saladin saw that both men were listless with thirst and had a servant give Guy a bowl of cool, refreshing water. Guy drank his fill, wiped his sleeve and then passed the bowl on to his parched and panting comrade. It was a "poisoned chalice". Saladin told them that he was shocked at their breach of etiquette and stormed out. Death remained imminent.

On his return, he explained that for Raynald not to request permission before drinking was the height of discourtesy. Saladin had the offender dragged before him and then, according to one eyewitness, "struck him between the neck and the shoulder-blade." For Guy, death must have seemed a certainty, but after a while he was allowed to go home. "Kings don't kill kings," Saladin explained.

# JULY 5

## ❈ 1764: Ivan VI, tsar of Russia
† *Cause of Death: Guards*

A mildly deranged Ukrainian army officer finagled his way into the dungeons of the fortress at Schlüsselburg, and tried to liberate "nameless prisoner Number 1", as Ivan was officially known. The tsar's gaolers killed the officer in a trice and then turned their daggers on their anonymous but precious charge.

## ❈ 2006: Tu'ipelehake and Kaimana, prince and princess of Tonga
† *Cause of Death: Mustang*

Eighteen-year-old Edith Delgado from Redwood City, California, was burning rubber down Highway 101 in her dad's Ford Mustang. One witness reported how the teenager, travelling in excess of 80 mph, tried to "shoot the gap" between two cars ... but miscalculated and sideswiped a red 4x4. The clipped Ford Explorer cartwheeled crazily before ending up on its roof, and despite wearing seatbelts, all three occupants – the royal couple and their driver – were killed. Edith Delgado was sentenced to two years imprisonment for vehicular manslaughter.

# JULY 6

## ❋ 1189: Henry II, king of England
† *Cause of Death: Depression*

Henry reluctantly signed a peace treaty with King Philip Augustus of France, but as he set off on Crusade, was damned if he wasn't going to make those who sided with the enemy pay for their treachery. Pausing at Chinon in France, he made Master Roger, the Keeper of the Seal, copy out the names of those who had deserted his cause. "Sire," Master Roger glumly reported, "the first name on the roll is that of your son, John."

HENRY II.

For Henry, who was predisposed to bouts of manic depression, this was the last straw. "You have said enough," the king replied and, trembling like a leaf, turned over in his bed, cursed the day he had been born, and died.

## ❋ 1758: George, Lord Howe
† *Cause of Death: Lousy French Accent*

At the outset of the British invasion of French Canada, Howe led a troop of about 200 men on a reconnaissance mission at the north end of Lake George. As the party passed in front of a thick-wooded copse, a voice from within shouted "Qui vive?" ("Who goes there?") In reply, a voice, probably belonging to a member of the First Connecticut regiment, said something like "Freeaansaaay". The small group of French soldiers hidden in the wood wasn't fooled for a moment and opened fire. As luck would have it, one of their bullets slammed into Howe, who collapsed and died almost instantly.

His untimely passing meant that the war would not be led by a thoughtful, strategic mind, but by that belonging to Lord Abercrombie, the military equivalent of an old duffer. An officer ruefully noted that the offensive was over almost before it began. "The death of one man," he remarked, "was the ruin of fifteen thousand."

# JULY 7

## ❀ 1307: Edward I, king of England
† *Cause of Death: Dysentery*

Edward led a charmed life: when he was a boy, falling masonry missed him by inches; while on Crusade a would-be assassin scratched him in the forehead with his dagger, but his wife Eleanor of Castile was on hand to suck out any poison; and when he was laying siege to Stirling Castle in 1304, a crossbowman fired a shot from the ramparts that ripped through his clothing but then lodged harmlessly in his saddle.

Edward's death was anything but charming. Suffering from a horrendous form of dysentery (some suggest it was cancer of the rectum), he resorted to unorthodox medicine to stave off the Grim Reaper. He drank pomegranate wine and a potion that included amber, jacinth and musk. He took herbal baths. He ate sugar rosettes made with coral and pearl. Nothing worked and he died, a mess, while travelling north towards Scotland, his lifelong enemy.

## ❀ 1930: Sir Arthur Conan Doyle, author
† *Cause of Death: Illicit Gardening*

On March 15, 1897, Conan Doyle met and fell in love with Jean Leckie, the beautiful daughter of a wealthy city trader. During those first few hours together, he gave her a snowdrop as a token of his affection, and for the next decade – while remaining married to his sick wife Louise – he secretly sent Jean a snowdrop on the same date each year. Following Louise's death, he married Jean, and continued to show his love for her with his unusual floral "anniversary present".

March 15, 1930, started cold and cheerless. Although confined to his bed with angina, Sir Arthur worked his way into his dressing gown and stole out into his garden. A few minutes later, the butler heard a crash in the hallway. He found his master crumpled on the floor, clutching his chest with one hand and a snowdrop with the other.

The creator of Sherlock Holmes remained bedridden for the rest of his life. His last written words were for his adoring public. "The reader will judge that I have had many adventures. The greatest and most glorious awaits me now." His last spoken words were reserved solely for his wife. "You are wonderful," he whispered.

## JULY 8

❁ 1898: Soapy Smith, "King of the Frontier Con-Men"
† *Cause of Death: 1 of the 101*

Jefferson Smith was the most slippery of swindlers, basing his criminal operations initially in Colorado and later in Alaska during the Klondike Gold Rush. From such simple cons as the "shell-game" and "three-card monte" to more elaborate hoaxes like rigged poker games and fraudulent lotteries, he did his best to separate a gold-digger from his gold.

The good folk of Skagway eventually had enough of the man known as "King Con" and "The King of Frontier Con-Men" and formed a vigilante group – "The Committee of 101" – to put an end to his racket. Soapy learned that they were holding a private meeting on Juneau Wharf and hurried there to put forward his case, with a .44 Winchester rifle in hand to press his point home. As he stormed up the boardwalk, a man called Frank Reid blocked his way, brandishing a revolver. The two men argued, scuffled, fired their guns and fell, and the committee headed home, their mission accomplished earlier than they had expected.

## JULY 9

❁ 1746: Philip V, king of Spain
† *Cause of Death: Madness*

According to the diplomat Benjamin Keene, Philip was "disordered in the head" as early as 1738. Manifestations of his malady included

1.  His timetable. Philip woke up at noon, heard Mass at 3, conducted any matters of state in the early hours of the morning and went to bed after a dawn supper.
2.  His silence. Philip padded around his palace without a sound, in the belief he was already dead.

3. His lack of hygiene. Philip did not wash for six years, and when he really did die, his servants had a devil of a time trying to peel his clothes away from his body.

# JULY 10

## ✽ 1559: Henry II, king of France
† *Cause of Death: Lance*

Henry enjoyed all sports but absolutely loved jousting, and wouldn't allow anyone to go easy on him just because he was king. During a five-day tournament to celebrate a couple of royal marriages, he faced Gabriel de Montgommery, captain of the Scottish guards. In the first pass Henry was almost unseated. In the second, the two contestants charged at each other like men possessed and both shattered their lances on the other's shield. As he lifted up what remained of his weapon, Montgommery somehow unhinged and flipped up Henry's visor, and drove a long splinter of wood into the king's forehead. Henry immediately fainted from what was ultimately a fatal wound, but regained consciousness to forgive Montgommery for what was clearly an accident and to commend him for his valour.

*Jousting.*

## ✽ 1920: Jackie Fisher, baron of Kilverstone
† *Cause of Death: Cancer*

The First Sea Lord's funeral instructions were found on a single sheet of paper in an envelope marked "Private: To be opened when necessary":

> The nearest cemetery
> No flowers
> No one invited except relatives
> No mourning

For once, his orders were not obeyed. Three days later Westminster Abbey was filled to the rafters as a nation paid its last respects to a man widely held to be the greatest admiral since Nelson.

# JULY 11

❋ 1665: Sir Kenelm Digby, English nobleman
† *Cause of Death: Fever*

Richard Ferrar recorded in verse how Sir Kenelm was born, won a naval victory in the Adriatic off what is now Iskenderun in modern-day Turkey, and died, all on the same date:

> Born on the day he died, th'eleventh of June
> On which he fought bravely at Scanderoon
> 'Tis rare that one and self-same day should be
> His day of birth, of death, of victory.

Poetic quality aside, there is the small problem that Digby actually died on th'eleventh of July.

# JULY 12

❋ 1926: Gertrude Bell, English noblewoman
† *Cause of Death: Dial*

One of Britain's most intrepid agents in Arabia took a no-nonsense approach to life. Following a trip to England during which she learned that her family's fortunes were in a parlous state, and that both she and her brother were terminally ill, she took her life – and death – into her own hands. Back in Baghdad, after an evening swim with some friends, Gertrude went home and told her maid that she was going to bed, and that on no account was she to be woken up until the next morning. As she had planned, there was no next morning. Her death certificate recorded that she had died of "Dial poisoning" – "Dial" being the common name for diallylbarbituric acid, a highly potent sedative.

## JULY 13

❀ **1842: Ferdinand Philip, duke of Orleans**
† *Cause of Death: Coach Crash*

It was on the aptly named Rue de la Revolte on the outskirts of Paris that the duke's horses bolted. With his carriage careering out of control, there was little he could do but leap out and hope for the best, but unfortunately he landed with the worst possible result. Horrified onlookers carried his rag doll of a body to a nearby grocer's where he passed away between the peas and carrots.

## JULY 14

❀ **1824: Kamehameha II, king of Hawaii**
† *Cause of Death: Measles*

Nervous about American designs on his islands, Kamehameha boarded a whaling vessel with his wife Kumamalu and sailed to England to ask King George IV for help. The ship may have been smelly but it did have cabins spacious enough to cater the sizeable king and his equally sizeable queen. They arrived some six months later in an England, and among a metropolitan glitterati, that had never seen the like of their Pacific visitors and revelled in their curious customs and colourful clothing. For their part, the royal couple couldn't get enough of city life, especially the theatre, which they attended as often as possible.

But then the measles struck. Like the rest of her nation, Kumamalu had no resistance to the white man's disease and soon perished. Repeating his late wife's name to the end, Kamehameha soon slipped into a coma as well, and died a few days later. The couple then made the return journey to Hawaii. Their transport, a royal navy frigate, was certainly a step up from a whaling ship, but their accommodation – the storage hold – was more basic.

## JULY 15

✿ 1685: James, duke of Monmouth
† *Cause of Death: Axe*

Jack Ketch, the executioner at Tower Hill, had a bad day at the office. It is said that it took several blows – one report says eight – to sever Monmouth's head from his body. This botch job made piecing the duke's body back together again all the more cumbersome, but piece it back together they did when it was realised that he had never sat for an official portrait. Traitor he may have been, but he had still been the son of a king, Charles II, and a proper painting was required. Accordingly they exhumed the body, dressed it in fine clothes, and painstakingly sewed the head back on, so the duke could pose for posterity.

## JULY 16

✿ 1546: Anne Askew, English noblewoman
† *Cause of Death: Flames*

Martin Luther would have been proud of his disciple who campaigned against Catholicism with such fervour and, when tortured on the rack in the Tower of London, refused to divulge the names of any fellow Protestants. King Henry VIII's Lord Chancellor, Thomas Wriothesley, personally oversaw her ordeal – the only time such a punishment was meted out in the Tower to a woman – and, as evidenced by her ability to write letters home, may have lessened the agony a smidge. It was agony enough, however, for her to be unable to walk, and she was carried to the stake at Smithfield where, according to ecclesiastic historian Thomas Fuller, she "went to heaven in a chariot of fire".

## JULY 17

✿ 1676: Marie-Madeleine-Marguerite, marquise de Brinvilliers
† *Cause of Death: Two Questions and a Blade*

The marchioness just couldn't help poisoning people. First she poisoned her father, brother and two sisters, and then, when she visited the poor in hospital, she would slip them some poison too. For her extraordinary behaviour, she was given an extraordinary punishment.

First there was the "Ordinary Question". This entailed de Brinvilliers being stripped naked and stretched backwards over a wooden trestle, with her ankles attached to a ring on the floor and her hands chained to rings on the wall behind her. Then ten pints of water – in two-pint units called "coquemards" – were poured through a cow's horn down her gullet. Then came the "Extraordinary Question", where the trestle legs were extended so her body was even more arched and contorted. Again ten pints were funnelled into her.

A few hours later, a tumbrel rolled her to the Place de Grève where, in front of tens of thousands of onlookers, the executioner painstakingly shaved her head and then, in a flash of steel, severed it from the rest of her body. At first, nobody was quite sure if she had actually been executed, since her body appeared perfectly intact. But it was soon evident that the executioner had done an expert job. In the slight breeze, the head slowly wobbled and fell to the floor.

## ❁ 1918: Nicholas II, tsar of Russia
† *Cause of Death: Bolsheviks*

The ex-tsar and his family were hurried down to the basement of their prison-house in Yekaterinburg on the pretence that they might be under attack. Once there, the "house commander" read out the death sentence, and assured them all there was no hope. A moment of dumbfounded silence followed. Nicholas then rose from his chair and asked "Wha...?" but was abruptly shot before he could say any more. His wife, their five children and four members of the household were then quickly shot or speared with bayonets, and their bodies were carted off to a disused mine for disposal.

## JULY 18

## ❁ 1918: Sergei, grand duke of Russia
† *Cause of Death: More Bolsheviks*

Lenin's eradication of the Romanovs continued into a second day.

As he and several members of his family were being driven away to be murdered, Sergei knew it was pointless to plead for mercy. Instead he asked his guards a rhetorical question. "We are all going to die. But tell me why? I have never been involved in politics in my life. I like sports for heaven's sake! I play billiards!

*Grand duke Sergei, tossed down Shaft Number 7.*

I collect coins!" Unmoved, his captors shot him and threw him down Shaft Number 7 of a disused mine outside the town of Alapayevsk. The remainder of the family was then tossed down the shaft alive. Some survived the sixty-foot fall and began singing hymns. The Bolsheviks lobbed in grenades.

## JULY 19

❋ 1850: Margaret Fuller, marchioness Ossoli
† *Cause of Death: Shipwreck*

A feisty Boston-born bluestocking who made a name for herself as a journalist on the *New York Tribune*, Margaret sailed to Europe to meet the literary greats of the time. She drank tea with Carlyle and Wordsworth in England, sipped coffee with George Sand in Paris, and discussed poetry over a glass of wine in Italy with Robert and Elizabeth Barrett Browning. While in Rome she also met and later married the young, handsome, though penniless marquis Angelo Ossoli.

With her husband, Margaret became a republican activist, and while in self-imposed exile in Florence, wrote a definitive history of the unsuccessful "Roman Revolution". The couple, together with their small son Angelino, then set sail for America to find a publisher, but it was an ill-fated trip. The captain died of smallpox and just one day away from docking in New York, their ship foundered in a storm off Fire Island. The little boy's body was washed ashore but the marquis, his American bride and her manuscript were never seen again.

# JULY 20

## ❋ 1951: William, crown prince of the German empire
† *Cause of Death: Camels*

Care packages of silk underwear, champagne and caviar did little to raise William's spirits. Having forfeited the family estates in Brandenburg – lands that represented centuries of Prussian and German dominion – the son of the Kaiser lived out his post-war years in a rented house in faraway Hechingen. Lonely, disillusioned and utterly defeated, he took to the bottle and chain-smoked his way through box upon box of Camel cigarettes. His only pleasure was to sit with his shepherd dog Argo in the garden of the town's castle, and gaze over the Swabian countryside, puffing his way to oblivion.

# JULY 21

## ❋ 1719: Mary Louise Elizabeth, duchess of Berry
† *Cause of Death: Gluttony*

- ❀ Plump at 18, Mary preferred sedentary pursuits.
- ❀ Obese at 19, when she said she could eat a horse, she meant it.
- ❀ Bulbous at 20, she was so heavy she couldn't mount a horse.
- ❀ Elephantine at 21, she drank her peers under the table.
- ❀ Gargantuan at 22, she rarely got up from the table.
- ❀ Spherical at 23, she devoted the rest of her life to gluttony.
- ❀ Dead at 24, her coroner recorded that she ate herself to death.

## ❋ 1723: Anthony Grey, Baron Lucas
† *Cause of Death: Ear*

Anthony Grey, commonly styled "Earl Harold" was Lord of the Bedchamber to King George II, and had a promising career ahead of him when he "choked to death on an ear of barley he inadvertently put in his mouth".

## JULY 22

❀ 1274: Henry I, king of Navarre
† *Cause of Death: Fat*

"Henry the Fat", also known as "Enrique el Gordo" and "Henri le Gros" was really, really fat. How fat? He was so fat that he suffocated to death on his own fat.

❀ 1461: Charles VII, king of France
† *Cause of Death: Starvation*

A terrible mouth infection meant that Charles couldn't eat a sausage, or anything else for that matter, and soon he found himself receiving the last rites. According to the *Chronique Martinienne*, he asked what day it was, to which his councillors replied that it was St Mary Magdalene's Day. Charles nodded and whispered that it was only fitting that he, the greatest male sinner of all time, should die on the feast day of the greatest female sinner.

## JULY 23

❀ 1942: Andrew Ducat, player at Lord's
† *Cause of Death: Yorker*

Ducat squeaks into this "noble" book because his surname derives from the Latin word for "duke", and he died while in the middle at "Lord's," the home of cricket.

One of the few men to represent England in both cricket and football, his one Test appearance is notable for his double dismissal with the same delivery. Fast bowler Ted Macdonald fired in a humdinger that disintegrated Ducat's bat and the ball ballooned to slip and was caught. A splinter from his former bat, meanwhile, spun onto the stumps and dislodged a bail.

His death came during a morale-boosting wartime match between the Home Guard teams of Sussex and Surrey. He had reached 29 when he chopped his bat down on a Yorker. As the ball rolled harmlessly to mid-on, Ducat gasped and crumpled to the crease as if he had been felled by a beamer. His fellow batsman gave his heart a couple of thumps and took out his false teeth, but to no avail. At 56, it had been a decent, if not a long innings.

## JULY 24

❋ 1568: Carlos, prince of Spain
† *Cause of Death: Blow to the Head*

While up at university, Carlos fell downstairs. The story goes that he was chasing the daughter of a porter when he tripped, took a tumble and smashed his head against a door. From that day on, he became, to put it mildly, a little odd. His behaviour included:

- ❊ Roaming the streets of Madrid randomly kissing girls.
- ❊ Sitting really, really close to a fire for hours and then rushing off and have a long cold shower.
- ❊ Interspersing hunger strikes with bouts of gluttony.
- ❊ Shovelling ice down his bed in hot weather
- ❊ Wearing oversize boots in which he kept a pair of pistols.

Finally, after launching himself upon a senior official with his dagger, he had to be confined to his chambers, where he died aged 23.

## JULY 25

❋ 1643: Robert, earl of Kingston upon Hull
† *Cause of Death: Slipping out of Neutral*

Refusing to lend his support to either cause during the English Civil War, Robert told both parties that "when ... I take arms with the King against Parliament, or with the Parliament against the King, let a cannonball divide me between them". No sooner had he professed his neutrality, however, than he was seen leading a royalist force in the capture of the Lincolnshire town of Gainsborough.

Roundheads quickly retook the position and were rowing him to a prison across the Humber when his boat was smashed to kindling ... by a royalist cannonball.

## JULY 26

### ✿ 1680: John, earl of Rochester
† *Cause of Death: Excess*

Dr Alexander Bendo opened up a surgery in London's busy Tower Street specialising in skin disorders. He quickly developed a reputation for dispensing bizarre medical advice and conducting abnormally in-depth physical examinations, especially if his patients were young women, and it wasn't long before "Dr Bendo" was discovered to be none other than John Wilmot, the earl of Rochester, the most dissolute member of the court of King Charles II.

Wilmot's own body was hardly a picture of health. A lifetime of debauchery (by his own admission he had not been sober for five years) had left it completely clapped out, and when he took to his bed, senior churchmen waved their fingers at him and warned him to prepare to meet his Maker. To their surprise, he did. Wilmot read Bishop Gilbert Burnet's *History of the Reformation* and, between increasingly shallow breaths, held theological discussions with the author. The bishop left his dying "patient" to tell Wilmot's concerned friends that even though the earl's body was unsalvageable, his soul was in a healthier condition than one might have expected.

## JULY 27

### ✿ 1828: Radama I, king of Madagascar
† *Cause of Death: Excess*

Christian missionaries were delighted when Radama allowed them into his country to share their faith with the Malagasy heathen, but were deeply frustrated that the king's personal response to the story of the crucifixion was not one of thanksgiving for God's saving grace, but a practical interest in the novel form of execution. They were similarly frustrated at his encouragement of vast public orgies on days of royal celebration, and at his habit of sleeping with any girl who took his fancy. At least they could take some comfort in their one small victory – his decree that the only music his band could play on the Sabbath was "God save the King".

Radama died in his thirties, sozzled with drink and riddled with disease.

## JULY 28

### ❀ 1835: Edward, duke of Treviso
† *Cause of Death: Infernal Machine*

Edward was one of Napoleon's finest generals, but following the Restoration, loyally served King Louis-Philippe as ambassador and president of the council of ministers. He was with the monarch on a busy Parisian street corner when a bullet from an "infernal machine" scythed him down. The machine – also called a ribauldequin – was a contraption made up of twenty gun barrels that fired simultaneously, and considered by some as a precursor of the machine gun. It had been fired by a deranged criminal called Giuseppe Fieschi who managed to kill a dozen people but somehow missed his main target.

## JULY 29

### ❀ 1108: Philip I, king of France
† *Cause of Death: Bertrade*

William of Malmesbury describes Bertrade de Montfort as "charming to men" and she certainly had a Circe-like effect upon Philip. After marrying him in 1092 – even though they both were already married – she sapped him of so much energy that he gave up on all affairs of state, and allowed the country to go to ruin. Of greater concern to the contemporary Abbot Suger was that he allowed the Church to go to ruin too. Simony was rife. The Bishop of Beauvais, for example, was an illiterate drunk, the Abbot of Saint Medard de Soissons an embezzler, and the abbot of St Denis a sensualist who tortured anyone who complained about it.

Philip also allowed himself to go to ruin, growing fatter and fatter until, as Suger neatly puts it, he "ceased to be king, breathing his last breath at the castle of Melun-sur-Seine". And what of Bertrade? According William of Malmesbury, she became a nun, "pleasing to God, and like an angel".

## JULY 30

❀ 1683: Maria Theresa, queen consort of France
† *Cause of Death: Tumour*

As long as she had her collection of dwarves, her hot chocolate and someone to play cards with, Maria Theresa was happy to ignore the multiple mistresses of her husband, Louis XIV. For his part, the king found life with his dumpy queen to be rather comforting, even though her statement "Let them eat cake" (wrongly attributed to Marie Antoinette) did ruffle a few feathers. When she died (a tumour in her armpit suggests some form of cancer) Louis remarked, "This is the only way in which she has displeased me."

## JULY 31

❀ 1944: Antoine de Saint-Exupery, French nobleman
† *Cause of Death: Plane Crash*

> "What! You dropped down from the sky?"
> "Yes," I answered, modestly.
> "Oh! That is funny!"

Saint-Exupery left us with a fable and a mystery. The fable is his bestselling work, *The Little Prince*, the story of the encounter between a little boy and an airman who has crash-landed his plane. The mystery is the circumstances of his death. We now know that that the plane he was piloting on a reconnaissance mission plunged into the Mediterranean, but the question of why remains unanswered. There are currently three theories doing the rounds. First, his American P-38 Lightning suffered catastrophic engine failure. Second, a German Messerschmitt pilot shot him down (an eighty-eight-year-old former aviator recently came forward claiming he was to blame). Third – and a suggestion that his family are understandably keen to dismiss – he committed suicide. A natural tendency to melancholy, a failed marriage, increasing ill-health and what he considered Europe's miserable post-war prospects perhaps all contributed to his dropping from the sky.

# AUGUST

## AUGUST I

✤ 1714: Anne, queen of England
† *Cause of Death: Lupus*

When she was a child, Anne was a slip of a thing, but by her late thirties, she had ballooned into a gargantuan mass of blubber. The doctors of the time were at a loss to explain how their petite princess had swollen into a jumbo queen. Many suspected her to be a closet binge drinker and dubbed her "Brandy Nan". Today we know her condition to have been lupus erythematosus, a disease in which the immune system goes into overdrive. As the lupus developed, so Anne piled on the pounds, and when she died her coffin was almost square.

## AUGUST 2

✤ 1100: William II, king of England
† *Cause of Death: Arrow*

"Shoot damn you!" barked William Rufus to his hunting companion William Tyrrel as a stag leaped out from a New Forest thicket. Tyrrel dutifully shot. Unfortunately for the two Williams (but fortunately for an England with nothing but contempt for its monarch) the arrow fizzed past its target, ricocheted off a tree and slammed into the king's chest. A shocked Rufus snapped off the shaft, only to faint and fall on the rest of the arrow, making things a lot worse. Tyrrel raced to his side, saw the damage and raced away to the Continent, never to be seen again.

❋ 1589: Henry III, king of France
† *Cause of Death: Monk*

Wearing nothing more than a pair of breeches and a dressing gown, Henry had his first audience of the day with a Dominican monk, who was wearing nothing more than a white habit. The monk, a fanatical Jacobin who considered Henry a monster and an enemy of the Church, drew a knife from his sleeve and plunged it into the king's belly.

## AUGUST 3

❋ 1460: James II, king of Scotland
† *Cause of Death: Cannon*

While laying siege to Roxburgh Castle, James was standing rather too close to one of his newfangled cannons when, according to Robert Lindsay of Pitscottie, "his thigh-bone was dug into two with a piece of misframed gun that broke in shooting, by which he was stricken to the ground and died hastily".

❋ 1916: Sir Roger Casement, revolutionary
† *Cause of Death: Comma*

In her book *Eats, Shoots and Leaves*, Lynne Truss shows us how a misplaced comma can significantly alter the meaning of a sentence. Prosecutors of Roger Casement demanded that a comma that wasn't there should be "read into" the medieval Treason Act, thus smoothing the way for the British diplomat turned Irish Republican to be tried for activities against the crown, even though they were not conducted on British soil. Casement was found guilty and famously "hanged by a comma" for his crimes.

## AUGUST 4

❋ 1578: Sebastian, king of Portugal
† *Cause of Death: High Visibility*

A strict Jesuit education left Sebastian convinced that his mission in life was to be Christ's captain in a crusade against the African Muslims, and as soon as he was of age, he started to make plans for a campaign in Morocco. It was an utterly mad idea, fuelled by obsession for military glory rather than by reason, and everyone tried to talk him out of it. Despite the protestations, a Portuguese force led by the king landed on African soil and headed inland to engage with Muslim troops from the city of Fez.

It is here that historical fact and legend blur. In the ensuing battle it is widely recorded that Sebastian deliberately dressed in green armour in order that he might be clearly visible to one and all. Awed by such recklessness, the enemy repeatedly promised to spare his life if he would surrender. But the king refused ... and was duly hacked down.

Or was he? A cult has evolved around "Sebastian the Madman" with many believing that he cheated death and will one day return to claim the Portuguese throne. Over the centuries a bevy of pretenders have maintained that they were Sebastian. All have been examined, and all have been dismissed as complete nutcases.

# AUGUST 5

## ❋ 1881: Spotted Tail, Sioux chief
† *Cause of Death: Crow Dog*

An idealistic dove in a time of hawkish distrust, Spotted Tail advocated accommodation with the white settlers, but his dreams of peaceful coexistence were shattered when the US government drove his people off their traditional hunting grounds and onto reservations. On one such reservation, Spotted Tail was assassinated by a fellow Sioux called Crow Dog, widely acknowledged as being an agent for the Bureau of Indian Affairs, an organisation bent on toppling any semblance of an Indian powerbase once and for all.

❀ **1962: Norma, queen of the artichokes**
† *Cause of Death: Barbiturates*

In 1948, a photogenic twenty-one-year-old called Norma Jeane Mortensen was crowned "Queen of the Artichokes" at a festival in the Californian town of Castroville. Fifteen years later, Marilyn Monroe, sex bomb and queen of the silver screen, died in her Los Angeles mansion from an overdose of sleeping pills. The scant details from her post-mortem have fuelled speculation that she did not kill herself – accidentally or otherwise – but that she was murdered on government orders. One undisputed detail about her death has been immortalised in Elton John's tribute song "Candle in the Wind". Marilyn was found in the nude.

## AUGUST 6

❀ **2006: Christoph von Hohenlohe, European prince**
† *Cause of Death: Poor Penmanship*

Millionaire playboy Christoph "Kiko" von Hohenlohe spent his last days at the Bangkok Hilton – not the hotel, you understand, but the notorious city jail where up to forty prisoners share a cell of unspeakable squalor. Just how von Hohenlohe ended up checking into the Klongprem Central Prison (and never checking out) is a bit of a mystery. It seems that the jet-setting Lichtenstein nobleman had flown to Thailand to lose some weight at an exclusive health spa. When he realised that he had stayed a few days longer in the country than his tourist visa allowed, he temporarily lost his senses, took out his biro and changed the departure date in his passport from July 20 to July 29. At Bangkok airport, a trim, fragrant and tanned Kiko tried to board a plane for Hawaii, but officials spotted the alteration and hauled him off to the "hotel", where the heat, stench and filth proved too much.

## AUGUST 7

❀ **1817: Pierre du Pont, French nobleman**
† *Cause of Death: Exhaustion*

The aristocratic du Pont family escaped Napoleonic France and settled in America on the banks of Delaware's Brandywine River, where they invested in a couple of gunpowder factories. A fire in a charcoal house nearly put an end to their commercial aspirations, but the entire clan, including the frail seventy-seven-year-old Pierre, pulled together and managed to extinguish the flames. Such exertions came at a cost, though, with Pierre (or "Bon-Papa" as he was affectionately called) suddenly falling into a coma from which he never awoke. The du Pont business, on the other hand, went from strength to strength to become one of the world's leading industrial companies.

## AUGUST 8

❀ 1821: Caroline, queen of Brunswick
† *Cause of Death: Humiliation*

Banned from court she may have been, banned from going to her former husband's coronation she may have been, but Caroline could not be banned from taking in a show. At the end of a performance at the Drury Lane Theatre – a re-enactment of George IV's big day – she curtsied to her fellow theatre-goers and then suddenly doubled up in pain. Her doctor, Henry Holland, was sure her stomach ailment was psychosomatic – brought on by the public humiliation of having the doors of Westminster Abbey literally slammed in her face – and prescribed regular doses of calomel, topped up with "a quantity of castor oil that would have turned the stomach of a horse." It didn't work.

Surprisingly large crowds lined the streets as her coffin made its journey from London to Harwich and on to Germany. Public perception, as opposed to the judgement of those in power, was yes, as Princess of Wales, Caroline may have gossiped too much, flirted too much, and eaten too many raw onions for polite society, but she was a royal, nevertheless, and deserved a good send-off.

## AUGUST 9

❀ 1250: Eric IV, king of Denmark
† *Cause of Death: Axe*

Danish peasants shook their heads in disbelief at Eric's crippling tax on ploughs and many joined Abel, duke of Schleswig, in his rebellion against their king. One evening some of the duke's men grabbed Eric, threw him into a dinghy and rowed him out into the middle of a river. Eric soon realised that this was no fishing trip and asked, since he was about to die, to make his confession to a priest. The ruffians duly rowed him back to shore and found a minister. They then rowed their prisoner – now in a state of grace – back into the middle of the river and chopped his head off.

Abel, who just happened to be Eric's brother, denied any part in the murder, but those Danes with a working knowledge of the Book of Genesis knew a regicide when they saw one and nodded sagely to each other, saying "Abel by name, Cain by nature".

# AUGUST 10

## ✸ 1759: Ferdinand VI, king of Spain
† *Cause of Death: Grief*

Horribly fat, hideously ugly and horrendously asthmatic (William Coxe more kindly describes her as "homely"), Barbara of Portugal was well past her sell-by-date, but from the moment his wife died, Ferdinand lost interest in living. He slumped back to his palace and refused to eat, sleep, wash, shave or even change his clothes. Wearing nothing but a filthy nightshirt, he would roam the corridors begging his servants to give him a lethal dose of poison, and when they refused, he would beat them. Once he tried to stab himself with a pair of household scissors but just hurt his chest. With a quick and dramatic suicide clearly denied him, he sank into a melancholic stupor and died of "natural causes" almost a year after his bride.

# AUGUST 11

## ✸ 480 BC: Leonidas, king of Sparta
† *Cause of Death: Desire for Glory*

Leonidas was one of 299 Spartans to die at the Battle of Thermopylae. Supported by forces from other Greek city states, he withstood an immense army of some 250,000 Persians under the command of Xerxes for two days, until they were outmanoeuvred and overpowered. Before they were completely surrounded, most of the Greeks headed home, leaving a token force comprising a thousand or so Thespians and Helots and the king's 300 elite bodyguards (all with sons, so when they died their name would be carried on) to fight for their honour. Rather than passively submit to the inevitable, these warriors took the game to the enemy. They attacked with spears, and when their spears shattered, with swords, and when their swords shattered, with their bare hands. And to the last man, they died.

Three hundred Spartans initially took to the field with their king, and in a way all three hundred were casualties of the lopsided encounter. Of the two survivors of the battle itself, Aristodemus (who was sent back to Sparta because of a serious eye infection) redeemed his honour by fighting and dying like a true hero in a later battle, while Pantites (who had taken a message to Thessaly and returned too late to take part) hanged himself, unable to suffer the disgrace of being considered a "trembler".

# AUGUST 12

## ✿ 30 BC: Cleopatra VII, queen of Egypt
✝ *Cause of Death: Naja haje?*

You just can't make a reluctant snake bite you, but in the absence of any credible alternative, we have to believe the accounts of Cassius Dio, Plutarch and others, who claim that Cleopatra smuggled an asp into her chambers and held it to her breast. The snake (the *naje haje* or Egyptian cobra, is particularly venomous for those considering such an exotic exit) dutifully bit her, and the queen serenely bit the dust. The accommodating cobra then bit the queen's two maids, so that when Octavian's men burst into her bedroom, they found three women sprawled *in extremis* on or beside the bed. Libyan snake charmers called psylli, specialists in sucking out venom, did their best, but Cleopatra was history.

*Augustus Caesar finds Cleopatra.*

## ❀ 1676: Philip, sachem of the Wampanaog
† *Cause of Death: Alderman*

In the misguided belief that he was docile and subservient, British settlers conferred an English name upon "Metacom", the tribal chief of a region comprising the south of modern-day New England. To their chagrin, they found that Philip was in fact the William Wallace of the Eastern Seaboard, and were forced to hire local native men to track the rebel down.

The biblically knowledgeable Colonel Benjamin Church was on hand when "Alderman", an informer from the Awashonk tribe, found his prey. A terrified Philip, he recounted, wearing nothing but his breeches and moccasins, plunged into a nearby swamp, whereupon Alderman chased after him and shot him twice "where Joab thrust his darts into rebellious Absolom". The sachem was dead before he sank into the mud. His body, "a doleful, great naked dirty beast", was lugged out of the bog, and then (mirroring the final fate of traitors like Wallace) beheaded and quartered "like as Agog was hewn to pieces before the Lord". Philip's head was displayed on a pole in Plymouth, Massachusetts, for nearly a quarter of a century. One of his hands was given to Alderman, who preserved it in rum and, for a small fee, would show it to curious new arrivals from England.

## ❀ 1822: Robert Stewart, Viscount Castlereagh
† *Cause of Death: Letter Opener*

Terrified that he was going to be "outed" as a homosexual, Britain's Foreign Secretary went home, took a letter opener from a desk drawer and sliced through his carotid artery. The government declared that at the moment he took his own life he was temporarily insane, and consequently eligible for a state funeral. It was not a popular decision. Hundreds jeered as the funeral cortege passed by, and cheered as the coffin was carried into Westminster Abbey. A little while later, Lord Byron summed up a nation's contempt when he wrote this mock epitaph for the viscount's grave:

> Posterity will ne'er survey
> A nobler grave than this:
> Here lie the bones of Castlereagh
> Stop, traveller, and piss.

## AUGUST 13

❀ 1958: Otto I, king of Albania
† *Cause of Death: Cirrhosis of the Liver*

Otto Witte was a member of a circus troupe travelling through the politically chaotic Balkans just prior to the First World War. He was an acrobat and a juggler but above all a master of illusion; when a sword-swallowing colleague suggested that, with his white hair and bushy moustache, he was the spitting image of one of the candidates for the leadership of the newly independent Albania, Otto decided to work a little magic of his own. Telegrams, purportedly from Constantinople, arrived in the city of Dorazzo claiming that Prince Halim Eddine was on his way to claim the throne, and a few days later, Otto rode into town dressed to the nines in fancy-dress regalia borrowed from his workmates. The people of Durazzo were completely taken in, and were so delighted with his suggestion that his army might soon attack Belgrade, that they immediately crowned him king. In an act of true humility to his many European subjects, the Turkish prince chose the regnal name of Otto.

For a few days everything went swimmingly. King Otto I set all prisoners free and enjoyed the privileges of his position, including his harem of twenty-five girls. But then genuine cables started to arrive from Constantinople, and Albania's first monarch, his pockets stuffed with gold, quietly left for his native Germany, where he died after a long, happy and comfortable retirement.

## AUGUST 14

❀ 1464: Aeneas Piccolomini, Italian nobleman
† *Cause of Death: Gout*

Aeneas Silvyus Piccolomini, born of noble though impoverished Sienese stock, liked a rude joke as much as the next man, was the father to two illegitimate children, and wrote an obscene play called *Chrysis* and an erotic novel called *The Tale of Two Lovers*. Bawdy literature and loose living were not uncommon in fifteenth-century Italy – even for popes.

In his *Commentaries*, Aeneas – or Pope Pius II as he was now called – writes of his dream "of rousing Christians against the Turks and declaring war upon them", and despite his crippling gout, he called for princes and peasants alike to meet him at the seaport of Ancona to begin a glorious journey to face the infidel. Thousands of peasants, albeit unarmed and untrained, waited for him at the dockside, but of princes and professional soldiers there was not a soul, and a despondent Pius knew it was a lost cause. Within days, his life force, like his supporters, quietly ebbed away.

## AUGUST 15

**❋ 1196: Conrad II, duke of Swabia**
† *Cause of Death: Bite*

An anonymous chronicle describes Conrad as being as "a man thoroughly given to adultery, fornication, defilement, and every foulness". He died, it is said, after being bitten in the eye by a virgin he was trying to rape.

## AUGUST 16

**❋ 1419: Wenceslas IV, king of Bohemia**
† *Cause of Death: Defenestration*

Following a fiery sermon on the Second Coming, and how to get ready for it, an excited crowd of religious zealots marched in procession through the streets of Prague. As they passed through the cosmopolitan district of New Town, some of the local councillors leant out of their offices and mocked both them and their faith. Enraged by such abuse, some of the Christians ran upstairs, grabbed the councillors by the scruff of their necks and slung them out of the windows. When news of the defenestration reached court, King Wenceslas was incandescent with fury. He turned red, then white, like a human Belisha beacon, before keeling over backwards with a terrible roar.

**❋ 1861: Ranavalona, queen of Madagascar**
† *Cause of Death: Old Age*

Whereas her husband and cousin Radama I welcomed Christian missionaries (*see* July 27), Ranavalona had them tied naked to poles and speared to death. Island converts to the faith fared no better – twenty were stoned within an inch of their lives and then had their heads lopped off, while one elderly woman was memorably dragged to the market place where "her backbone was sawn asunder".

The queen's last years and death were rather quiet affairs, but her funeral – at which two soldiers died when the cannon they were manning exploded and a further eighty were blown to bits when a powder magazine caught fire – was a fitting, bloody end to a frightful, bloody reign.

# AUGUST 17

❊ 1153: Eustace IV, count of Boulogne
† *Cause of Death: Eel*

The son of King Stephen barrelled up to the abbey at Bury St Edmunds and demanded money. The abbot politely but firmly declined and, in reaction, Eustace "ordered all the country round about, and especially St Edmund's harvests, to be plundered". That night he sat down before his favourite dish of eels and choked to death on his first bite.

❊ 1786: Frederick II, king of Prussia
† *Cause of Death: Dropsy*

Frederick the Great died with his boots on. He also died wearing a pale blue satin nightgown stained yellow and brown from snuff, his legs bloated with dropsy, his fingers distorted by gout. Such an ignominious end, mercifully behind the doors of his palace of Sans Souci – which itself had descended into being little more than a vast, heavily-soiled kennel for his dogs – could not detract from a glittering career. In his assessment of the man, an effusive Count Mirabeau could hardly contain himself. "One of the greatest characters that ever occupied a throne is no more," he declared, "and one of the most perfect moulds, which nature ever formed or organised, is broken."

# AUGUST 18

❋ 1852: Alexander, duke of Hamilton
† *Cause of Death: Old Age*

The mausoleum had been built on his Lanarkshire estate and the embalmers had been notified. All Hamilton now required to fulfil his dream of being buried like a pharaoh was a suitable coffin. As luck would have it, a sarcophagus, previously occupied by an Egyptian princess, came onto the market, and he bought it, outbidding the British Museum, for a dizzying £11,000. The princess turned out to have been a short woman and, when the duke died, his feet had to be chopped off and placed beside him. To add insult to injury, archaeologists re-examined the coffin in 1927 and declared that it was not that of an Egyptian princess after all, but a court jester.

# AUGUST 19

❋ 14: Augustus Caesar, Roman emperor
† *Cause of Death: Figs?*

All the world was a stage for Augustus, and he played his last scene with panache. Although in agony from acute diarrhoea, he carefully combed his hair in front of a mirror and then invited his friends to come round and applaud him as he bowed out of what he termed the "comedy of life". But did his wife have the last laugh? Some suggest that Livia murdered her husband by having him stroll through an orchard and pluck and then eat some figs that she had earlier smeared with poison.

# AUGUST 20

❋ 2007: Leona, "Queen of Mean"
† *Cause of Death: Congestive Heart Failure*

Leona Helmsley and her husband Harry (whom she referred to as "snooky wooky dooky") were American billionaire property tycoons, with a vast portfolio that included the Empire State Building. In 1986 they were indicted for tax evasion, and at her trial the jury heard how Leona had apparently told her housekeeper, "We don't pay taxes. Only little people pay taxes."

The press rejoiced in her sentence of four years and dubbed her "The Queen of Mean", an epithet she appeared to substantiate when, in her will, she left millions of dollars to only two of her four grandchildren. The lucky two received their money on the proviso that they visited their father's grave once a year. The other two she cut out completely, bequeathing $12 million instead to "Trouble", her beloved Maltese poodle.

## AUGUST 21

### ❁ 1814: Benjamin Thompson, count Rumford
† *Cause of Death: Fever*

Revolutionary America did not take kindly to its native son. The people of Concord, New Hampshire, in particular, could not tolerate the pro-British leanings of their local landowner and summoned him to answer charges of "being unfriendly to the cause of Liberty". On learning that he would be tarred and feathered, Thompson borrowed his brother's best horse and galloped out of town.

Bavaria found him far more to their liking. For his assistance to the services of the nation, both civil and military, the Elector made him a "Count of the Holy Roman Empire". Thompson chose the title "Count Rumford" after the old name of Concord, a place that he clearly held in higher regard than it held him.

*The Comforts of a Rumford Stove.*

England found him insufferable. Senior members of the Royal Institution, which he helped establish, were appalled at his high-handedness and prised him out of office. Thompson huffily retired to Paris where he died of a "sudden violent fever".

The world, however, owes a debt of gratitude to Rumford. Cold, arrogant and unfeeling he may have been, but he designed a fireplace that retained heat like nothing before, and invented both the first drip coffee pot and thermal underwear.

❋ 1982: Sobhuza II, king of Swaziland
† *Cause of Death: Leukaemia*

The embalmed body of the world's longest-reigning monarch was carried upright in a sedan chair to create the illusion that he was still alive. Given that it was his funeral, it was a hard sell.

## AUGUST 22

❋ 1485: Richard III, king of England
† *Cause of Death: Northumberland*

Three men stood in the way of Richard III killing his adversary, Henry Tudor, at the Battle of Bosworth Field. The first was the man mountain they called Sir John Cheyney. Richard hacked him down. The second was the shorter but equally fierce rebel standard-bearer William Brandon. Richard hacked him down. The third was Henry Percy, the Duke of Northumberland, who had promised to give him backup if the need arose. Richard was only a few yards away from Henry Tudor, the man he derided as "that Welsh milksop", and with the battle intensifying on one of his flanks, this was the moment for Northumberland and his seasoned troops to intervene.

Percy did nothing. Instead he watched from a nearby hill as his king gasped "Traitor! Traitor!" and slumped under a torrent of blows.

*Richard III at Bosworth Field.*

# AUGUST 23

## ❁ 1628: George Villiers, duke of Buckingham
† *Cause of Death: "Frenchman"*

While staying at the Greyhound Inn in Portsmouth, Buckingham was told (falsely as it turned out) that there was no need for him to lead a military force against the French city of La Rochelle, as it had already been relieved. The duke, who thought that the venture might well end in failure, was delighted at the news, and called for his coach in order to tell King Charles personally. Just as he was heading out the door, one of his colonels stopped him for a few words and, as they were both bowing deeply to each other, someone jumped out of the shadows and stabbed him in the chest.

*John Felton, assassin.*

His killer, a lieutenant called John Felton who was furious that he had been deprived of promotion, fled down into the kitchens, and would have made good his escape had his hearing not let him down. Buckingham's men were sure that the murderer was an agent of Louis XIII, and careered round the lower floors of the inn yelling "A Frenchman! A Frenchman!" Felton misheard their shouts and thought they were calling his name, and stepped forward between the pots and pans with his hands up. Buckingham died within minutes upstairs in the hallway. Felton died at Tyburn a few months later.

# AUGUST 24

## ❁ 1572: Gaspard II of Coligny, French nobleman
† *Cause of Death: Pavement*

August 24 is St Bartholomew's Day – a day remembered by most historians not for the good deeds of one of Christ's disciples, but for the vile deeds of a French king. Under massive pressure from a council including his mother, Catherine de Medici, the French King Charles IX agreed to the assassination of half a dozen Huguenot leaders. But what Charles understood to be a small-scale murder turned into a full-scale massacre. Thousands were cut down, drowned or hanged for their Protestant beliefs. And the first to die was Coligny.

Woken by the clumping of soldiers up his stairs, Coligny only had time to slip out of bed and into his dressing gown before a rough-hewn thug of a soldier called Besme ran him through. As he lay curled up in agony on the floor, Besme and his mates repeatedly thrust at him with their swords until he lay motionless. "Is it done?" cried a voice from the courtyard below. It was the duke of Guise, the man put in charge of the murder. "Yes," one of the soldiers replied. "Well, throw him out, then." The "corpse" was duly tossed through an open window, but Coligny, who was alive but only just, reached out and clung onto the ledge. A soldier prised his fingers away and he fell onto the pavement below with a thud.

That morning, five of the six intended victims were hunted down and murdered. But it was the scores of others who also perished in the St Bartholomew's Day Massacre that make the date so memorable.

# AUGUST 25

## ✻ 1330: James Douglas, lord of Douglas
† *Cause of Death: Heart Attack*

Four fourteenth-century chroniclers write in some detail about the death of Robert the Bruce's right-hand man, stating that while besieging a castle between Granada and Seville, he was overwhelmed and cut down by Moorish forces. None recall the anecdote of the "Thrown Heart" because, in all likelihood, it's utter balderdash.

The fifteenth-century poem "The Buke of the Howlat" bubbles over in its description of the moment when James, who had been commissioned to go on crusade carrying the heart of Robert the Bruce in a small silver casket around his neck, realised that he was outnumbered and his number was up. The nobleman, the poem relates, yelled "Go first as thou was wont to do and Douglas will follow thee or die!" and then "the hert hardeley he slang" among his enemy. He ran after it, reverently picked it up and was chopped down.

Romantic piffle maybe, but a cracking yarn.

## ✻ 1942: George, duke of Kent
† *Cause of Death: Fifteen Degrees*

That an attaché case, stuffed with bundles of hundred-kroner notes, was found handcuffed to the duke's charred corpse was, in itself, mildly perplexing. More perplexing, however, was how George's flying boat, en route to Iceland, came to crash fifteen degrees off course when it was a clear day and the crew contained four experienced navigators. Had the duke, who liked a drink, been at the controls? Had his colleagues been too sloshed to notice?

## AUGUST 26

❀ 1346: John, king of Bohemia
† *Cause of Death: Final Request*

Of all the many aristocratic deaths at the Battle of Crecy, that of King John is perhaps the most poignant. In his *Chronicles*, Froissart writes how the blind king called his knights together and begged them for one final favour. "Take me far enough forward," he asked, "for me to strike a blow with my sword." It was unquestionably a suicide mission, and not just for the king, but his men loyally hitched their reins to his, and rode as one into the thick of the fray. Froissart tells us that before he and his companions all died, John "fought bravely" and used his sword "more than four" times.

## AUGUST 27

❀ 1862: Albert, prince of Hawaii
† *Cause of Death: "Brain Fever"*

Four-year-old Albert threw a tantrum because he was made to wear a new pair of boots that he didn't like, and his father, King Kamehameha IV, scooped him up and held his head under a cold tap to cool him off. Later that same day, the youngster complained of a headache, wept uncontrollably and then died from what the doctors concluded was "Brain Fever". The king never forgave himself (*see* November 30).

❀ 1979: Louis, Lord Mountbatten of Burma
† *Cause of Death: IRA*

When the fishing boat *Shadow V* cleared the little harbour of Mullaghmore, its skipper, Lord Mountbatten, raced the engine and steered the craft towards some lobster pots across Donegal Bay. As he slowed down to examine his catch, a fifty-pound bomb, hidden beneath his feet, was detonated by remote control from the shore.

The villagers of Cliffoney and Bunduff, several miles from the blast, initially thought the noise that shook their windows must have come from the Finner Army Camp across the bay, but soon learned that another army was responsible. The Irish Republican Army coldly explained that it had "executed" Mountbatten for being a symbol of the imperialist establishment.


## AUGUST 28

❁ 1972: William, prince of Gloucester
† *Cause of Death: Pilot Error*

The yellow and white Piper Cherokee Arrow, piloted by Prince William, smoothly took off at an airport near Wolverhampton, gracefully banked left, and hit a tree.


## AUGUST 29

❁ 1533: Atahualpa, Incan emperor
† *Cause of Death: Garotte*

Condemned for revolting against the Spanish, Atahualpa was made an offer he could hardly refuse. If he converted to Christianity and allowed himself to be baptised, he would be strangled with a garotte. If he didn't, he would be slow-roasted at the stake. And verily it came to pass that, with his forehead still damp with holy water, the Incan Emperor – Christianity's newest member – had his throat slit.


## AUGUST 30

❁ 1483: Louis XI, king of France
† *Cause of Death: "Shingles", etc.*

Like Robert the Bruce (*see* June 7), Louis was convinced he was dying of leprosy, and like Robert he was wrong. He was actually suffering from a skin disease not unlike shingles which, coupled with gout, chills and basic old age, was making his life miserable. In his desperation, he sent for three things:

1. Giant tortoises from the Cape Verde Islands.
2. A ring belonging to Lorenzo de Medici.

3.  A holy man called Francis who lived under a rock in Calabria.

The first two were supposed cures for leprosy but, as one might expect, bathing in the tortoise blood and wearing the ring (originally worn by the fifth-century saint, Bishop Zenobius) proved useless – and so Louis summoned the hermit.

Francis eked out a living on a meagre diet of fruits and root vegetables, and in order to make him feel welcome, Louis had crates of oranges, lemons, pears and parsnips waiting for him. Accepting the parsnips, but spurning the fruit, the holy man then began a quiet vigil – sitting beside the king's bed day and night, offering occasional spiritual comfort. Many were surprised at the calm with which Louis made his confession and passed away, leading them to comment that Francis, unlike the blood and the ring, had really helped.

## AUGUST 31

### ❀ 1422: Henry V, king of England
† *Cause of Death: Something Saintly?*

Ever since their gloriously successful siege of Meaux in May 1422, nothing had gone right for Henry and his men. French contemporary Jean Juvenal des Ursins writes that the English forces spent the summer doubled up by a "marvellous pestilence of stomach flux", and that by the autumn their young king was clearly not long for this world. So who was to blame for this reversal of fortune and Henry's death? Step forward two holy contenders:

1.  St Fiacre. The Scottish historian John of Fordun posits that the lesser-known seventh-century missionary hermit took vengeance on Henry for allowing his troops to plunder a shrine and destroy some fields dedicated to his memory.

2.  St Anthony. The Burgundian chronicler Jean de Waurin is confident that Henry had contracted the terrifying and, at that time, untreatable "St Anthony's Fire" after eating some contaminated rye bread. Sufferers of this fungus-borne disease feel like they're being burned at the stake. They then

go completely mad. And it was this condition, claims de Waurin, which had seized Henry "in the fundament".

Dysentery, cancer of the rectum and "long and excessive labours" have also been proffered as causes of death, but whatever Henry's exact condition, his doctors knew there was nothing they could do but try to relieve his suffering. After he died, they steeped his emaciated corpse in aromatic herbs and balsam, wrapped it in waxed linen, and brought it back to England for burial in Westminster Abbey.

*The funeral procession of Henry V.*

## ❋ 1997: Diana, Princess of Wales
† *Cause of Death: Car Crash*

The driver was drunk.

# SEPTEMBER

## SEPTEMBER I

❋ 1715: Louis XIV, king of France
† *Cause of Death: Gangrene*

<u>Menu</u>

*Starter*

Soup (four bowls)

*Main Course*

Pheasant (whole)
Partridge (whole)
Ham
Mutton
Eggs
Bowl of Salad (large)

*Dessert*

Pastries (several)
Fruit

Louis liked to eat ... a lot. Before his teeth fell out he would think nothing of munching his way through a meal like the one above, and after they fell out, he dispensed with the inconvenience of chewing and simply gulped everything down whole, including globe artichokes and peas still in their

pods. His doctors, therefore, feared the worst when one day he told them he wasn't hungry. Unable to halt the march of gangrene in the old king's left leg, there was nothing they could do except bring a modicum of relief by bathing it daily in Burgundy.

*The deathbed of Louis XIV.*

## SEPTEMBER 2

### ❁ 1820: Jiaqing, emperor of China
† *Cause of Death: Lightning*

Ambling beside the Temple of Universal Joy in his summer palace in Chengde, the emperor drank in lungfuls of cool mountain air. He did not see the darkening clouds above. Strolling through the Temple of Universal Peace, he surveyed the vast imperial hunting grounds usually teeming with deer. He did not notice that all the animals had scampered for cover. Dawdling outside the Temple of Happiness and Longevity, he was zapped.

## SEPTEMBER 3

### ❁ 1792: Marie Therese, princess of Lamballe
† *Cause of Death: Mob*

Any friend of Marie Antoinette was an enemy of the people, and Lamballe was the queen's most loyal companion and confidante. When she refused to publicly denounce the monarchy, she was thrown out of La Force prison and onto the street for swift and brutal execution by the bloodthirsty mob.

Piranhas fed with fresh steak would have been less frenzied. They ripped off her clothes, gang-raped her, bludgeoned her with hammers and hacked at her flesh with axes and pikes. In a final act of savagery, they cut off her head, rammed it on a spike and paraded it through the streets until they reached Marie Antoinette's prison cell. The queen fainted when she learned what had happened, and while she lay unconscious on the floor, her fellow inmates were forced to watch the grisly horror show of Marie Therese's head jiggling before the bars, her blond, bloodied curls playfully bobbing up and down.

## SEPTEMBER 4

✾ 1199: Joan of England, queen of Sicily
† *Cause of Death: Things Left Undone which They Ought to Have Done*

Fearful of her abusive husband, Joan sought refuge at Fontevrault Abbey in the Loire Valley of France, and although unaccustomed to having a pregnant queen as one of their order, the nuns welcomed her with open arms. There, safe from the violent advances Raymond VI, she gave birth to Raymond VII, but with midwifery not exactly high on the list of skills required within a monastic community, it is perhaps of little surprise to learn that she died in labour.

## SEPTEMBER 5

✾ 1877: Crazy Horse, chief of the Lakota
† *Cause of Death: Recruit*

Bayoneted in the kidneys, Crazy Horse fell back into the arms of Little Big Man, and spent his last agonising hours tended by He Dog, Touch the Clouds and Worm. As his life ebbed away, he must have rued his decision to discuss terms with the US army. They had displaced his people from their ancestral land, forced them to live in grinding poverty on a reservation, and invited him to their barracks at Fort Robinson on false pretences.

Land rights were never on the agenda. In fact there was no agenda. Colonel Bradley and his men simply planned to arrest him and cart him off to a penal colony of the coast of Florida. The soldiers manning the southbound wagon were stood down, however, when a young recruit, frightened possibly by his imposing frame and feathers, slashed the muzzle of his rifle at him as he passed by.

## SEPTEMBER 6

❋ 1572: John, Lord Fleming
† *Cause of Death: Salute*

Fleming was a staunch supporter of Mary Queen of Scots, and as he was passing in front of Edinburgh Castle with a party of French soldiers, he commanded his men to salute the queen by firing their long-barrelled hagbuts into the ground. Their volley threw up a shower of stones, one of which smashed into his knee. He was taken by litter to the family seat at Biggar where he died of his wounds.

## SEPTEMBER 7

❋ 1312: Ferdinand IV, king of Castile
† *Cause of Death: Summons*

The similar circumstances of Ferdinand's death and that of Philip IV of France two years later (*see* November 29) suggest that chroniclers may have spiced up one or both stories for narrative effect. Ferdinand is said to have found a pair of brothers guilty of murder, despite the flimsiest of evidence, and sentenced them to be thrown off a cliff. As they stood on the edge of the precipice, the two condemned men vociferously protested their innocence and summoned Ferdinand to join them in death within thirty days to face the one and only Judge. Exactly thirty days later the king had a heart attack while getting ready for bed, and an alarmed Castilian people dubbed their late monarch "El Emplazado" or "The Summoned".

## SEPTEMBER 8

❋ 1397: Thomas, duke of Gloucester
† *Cause of Death: Mattress or Towel*

Two stories vie for the manner in which King Richard II got rid of his uncle Thomas.

1.  Thugs hauled him off to Calais where they told him "it was the king's will that he should die". The duke calmly answered that "if it was his will, it must be so," and made his last confession to a priest. Five valets then pinned him down on a bed and smothered him with a feather mattress.

2.  Thugs hauled him off to Calais and strangled him with a towel.

Either way it was rather cumbersome.

## ✤ 1650: Elizabeth, princess of England
† *Cause of Death: Rainstorm*

A prisoner at Carisbrooke Castle on the Isle of Wight, the frail teenage princess had two things to keep her company: her younger brother Henry and the Bible that her father Charles I had given her in a tearful meeting just before he met his end (*see* January 30). She was playing bowls with Henry when a violent rainstorm caught them by surprise and soaked them to the skin. A chill quickly developed into a raging fever and, within hours of the game, her attendants found her dead in bed, her hands clasped in prayer and her face resting on the pages of her precious book.

# SEPTEMBER 9

## ✤ 1087: William I, king of England
† *Cause of Death: Pommel*

Given his nickname of "the Fat", King Philip of France was hardly one to talk, but he nevertheless publicly joked that William's pot belly was so big that he looked pregnant. It was this belly that flopped over the front of his saddle and, according to William of Malmesbury, brought about the conqueror's downfall. He was pillaging the town of Mantes west of Paris, when his horse "reared in fright at a blazing timber and threw its ponderous

*A portly William I surveys his troops.*

rider against the iron of his saddle," fatally rupturing his internal organs. His retainers tried to squeeze his vast frame into a slightly undersized coffin, and horrifically his body burst open. The ensuing stink led to one of the quickest royal funerals in history.

❁ **1545: Charles, duke of Orleans**
† *Cause of Death: Feathers*

A nasty strain of influenza broke out near Charles's lodgings, but the duke declared that he would stay put, maintaining that "no son of a king of France ever died of plague". He and his brother Francis then went to inspect some houses that had been infected. There, in an act of bewildering bravado, he sliced open a quilt with his sword and threw the feathers in the air. A few days later, he hopped the twig.

## SEPTEMBER 10

❁ **210 BC: Shi Huangdi, emperor of China**
† *Cause of Death: Magic Formula*

The emperor drank a potion, a major ingredient of which was mercury, in the hope it would make him immortal. It made him go bonkers and then killed him.

❁ **1669: Henrietta Maria, queen consort of England**
† *Cause of Death: Monsieur Vallot's "Luckless Grains"*

Plagued by chronic insomnia, Henrietta Maria, the widow of Charles I, allowed a team of French physicians to check her over. Historian Thomas Birch writes that Monsieur Vallot, Louis XIV's personal doctor, declared that she was in fine fettle, but she should take three grains of laudanum to help her sleep, boasting that they were of a "particular composition" and would be definitely "conducive to her health".

The following day the queen went to bed and, as directed, took the three-grain sleeping draught mixed with an egg yolk. Soon she fell into a deep sleep . . . a very deep sleep. Monsieur Vallot's "luckless grains", as they came to be known, had done their job rather too well.

❀ **2006: Taufa'ahau Tupou IV, king of Tonga**
† *Cause of Death: Yams*

Weighing in at around 450 pounds, the king was, even by Tongan standards, on the heavy side. "I'm only allowed to eat three yams a day," he once complained to a reporter. "But" he then smiled, "a yam can be six feet long."

## SEPTEMBER 11

❀ **1971: Sylvia, ranee of Sarawak**
† *Cause of Death: Old Age*

Alone and unloved, Sylvia tried to commit suicide twice when just a girl. The first time she tried to contract ptomaine poisoning by eating rotting sardines. The second time she hoped to catch pneumonia by lying naked in the snow. Life dramatically improved when she met and married Vyner Brooke, heir to the throne of Sarawak, a jungle kingdom on the island of Borneo. After becoming rajah and ranee in 1916, the couple lived in unspeakable opulence, holding absolute sway over half a million subjects, including a tribe of head-hunting Dyaks. By her own admission, Sylvia's life had changed beyond recognition. She wrote to her friend George Bernard Shaw that she had servants at every turn and had become "a howling snob with a head as swelled as the largest coconut in the land".

   The British took over governance of the country after the Second World War and the former royal couple returned to England where they found their new status and London living decidedly dreary. Vyner moved into a separate house and began a string of affairs. He died in 1963, leaving Sylvia a very rich widow but, as in her early years, despondent, unloved and alone.

## SEPTEMBER 12

❀ **1185: Andronicus I Comnenus, Byzantine emperor**
† *Cause of Death: Swords*

The people of Constantinople showed no mercy to their deposed emperor. They ripped out his teeth and hair, gouged out an eye and severed his right hand. They then paraded him through the city streets sitting backwards in humiliation on a flea-ridden camel, as bystanders hurled excrement and abuse at him. Finally, they hung his naked body upside down and encouraged any spectator who had a sword to use him as target practice.

# SEPTEMBER 13

## ❋ 81: Titus, Roman emperor
† *Cause of Death: Excessive Bathing*

Just like his father (*see* June 23), Titus died of a fever after swimming overenthusiastically in the chilly waters of his local spa. His final words were: "I have made but one mistake." No one quite knows what he meant.

## ❋ 1598: Philip II, king of Spain
† *Cause of Death: Cancer*

A royal valet writes how Philip, a man who was fastidious about matters of personal hygiene, must have undergone "the worst torments imaginable" as, for fifty-three excruciating days and nights, he lay dying in his tiny study in the Escorial palace. He had lost control of his bowels, the sores covering his body gave off an "evil smell" and all he could do was lie there.

Upon his death, magistrates in Madrid decreed that everyone should wear the black of mourning. If they couldn't afford the black of mourning, they were to buy a special pointy hat called a "caperuza" and wear that. And if they couldn't afford a special pointy hat, they were to put on whatever hat they had, as long as it wasn't fancy.

# SEPTEMBER 14

## ❋ 1982: Princess Grace of Monaco
† *Cause of Death: Brake Failure?*

Princess Stephanie's refusal to talk publicly about the crash in which she received superficial injuries but her mother died, forces us to look elsewhere for clues as to its cause:

- ❋ The truck driver travelling behind the royal couple reports how the former movie star was honking her horn furiously and zigzagging wildly before careering over the edge of a ravine. Had the brakes failed?

- ❀ Palace gossips reveal that on the day of the accident Stephanie and Grace were having a right royal spat about Stephanie's boyfriend – an argument that was still ongoing when they got into their Rover. Was this a factor?
- ❀ Several eyewitnesses claim that it was Stephanie and not Grace who was driving. At the time Stephanie was 17, a year below the legal driving age. Was her inexperience behind the wheel to blame?

Several questions remain unanswered, but one indisputable fact is that Grace was not wearing a seatbelt.

# SEPTEMBER 15

## ❀ 668: Constans II, Byzantine emperor
† *Cause of Death: Cubicularius*

While the emperor was having a bath, his chamberlain hit him over the head with a marble soap dish.

## ❀ 929: Ludmilla, duchess of Bohemia
† *Cause of Death: Veil*

Two weeks before Boleslav and his men got rid of Good King Wenceslas (*see* September 28) they bumped off his grandmother by sneaking up behind her as she was praying and strangling her with her own veil.

## ❀ 1425: Bonne, countess of Nevers
† *Cause of Death: The Good Life*

In a society where outlandish clothing, boorish feasting and long bouts of intemperate drinking were the norm, Bonne was a gentle soul who dressed sensibly, ate sensibly and drank in moderation. And she died aged twenty-nine.

## SEPTEMBER 16

❋ 1701: James II, king of England
† *Cause of Death: Lamentations, Chapter 5*

After his withering defeat at the Battle of the Boyne, James fled to France where he took refuge in his religious devotions, hearing Mass twice a day. According to historian Lord Macaulay, the exiled monarch suffered a fit while listening to a choral anthem, the words of which were painfully appropriate to his own plight. "Remember O Lord, what is come upon us," declares the prophet Jeremiah in Lamentations 5. "Consider and behold our reproach. Our inheritance is turned to strangers, our houses to aliens; the crown is fallen from our head." For James it was all too much, and he toppled from his pew.

## SEPTEMBER 17

❋ 1665: Philip IV, king of Spain
† *Cause of Death: Disappointment*

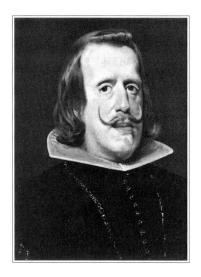

Philip took himself very seriously indeed. They say that he only laughed three times in his entire life. He also took his succession very seriously and was mightily relieved when his wife Elisabeth produced a son, Baltasar. To his dismay, however, his heir died aged sixteen, with chroniclers almost universally crediting his death to the dissolute lifestyle that his so-called tutors encouraged him to follow. Eleven years later, Philip's morose outlook on life brightened briefly when his second wife Margaret gave birth to a baby boy, but returned its default state of misery when little Philip died aged only four. Mercifully, a third son arrived that same year and the succession seemed to be safe. And safe it was except that this third male – the future Charles II of Spain – was physically deformed and mentally unstable, and certainly incapable of fathering any children himself. All too aware that the future of the country was in disarray, Philip died a broken-hearted, sullen sourpuss.

## SEPTEMBER 18

### ❁ 96: Domitian, Roman emperor
† *Cause of Death: List*

*Venerunt*

Worried that their emperor was considering a changing of the guard, a group of palace officials tiptoed into Domitian's study, hoping to find some clue as to his intentions.

*Viderunt*

There they chanced upon a writing tablet with the heading "People I am planning to bump off". Their names were at the top of the list.

*Vicerunt*

One of their number, a steward called Stephanus, walked around the imperial palace with his arm in a sling, feigning an injury, while in fact he was concealing a dagger in the bandages, just waiting for the right moment to arrive. And it arrived when Domitian summoned him to a private discussion about – of all things – a rumoured assassination attempt. As the two were bent over in conversation, Stephanus tried to whip the dagger from the sling, but fumbled in his excitement and gave his master time to spring back and make for the door.

Like two feral cats the emperor and his steward fought on the floor. Domitian wildly tried to scratch his servant's eyes out while Stephanus flayed away with his dagger, until eventually his co-conspirators shoved their way into the room and helped him finish the job.

## SEPTEMBER 19

❀ 1841: Charles, Baron Sydenham
† *Cause of Death: Business*

Sydenham lived, and died, by the adage "If you want
something done, ask a busy person." As Governor of Canada,
he worked at a feverish pace, implementing the Union Act
of 1840, ensuring financial independence from the United
States, and yet still finding time to write to a colleague who
was lax in his correspondence. "Of course you have no time,"
he wrote. "No one ever has who has nothing to do." His
hectic schedule stretched into his private life as well. While
entertaining a lady friend, he suddenly realised he had lost
track of time and was due for an important meeting. He made
his apologies, leaped onto his horse and raced away, but in his
haste fell from the saddle and shattered his thighbone. It took
him a whole fortnight to die from the resulting lockjaw.

## SEPTEMBER 20

❀ 1643: Lucius, Viscount Falkland
† *Cause of Death: Grief*

John Aubrey speculates that Cary committed suicide at the Battle of Newbury
because of the death of his mistress, one Mrs Moray "whom he loved above all
creatures". "At the fight," he writes, "my Lord Falkland being there, and having
nothing to do [decided] to charge; as the two armies were engaging, he rode in
like a madman (as he was) between them, and was shot." His mangled body was
only identifiable by a mole on his neck.

## SEPTEMBER 21

❀ 1588: Charles V, emperor of Austria
† *Cause of Death: Fever*

After enjoying a year of comfortable retirement at the convent of St Justus in
Estremadura, Charles made a fifty-eighth birthday promise to the archbishop of

Toledo. "I have lived fifty-seven years for the world," he pronounced, "[and] a year for my friends in this retreat, and I am determined, from this moment, to devote entirely to God the remainder of my life."

With unbridled religious zeal, he then embarked upon the most ascetic of monastic rules. He slept in a bare cell. He ate gruel. He subjected himself to the severest discipline with a whip of cords. Delighted with his exacting lot and fixated on death, he then decided to hold his own funeral.

His servants, wearing mourning dress and carrying black tapers, solemnly processed into the chapel. Charles, wearing his shroud, then followed and clambered into his own coffin, from where he joined in the hymns and prayers for the repose of his soul. At the end of the service, the congregation sorrowfully filed out and the doors of the chapel were quietly closed. Charles stayed in his coffin for a while, then climbed out and retired to his cell. Only a few months later, he developed a fever and died, and the liturgy had to be repeated, with one less voice than before.

# SEPTEMBER 22

❁ 1828: Shaka, Zulu king
† *Cause of Death: Dream*

Shaka woke from his midday nap and grumpily confided that he had dreamed that someone was trying to kill him. His half-brothers Dingane and Mhlangana, who were indeed plotting a coup, heard about his premonition, took it as a sign, and sprang into action.

That very evening a party of hunters came before their chief and presented him with their haul of exotic crane feathers and otter pelts, and Shaka, still tetchy from his dream, expressed mild dissatisfaction at the size of the booty. The king's personal attendant, and one of the conspirators, deliberately overreacted to his master's tut-tut and threw his spear to the ground, demanding the hunters' immediate execution. Everyone scarpered, with the exception of a few old and wizened councillors who sat and watched in horror as Dingane and Mhlangana stepped up and made Shaka's dream come true.

# SEPTEMBER 23

❋ **1531: Catherine, queen of Sweden**
† *Cause of Death: Hammer?*

Although she was queen of Sweden, Catherine irked her subjects by speaking only German. It is universally accepted that she also irked her husband, and was whispered in certain circles late at night that King Gustav, famous for his violent temper, did something unmentionable to her with a big hammer.

# SEPTEMBER 24

❋ **1891: Alexandra, grand duchess of Russia**
† *Cause of Death: Jumping into Boat*

A heavily pregnant Alexandra was walking along the Moskva River with some friends when the party decided to go for a boat trip. Instead of demurely stepping into the dinghy from the jetty, the high-spirited duchess leapt from the bank and fell awkwardly as she landed. The following evening she collapsed while dancing and went into premature labour. She died six days later, but baby Dmitri – born two months early and given little chance of survival – defied all odds and lived to a ripe old age.

# SEPTEMBER 25

❋ **1506: Philip I, king of Castile**
† *Cause of Death: Fever*

At just 28, Philip (universally known as "The Handsome") suddenly broke out in cold sweats and died. Upon his untimely demise, his widow Joan (universally known as "The Mad") completely lost the plot and refused to leave her late husband's side, regularly opening his coffin and stroking his slowly decaying corpse. After a funeral procession that lasted several months, during which Joan avoided nunneries, fearful that a nun might fall in love with her deceased partner, the royal couple reached Granada, where they were forcibly separated. Philip was buried and Joan was locked up.

## SEPTEMBER 26

❀ 1620: Zhu Chanluo, emperor of China
† *Cause of Death: That Second Red Pill*

Ten days after becoming emperor, Zuo Chanluo was poleaxed by the double whammy of acute constipation and exhaustion, brought on by excessive sexual activity with eight servant girls given to him as a coronation present. To counter the constipation, he took a laxative, which worked a little too well. To counter the exhaustion (and diarrhoea), he took a red pill, an alleged aphrodisiac and energy booster containing, among other things, "red lead" (dried menstrual blood) and "autumn stone" (crystallized urinal salts). It worked wonders and Zuo Chanluo praised its manufacturer as an official "Loyal Subject". Refreshed and rejuvenated, he took a second pill … and within hours his internal organs collectively imploded.

## SEPTEMBER 27

❀ 1615: Arbella Stuart, English noblewoman
† *Cause of Death: Starvation*

But for the interference of two Secretaries of State, Arbella could have been queen of England. Lord Burghley and his son Sir Robert Cecil deflected attention away from the claim of Arbella Stuart, a cousin to Elizabeth I, and ensured that a first cousin twice removed – James Charles Stuart – was first in line instead.

On Elizabeth's death (*see* March 24), King James I initially welcomed Arbella into his court, but a few years later, when she fell head over heels in love with the dashing William Seymour, the son of the Earl of Hertford, he refused to allow them to marry because their "combination of titles" posed a potential rival dynasty. They married anyway … and James threw them in separate jails.

Both managed to escape – Arbella disguised as a man and William as a carter's apprentice. Arbella's hopes for a romantic elopement to the Continent were soon dashed, however, when royal police arrested her as her ship was nearing Calais. They brought her back to England and slung her in the Tower of London where, deprived of her freedom and the company of her husband, she lost the will to live, refused all food, and shrivelled away.

## SEPTEMBER 28

❀ 929: Wenceslas I, duke of Bohemia
† *Cause of Death: Daggers*

Good King Wenceslas looked out on the feast of Leoba, and decided that, even though his younger brother Boleslav was a nasty piece of work, he would go to his party to celebrate the birth of his son. The celebration went on into the small hours, and Wenceslas slipped away to his brother's private chapel to say his prayers. Boleslav and seven colleagues tiptoed up behind him while he was kneeling before the altar, and peppered him with thrusts of their daggers.

## SEPTEMBER 29

❀ 1976: "Sheikh Ali" Wadi Ayoub
† *Cause of Death: Cancer*

"Sheik Ali" was famous for his head butts. The mere thought of one would make noble opponents like "Prince Kumali" and "Earl McCready", let alone plebeian grapplers like "Big Bad John" and "Abdullah the Butcher" quake in their wrestling boots. The Australian-based "matman", who enjoyed a massive fan base far beyond his native Lebanon, lost his battle with cancer just before a sell-out tour of Singapore.

## SEPTEMBER 30

❀ 1628: Fulke Greville, Lord Brooke
† *Cause of Death: Will*

During a trip to London, Lord Brooke was "coming from stool" and allowing his old retainer John Hayward to "truss up his points" (fasten his breeches to his doublet), when the servant rammed a knife a couple of times into his ribs. It appears that a few weeks before, Hayward had been asked to witness his lord's will, and had noted that despite many years of loyal service, he had only been left a year's wages – a sum he considered woefully inadequate to see him spend his dotage in comfort. John Aubrey and others record that a little later Brooke sweetened the pot to £20 a year for life, but it was clearly a case of too little too late.

# OCTOBER

## OCTOBER 1

❀ 1868: Mongkut, king of Siam
† *Cause of Death: Tsetse Fly*

The Siamese court was really impressed when their king, a keen astronomer, correctly calculated the exact day on which his people would have a once-in-a-lifetime chance to see a solar eclipse. It was less impressed when he declared that the only place to properly observe it was from the middle of a mosquito-infested bog. But he was king – the authoritarian monarch portrayed in the Rogers and Hammerstein musical *The King and I* – and whatever he said, went. And so it was that a sullen prince Chulalongkorn, some concerned British consuls and a clutch of hesitant courtiers nervously traipsed after him into the steaming swamp to watch the show.

Sure enough, the view of the eclipse was terrific. And sure enough, the king rapidly contracted malaria and died.

## OCTOBER 2

❀ 1780: John Andre, British "nobleman"
† *Cause of Death: Disguise*

The James Bond of the eighteenth-century, Andre was a cultivated and charming British spy who melted the hearts of high society with his rugged looks, sparkling wit and impeccable manners. During the American War of Independence, a group of soldiers captured him behind enemy lines carrying a fake passport and incriminating papers hidden in his boot; a panel of senior officers, headed by George Washington, found him guilty of travelling during wartime "under a feigned name and in a disguised habit", and sentenced him to death.

Andre was crestfallen when he learned that, out of spite, his mode of execution was to be hanging rather than firing squad (the norm for a soldier) and many of his captors openly wept with shame as they watched him on the gallows using his handkerchief as a blindfold and then placing the noose around his neck. In the moments before the drop, Andre calmly told those near him that he hoped he died as became a British officer, "while the manner of my death must reflect disgrace on your Commander."

Noble in life and death, John was a true "nobleman" only by extension. King George III made his brother, William, a baronet in his memory.

## OCTOBER 3

✿ 1873: Kintpuash, chief of the Modoc
† *Cause of Death: Rope*

Eager to get their hands on quality real estate, white settlers displaced the Modoc tribe from their ancestral lands on the California-Oregon border, and forced them to merge with the Klamath tribe to the north. Chief Kintpuash, commonly known as "Captain Jack", led a successful resistance movement but was eventually persuaded to engage in peace talks with the American army. If the Federal peace commission expected to reach a deal over a quiet handshake, they were in for a surprise. Kintpuash got it into his head that if he killed the army's "chief", the rest of his men would surely go away. At the negotiating table, therefore, he stood up, shot General Canby the senior officer smack between the eyes, and fled.

Eager to get their hands on Captain Jack, the army persuaded several Modoc, including "Shacknasty Jim", "Bogus Charley" and "Steamboat Frank" to turn their leader in. The thousand or more soldiers were expecting a final shoot-out, but again were in for a surprise. With only a few loyal, worn-out braves by his side, Kintpuash ceremonially laid down his rifle and went quietly to Fort Klamath to be hanged. His head was then shipped off to the Smithsonian Institution in Washington where, until it was recently reclaimed by some of his descendants, a junior scientist was using it as a paperweight.

# OCTOBER 4

❋ 1497: Juan, prince of Asturias
† *Cause of Death: Margaret?*

Delicate in appearance, but clearly not in bed, the only son of Spanish monarchs Ferdinand of Aragon and Isabella of Castile married Margaret of Austria in the spring of 1497. The marriage between the two teenagers was an important dynastic union and, by all accounts, one into which both parties enthusiastically entered. But it all ended in tears when, six months later, Juan died – a death often referred to as "the most important thing of his life", and traditionally ascribed to his physical passion for his young bride.

❋ 1597: Sarsa Dengel, Ethiopian king
† *Cause of Death: Fish and Folly*

When Sarsa Dengel declared that he was going to lead a Christian mission into Ethiopia's interior, a group of worried monks warned him to steer clear of the Maca, a tribe that brought nothing but trouble. And if he did visit the Maca, he must not, on any account, eat the fish from the local river. Sarsa Dengel thanked them for their advice, and set off inland. While visiting the Maca people, he ate fish from the local river and died.

# OCTOBER 5

❋ 578: Justin II, Byzantine Emperor
† *Cause of Death: Madness*

John of Ephesus, a contemporary historian, tells us how Justin's temporary bouts of insanity finally developed into full-blown madness. During his last days, the emperor demanded that organ music should be played constantly to soothe his soul, and made his attendants wheel him about on a portable throne from which he would suddenly pounce and bite unsuspecting courtiers. There is a rumour that Justin did more than just bite some of his servants: John reports that he actually ate two of them.

✿ 1760: Sir Robert Brown, baronet
† *Cause of Death: Parsimony*

Brown was more than just prudent with his finances. He was a tightwad, who held onto his vast wealth with a vice-like grip, even at the expense of his own family. When, for example, doctors told his sick daughter that she should go out riding to bring colour back to her cheeks, he provided her with a map that showed her only those roads that had no toll gates. When she eventually died, he tried to bargain with the undertaker. When he eventually died, he left everything – including his avarice, Horace Walpole writes – to his long-suffering wife.

## OCTOBER 6

✿ 1014: Samuel, tsar of the Bulgars
† *Cause of Death: 27,860 Bloody Eye Sockets*

The milk of human kindness wasn't exactly pumping through the veins of Basil I, the Byzantine emperor, when he captured 14,000 of Samuel's troops. Rather than slapping the prisoners on the wrist and sending them packing, he had them all blinded. Well, not all of them. He graced every hundredth man with the sight of one eye so he could lead the others home. On seeing his sightless soldiers, Samuel suffered a stroke.

## OCTOBER 7

✿ 1871: Sir John Fox Burgoyne, baronet
† *Cause of Death: Melancholy*

Sir John, a senior member of Lord Raglan's staff in the Crimean War, almost fell out of his chair laughing when he read his own obituary, mistakenly published when Sir John Montagu Burgoyne died in 1858. Nothing could lighten his spirits, however, when he learned of the death of his only son Hugh, drowned when his ship HMS *Captain* capsized off Cape Finisterre. His updated obituary appeared the following year.

## OCTOBER 8

❀ 1735: Yung-cheng, emperor of China
† *Cause of Death: Irrelevance*

On this day, Yung-cheng "The Immortal" died.

❀ 1820: Henry, king of Haiti
† *Cause of Death: The Enemy Within*

It was backbreaking work, and many perished in its construction, but after fifteen years of toil it was finally finished. For Henry, the self-proclaimed king of the newly independent Haiti, "La Coidavid" or "The Citadel" served a dual purpose. First and foremost, the vast fortress, thrusting out over the Caribbean like the prow of a huge stone ship, defended his realm from a French invasion by sea, and he was regularly seen standing on the ramparts nervously scanning the horizon for the tricolour. Second, the massive structure, with its palace, towers, batteries of cannon and barracks for thousands of soldiers, proved that black men, under the command of a black king, could produce anything equal to their white counterparts.

Henry should have turned his telescope 180 degrees, as his end came not from the sea, but from inland. When he suffered a mild stroke, his political enemies, including his eventual successor Jean-Pierre Boyer, considered the time ripe for revolution against his oppressive regime. Henry refused to go quietly and shot himself through the heart, maintaining his "royal" status to the bitter end by using a bullet of solid silver.

## OCTOBER 9

❀ 1953: Hastings Russell, duke of Bedford
† *Cause of Death: Gunshot*

Russell was an "arachnophile" and had one particular pet spider which he fed on roast beef and Yorkshire Pudding. He was also a keen "psittacophile" and once claimed to have bred a species of "homing budgerigar" that, since it could be taught to talk, could receive and deliver messages orally. Russell was, above all, a "vectigalophobe", detesting the British system of taxation that was so crippling to a wealthy family such as his. When he was found in the undergrowth near his home dead from a gunshot wound, many suspected that it had not been a hunting accident but a dramatic means of evading death duties.

# OCTOBER 10

## ❉ 1806: Louis Ferdinand, prince of Prussia
† *Cause of Death: Quartermaster*

At the Battle of Saalfeld, Louis suddenly found himself face to face with Guindet, the quartermaster of the French 10th Hussars. The Frenchman recognised his royal opponent and offered the prince quarter, but Louis was having none of it, and slashed out with his sword. Despite a nasty wound to his face, the nimble Guindet was able to counterblow and run the prince through, killing him almost instantly.

With his death the Prussian court lost a fine leader, the military fraternity an extremely able soldier, and the music community a highly gifted composer and pianist, upon whom Beethoven had conferred the great honour of dedicating his third piano concerto.

# OCTOBER 11

## ❉ 1424: John Ziska, Bohemian nobleman
† *Cause of Death: Plague*

The Hussites were a testosterone-fuelled peasant army who literally turned ploughshares into swords as they waged war against the forces of King Sigismund of Germany. Their leader was the diminutive but imposing figure of John Ziska, a true warrior's warrior whose long red moustache, bald head and one eye (he lost the other in a childhood fight) put the fear of God into many a foe.

When he lost the other eye in yet another clash with the royal forces, he demanded that he continue leading his troops from the front, and a violent, bloody death akin to his Bohemian namesake at the Battle of Crecy (*see* August 26) seemed on the cards. In fact, he fell to the ravages of the Black Death while besieging a small town on the Moravian border. His dying wish was for his soldiers to peel off his skin and use it to make drums, so he might accompany his troops into battle even after death.

## OCTOBER 12

❀ 1678: Sir Edmundbury Godfrey, English lawyer
† *Cause of Death: Greenberry Hill?*

*The Victim*: The exotically christened London magistrate Edmundbury Godfrey, a brilliant if sour-faced lawyer who had recently heard the deposition of Titus Oates, commonly denounced as the fabricator of a "Popish Plot" to murder Charles II.

*The Scene of the Crime*: Somewhere other than Primrose Hill where his body was found, impaled with a sword.

*The Clues*: The ditch was dry. Godfrey's shoes were clean. Money and jewellery were still on his body. There were bruises and a livid red line on his neck. There was no blood around the entry wound of the sword. Spots of white candle wax, exclusively used by persons of extremely high office – and priests – were spattered on his clothes.

*The Verdict*: Ironically, a Popish plot. Three Catholic priests, Robert Green, Henry Berry and Lawrence Hill by name, were arrested and found guilty of strangling him and dumping his body.

*The Punishment*: This may be hard to credit, but we are reliably informed that Fathers Green, Berry and Hill were hanged at a place called Greenberry Hill.

*The Truth?*: Two twentieth-century historians deduce that the real killer was Philip Herbert, the earl of Pembroke. Herbert choked Godfrey to death for putting him on trial for an earlier murder.

## OCTOBER 13

❀ 54: Claudius, Roman emperor
† *Cause of Death: Mushroom*

Perhaps it was an accident. Many people have apparently confused – to their cost – the harmless mushroom *boletus edulis* with the fatal *amanita phalloides*, and perhaps Agrippina gave one to her husband in good faith. Perhaps not.

Perhaps Agrippina, in a bid to replace Claudius with the young, strapping Nero, had her poisoner Locusta sprinkle something deadly on an especially tasty mushroom. And when Claudius had eaten it and clutched his stomach in agony, perhaps she had the imperial physician Xenophon drop a second dose of the poison on the very feather that was supposed to help him vomit.

## OCTOBER 14

❋ 1066: Harold, king of the Anglo-Saxons
† *Cause of Death: Arrow and Sword*

The Bayeux Tapestry, depicting Harold with an arrow in his eye, is actually a fair representation of events at the battle of Hastings. About noon, the Norman archers "fired high" and one of their arrows hit the king in the face. Some of William the Conqueror's cavalrymen then followed up this aerial assault and polished him off.

In the evening, French soldiers stripped and plundered the dead, making identification of Harold something of a challenge. Monks compared corpses in the area where he was last seen, but had to admit they couldn't single him out. For a while it looked as if a proper burial wouldn't be possible, but then a woman called "Edith the Swan-Necked" came to the rescue, spotting him immediately from a physical feature that only the most intimate of friends would recognise.

## OCTOBER 15

❋ 1839: Frances Mary, marchioness of Salisbury
† *Cause of Death: Coiffure*

The fire that destroyed Hatfield House in Hertfordshire started just after supper. Even into her eighties, the marchioness liked to wear her hair piled high and adorned with feathers. One evening as she got up from the dining table, she moved too close to a chandelier and a feather caught fire. Soon the marchioness's hair caught alight and, before you knew it, the marchioness herself and her mansion were burned to a crisp.

# OCTOBER 16

## ❋ 1793: Marie Antoinette, queen of France
† *Cause of Death: Guillotine*

The tumbrel ferrying the queen to the Place de la Revolution took a circuitous route to allow as many people as possible to vent their emotions against her. Head shaved, hands tied behind her back, she spent the miserable journey sitting as motionless and emotionless as possible, refusing to be affected by the jeers and insults as she passed. Even as she climbed the steps of the scaffold she maintained a serene composure. The historian Lacretelle the Younger famously described her deportment on the gallows not as that of a condemned traitor but of a queen about to take her place on a throne next to her husband. The only time she allowed her true trepidation to show was when she accidentally stepped on the executioner's foot. It was a momentary lapse, however, and her last action on earth, before being manhandled onto the board and shoved into position, was to apologise.

# OCTOBER 17

## ❋ 1586: Sir Philip Sidney, English nobleman
† *Cause of Death: Lack of Protection*

Sidney took part in a skirmish against the Spanish at Zutphen in the Netherlands, and received a bullet wound that shattered his thighbone. He would have survived had he been wearing his "greaves" or leg armour, but had put them to one side in sympathy with his colleague Sir William Pelham, who had left his at home

*The funeral of Sir Philip Sidney.*

but nevertheless ventured into the fray. Sidney's generous spirit continued until his last breath. He is said to have refused a drink of water in favour of a dying comrade, saying: "His need is greater than mine."

## OCTOBER 18

### ❋ 1865: Henry, Lord Palmerston
### † *Cause of Death: Fever*

In 1863 a society belle by the name of Mrs O'Kane paid a visit to the Prime Minister in the House of Commons. Later she claimed to have slept with him and her husband cited him in a divorce case, demanding £20,000 in damages. That Palmerston was seventy-eight years old at the time solicited admiration from some circles and gave rise to a new joke: "While the lady was certainly Kane, was Palmerston Abel?"

The case was thrown out. Mr O'Kane sailed off to Australia and Palmerston sailed on in his political career, relishing his increased popularity and reputation for indestructibility. When, a couple of years later, he caught a nasty chill, he dismissed his doctor's concerns that it might develop into a fatal fever with the last words: "Die, my dear doctor? That's the last thing I shall do!"

## OCTOBER 19

### ❋ 1216: John, king of England
### † *Cause of Death: The Welland and Peaches*

John's hyperactive personality, which possibly drove him to kill Prince Arthur (*see* April 3), intensified following his signing of the Magna Carta, and several chronicles describe his post-charter behaviour as that of a madman, routinely gnashing his teeth, rolling his eyes and gnawing on sticks. It was with characteristic "hot haste", therefore, that he and his men raced south to London to put down an uprising spearheaded by the French dauphin. When he reached The Wash, he had two options. He could either march across the shallow bay at Cross Keys, the shortest but most treacherous route, or take a nine-mile danger-free detour. True to psychological profile, he chose the former.

The king had just made it to the other side when the tide turned. As if on cue, the waters of the River Welland suddenly surged up and engulfed the royal baggage train behind him in a terrifying whirlpool – carriages, horses, treasures, men, the lot. Mortified at the loss, John sped on to Swinshed Abbey where, according to Matthew Paris, he drowned his sorrows, "indulging too freely in peaches and copious draughts of new cider". The morning after the night before, as he put his foot in his horse's stirrups, he fell back "afflicted with fever and burning pain" and was carried to the abbey at Newark-on-Trent where, with characteristic speed, he died.

Paris attributes John's demise to an excess of fruit and depression at the loss of so much of his retinue. But the chronicler makes it clear we should feel no sympathy for the man. "Foul as it is", he wrote, "hell is made even fouler with him in it".

## OCTOBER 20

❉ 1740: Charles VI, Holy Roman Emperor
† *Cause of Death: Mushroom*

Charles was suddenly taken ill while on a hunting holiday in Hungary. Like Claudius, his imperial forebear (*see* October 13), he was poisoned, either by accident or deliberately, by a dish of mushrooms – a "plat de champignons" that Voltaire maintained altered the destiny of Europe. Even as he groaned his last groans, Charles's sense of imperial propriety did not desert him. As a priest was giving him his last rites, he admonished a courtier for lighting only two candles when, for the sacrament of extreme unction of an emperor, there should of course be four.

## OCTOBER 21

❉ 1871: Josiah, prince of Ghor
† *Cause of Death: Tuberculosis*

San Francisco emergency services scooped up the crumpled body of Josiah Harlan off a city sidewalk and wheeled it to the morgue, where a doctor took little time in declaring that he had died from TB. Little did they know that the old man with a long white beard and leathery skin was once a Persian potentate.

Jilted by his one and only love, Harlan had left America in 1824, vowing never to return. After a short spell as a doctor with the East India Company, he made his way to the unmapped expanse of Afghanistan where, through a combination of steely ambition and almost lunatic courage, he ended up being appointed commander-in-chief of the national army. Like Alexander the Great, he led his men across the Hindu Kush atop an elephant, and like Alexander the Great, he enjoyed absolute power over a sizeable part of the planet ... until the British arrived.

The British pitched up in Kabul in 1839 and saw no place for Josiah in their "Great Game", summarily removing this strange and rather cantankerous "Prince of Ghor" from his throne. Harlan left without fanfare, and after a spell in Russia returned to the land he hoped never to see again. His attempts to educate an intrigued but bemused America on the proper use of camels in warfare and nutritional value of Afghan grapes were stymied by the outbreak of the Civil War, and he eventually headed to California where he died as just another statistic – another San Francisco crackpot, gabbling about past "glories" and coughing up his lungs on West and 22nd.

# OCTOBER 22

✳ 1792: Guillaume le Gentil, French nobleman
† *Cause of Death: Old Age*

There is an astronomical phenomenon known as the "transit of Venus" when the planet passes in front of the sun for a few hours. This happens twice in eight years but then not for another century, so stargazers have only two chances to see it, if they are lucky. And Guillaume le Gentil was not lucky.

As one of France's leading astronomers, he was despatched to observe the transit from the French colony of Pondicherry in India, but military activity in the area forced him to sail to the island of Mauritius. When the transit took place, he was still out in open water and infuriatingly the ship pitched and tossed in the swell so much that standing up on deck, let alone taking accurate readings, was nigh impossible.

Guillaume refused to be beaten, and determined to stay away from France until, as directed, he had successfully observed and recorded the transit out in the Far East. Accordingly he spent much of the following seven years mapping the east coast of Madagascar, before heading for Manila in the Philippines where he hoped to get a perfect view of the heavenly spectacle. The Spanish authorities, however, made it clear that he would not be welcome, and so he made his way once more to Ponidicherry. This time he was allowed to land, and he built a little observatory and waited for the big day.

Le Gentil was le Malheureux. Despite clear blue skies beforehand and afterwards, clouds obscured his view during the critical few hours of the transit and he didn't see a thing. And when he learned that his colleagues, who had been allowed to stay in Manila, had enjoyed brilliant sunshine, he almost went mad. Finally he pulled himself together and returned to France … only to find that he had been declared legally dead, and that his wife had remarried. It is at this moment, however, that Guillaume's fortunes finally changed. He met and married a lovely and fabulously rich woman, managed to persuade the Royal Academy of Sciences to give him his place back, and lived happily ever after, dying in retirement, feted as one of his nation's finest, if unluckiest scholars.

## OCTOBER 23

❀ 42 BC: Marcus Brutus, Roman nobleman
† *Cause of Death: Sword*

Everyone remembers "Et tu, Brute?" the supposed last words of Julius Caesar, as he collapsed in front of the Theatre of Pompey. Brutus' last words, before he launched himself on his sword, were less memorable. The statesman had just lost a decisive battle against Octavian and Antony and was mulling over his options as he rested on a riverbank not far from the battlefield. According to his friend, the philosopher Publius Volumnius, he spoke two lines of Greek. One was from Euripides' *Medea*: "Zeus, do not forget the author of these ills." And the other? Unfortunately for posterity, Volumnius was never able to remember it.

*Marcus Brutus falls on his sword.*

## OCTOBER 24

❁ 1920: Maria Alexandrovna, grand duchess of Russia
† *Cause of Death: Snobbery*

Additionally titled the "Duchess of Edinburgh" and "Duchess of Saxe-Coburg and Gotha", Maria collapsed in a hotel in Zurich, purportedly from shock after receiving a letter addressed to her merely as "Frau Coburg".

## OCTOBER 25

❁ 1760: George II, king of England
† *Cause of Death: Heart Attack*

6.00 a.m.: As was his custom, the king got out of bed and drank a cup of hot chocolate.

6.45 a.m.: As was his custom, the king went into the royal water closet and closed the door.

6.47 a.m.: Contrary to custom, the valet de chambre distinctly heard "a noise louder than the royal wind". He ran into the bathroom and found the king had fallen from his throne and was now sprawled lifeless on the floor.

❁ 1920: Alexander I, king of Greece
† *Cause of Death: Barbary Macaque*

A unique simian-induced fatality. Alexander was out walking in the Royal Gardens when Fritz, his dog, got into a fight with a pet monkey belonging to a local vineyard owner. Alexander tried to break it up and was bitten on his leg for his troubles. Try as they might, and they operated seven times, doctors could not prevent the resultant deadly infection.

❀ **2004: John Peel, margrave of the Marshes**
† *Cause of Death: The BBC?*

The veteran radio personality suffered a massive coronary while having drinks with "Pig", his wife, at the Monasterio Hotel in the high-altitude Peruvian city of Cuzco. The exotic location of his death rather bemused British listeners who so enjoyed his homespun style and who nicknamed him the "Margrave of the Marshes" because, countrary to the classic image of an urban clubbing DJ, he lived quietly with his family in boggy fenland. Fellow disc jockey Andy Kershaw asserted that the BBC could have been a factor in his death. He told the *Daily Mirror* that Peel confessed to him: "They have put my programme back further into the night and I feel marginalised. It's killing me." Most people agree, however, that he died, not from rescheduling, but from a dicky ticker.

## OCTOBER 26

❀ **1909: Ito, prince of Japan**
† *Cause of Death: Browning*

The prince was inspecting a company of crack Russian guards at the train station in Harbin. As he was raising his hat in salute, a man brandishing a Browning revolver sprang in front of him and shot him three times in the chest. Ito reeled backwards and was carried to his coach where he was given some brandy. When told that his assassin was a Korean, he replied, "The fellow is a fool."

*A cross-section of a turn-of-the-century Browning.*

## OCTOBER 27

❀ **1449: Ulugh Beg, Timurid Ruler**
† *Cause of Death: Son*

In his catalogue of 992 stars published in 1437, Sultan Ulugh Beg produced trigonometric tables where sin 1° was calculated to be

0.017452406437283571

when in fact, the correct approximation is of course

0.01745240643728351282.

Such precision demonstrates just how brilliant a mathematician and astronomer he was. His death suggests how such brilliance did not stretch to his parenting skills. His son, Abd al-Latif, defeated him in battle and then had his head chopped off.

## OCTOBER 28

❀ 1627: Jahangir, Moghul emperor
† *Cause of Death: Angelic Omen*

In his disarmingly frank diary, Jahangir writes of his first sip of sweet, yellow wine at age seventeen. He goes on to detail his descent into alcoholism, with his tipple of choice increasing in strength from wine to arrack, and then from arrack to double-distilled spirits. By his late twenties he was consuming up to twenty cups of the stuff, alongside a daily ration of opium, the "weight of fourteen berries."

His death, however, was not directly attributable to either drink or drugs, but from the sight of a servant falling from one of his palace turrets. The emperor considered it a sign from "the angel of death" that his number was up, and following three days of total abstinence, his fears were realized.

## OCTOBER 29

❀ 1268: Conradin, duke of Swabia
† *Cause of Death: Greed*

As well as duke of Swabia, Conradin was the titular king of Sicily, and in 1266 he marched over the Alps to wrest control of the island from Charles of Anjou. The two men's forces clashed at Tagliacozzo in central Italy. At a critical moment in the battle, the French appeared to retreat in disarray, and Conradin's forces – a job lot of Germans, Arabs, Spaniards and Italians – thought they had won the day and ran pell-mell towards the enemy camp in search of booty. As they scavenged, the French regrouped, marched up to the looters, and picked them off with ease. Conradin escaped but was caught trying to sail for Sicily and beheaded. He was sixteen.

## OCTOBER 30

❋ 1855: Emmeline, Lady Wortley
† *Cause of Death: The Road Less Travelled*

Emmeline was an enterprising if rather foolhardy traveller, and a successful if rather insipid travel writer. While in the Middle East, she insisted upon making a solo trek from Beirut to Aleppo, despite fracturing her leg during an encounter with a bad-tempered mule. If the journey up to Syria was reckless, the return trip, along a dangerous and unfrequented road, was madness. Somehow she managed to limp back to Beirut but died there, dehydrated and delirious.

## OCTOBER 31

❋ 1214: Leonora, queen of Castile
† *Cause of Death: Grief*

Leonora was the devoted sidekick of King Alfonso VIII of Castile, and when he died, she took to her bed and gave up the ghost within the month.

# NOVEMBER

## NOVEMBER I

✱ 1793: George, Lord Gordon
† *Cause of Death: Gaol Fever*

> *Ah! It'll be fine, it'll be fine, it'll be fine*
> *The aristocrats, we'll hang them!*

George, the third son of the third duke of Gordon, was a lifelong dissident, and the "Gordon Riots" of 1780, when for almost a week London was at the mercy of a wild, drunken Protestant mob, were named after him. Even though he instigated the uprising (and many were hanged for their participation in it) Gordon himself was acquitted of any treasonable act. That his last years were spent in Newgate Prison had, in fact, nothing to do with any attack, physical or otherwise, on the English establishment. His incarceration was instead the result of his libellous invective against the French ambassador and Queen Marie Antoinette, whom he charged with abuse of power and privilege.

Given his own wealth and privilege, his accommodation in Newgate was clean and spacious, and doctors urged him to remain in his quarters if he wished to guard himself against "gaol fever", the typhoid that killed hundreds of prisoners every year. True to form, however, Gordon paid little heed to those in authority. Eager to share his newfound Jewish faith, he converted his cell every Saturday into a makeshift synagogue, and invited all and sundry to come and worship with him. During the rest of the week, he assiduously spent his days visiting and offering words of spiritual comfort to his fellow inmates, many of whom were already sick with the disease.

The doctors were right to worry. As his maid massaged his feverish frame with hands that had been dipped in ice-cold water, Gordon's speech weakened until he could barely whisper. In awed silence, dozens of jailbirds listened intently as

*The Gordon Riots.*

this blue blood breathed out his last words – those of the "Ça Ira", the French revolutionary anthem of freedom:

*Ah! ça ira, ça ira, ça ira*
*Les aristocrates on les pendra!*

## NOVEMBER 2

❋ 1810: Amelia, princess of the United Kingdom
† *Cause of Death: Worthing?*

Every summer the young Princess Amelia spent a few weeks in the south coast resort of Worthing where her godfather, the Prince of Wales (later King George IV), had a house. And while she loved the company of the future monarch, she hated the wind off the sea that "hurts the drumsticks of my Ears". Her sister Princess Mary sympathised. "Nothing can be more dull than Worthing," she wrote, "confined to the couch and suffering so much pain." One day Prince George saw an alarming "eruption" on Amelia's face and had her whisked back to Windsor. There, despite constant medical supervision, the eruption slowly spread to her entire body and she died, aged 17, leaving her worldly goods to an equerry on whom she had a teenage crush.

# NOVEMBER 3

❀ 644: Umar I, Arabian Caliph
† *Cause of Death: Lulu*

A Persian slave called Abu Lulu complained to the caliph that at two dirhams a day he was being taxed too heavily. Umar replied that for someone so good with his hands (it was rumoured he was designing the first ever windmill) the amount was far from excessive. The following morning Abu Lulu stabbed the caliph while saying his prayers and then, on seeing Umar's fellow Muslims continue with their devotions, turned the knife on himself.

# NOVEMBER 4

❀ 1931: Charles, "King Bolden"
† *Cause of Death: Drink*

In the smoky back rooms of New Orleans dancehalls at the beginning of the twentieth century, a new kind of music was taking shape. It was loud, it was a little dangerous and its best practitioner was a cornettist called Charles "Buddy" Bolden. What precisely Bolden was doing differently, compared to his contemporaries, was difficult to pinpoint (his biographer Don Marquis termed it "ragging" with the music) but whatever it was, it sent the women wild.

With instant classics such as "Get Out of Here and Go Home" and "Funky Butt", Buddy acquired royal status, and "King Bolden", the father of jazz, reigned supreme until a fusion of hard liquor and acute schizophrenia bought him a one-way ticket to the asylum.

# NOVEMBER 5

❀ 1923: Jacques, Baron Adelswärd-Fersen
† *Cause of Death: Cocktail*

At first, Paris's social elite wallowed in the eccentricities of this poet-baron, and attended his salon parties mostly for the thrill of seeing nude "tableaux vivants" featuring local schoolboys. But after a while they saw him for what he really was – a smug, simpering pederast – and ostracised him to the isle of Capri where he slobbered at the island boys bathing and smoked himself into an opiate stupor.

His prodigious drug taking culminated one evening in drinking an unusual cocktail. The ingredients were champagne and lots of coke ... and there was not a drop of cola in sight.

## NOVEMBER 6

### ❋ 1612: Henry, prince of Wales
† *Cause of Death: Fever*

Henry was a Renaissance heartthrob, a strapping young prince with the looks of Adonis and brains to boot, and his sudden death at only eighteen shocked and baffled a nation. How exactly, everybody wanted to know, had he met his fate? The answer his doctors gave was, to say the least, unusual. They asserted that by removing his jacket to play a game of tennis, Henry had "allowed himself too much freedom of movement," leading to "violent and life-threatening over-exertion". To treat (unsuccessfully) the ensuing fever, these same physicians had then employed such unorthodox remedies as placing a pigeon on his head and a cockerel, split in half, against his feet. You cannot be serious.

### ❋ 1796: Catherine the Great, tsarina of Russia
† *Cause of Death: Stroke*

No, Catherine was not crushed to death by a horse whilst attempting to have sex with it. This was a completely prurient fabrication, probably spread by members of the French aristocracy, to sully her reputation. In actuality the tsarina suffered a stroke while in her privy closet, and died in bed some twelve hours later surrounded by animals exclusively of the two-legged variety.

### ❋ 1817: Charlotte, princess of England
† *Cause of Death: Lowering*

Charlotte's German doctor, Baron Stockmar, despaired at the medical treatment his charge was receiving at the hands of her English physician, Sir Richard Croft.

But this was the English court, and he knew his place. It was therefore with silent alarm that he looked on as Croft subjected the heavily pregnant princess to a "lowering treatment" of regular bleeding and underfeeding. Charlotte craved pork chops. Croft gave her tea and toast. And there was nothing Stockmar could do about it.

After giving birth to a stillborn boy, Charlotte started suffering spasms in the chest, and a concerned Croft finally consulted his colleague. Stockmar immediately went to her bedside, where he found her slightly drunk from a revised prescription of wine and brandy. "Schtocky! Schtocky!" slurred a terror-struck Charlotte before curling herself into the foetal position and following her son to the grave. A month later, Croft shot himself.

## NOVEMBER 7

❊ 1980: Terrence, "King of Cool"
† *Cause of Death: Cancer*

American doctors diagnosed mesothelemia, an uncommon cancer usually caused by exposure to asbestos, and told Terrence "Steve" McQueen, the unflappable anti-hero of such movies as *Bullitt* and *The Magnificent Seven*, that there was nothing they could do. McQueen, who possibly inhaled the carcinogenic fibres during his three-year stint as a Marine, decided to seek a second opinion and travelled south to the Chihuahua province of Mexico for some unorthodox medical treatment. There, he took laetrile, an experimental drug made from apricot pits, and underwent coffee enemas, but there was no escaping one of the most virulent forms of the disease.

## NOVEMBER 8

❊ 1226: Louis VIII, king of France
† *Cause of Death: Dysentery*

"In the mount of the belly shall the peaceable lion die." For some, not least the author of the *Grandes Chroniques de France*, the cryptic prophecy of King Arthur's wizard Merlin found fulfilment in Louis's death from acute dysentery. For his brave deeds, Louis was universally known as "The Lion", and the place of his death – Montpensier just north of Clermont-Ferrand – could, if you squinted and changed a couple of letters round, be the old French for "mount of the belly". The peaceable lion was less peaceable when the Archbishop of Bourbon arranged for a naked young woman to be slipped into his bed to keep him warm during his final hours. Louis kicked her out.

❊ 1793: Jeanne Marie Roland, viscountess de la Platiere
† *Cause of Death: Guillotine*

Unlike Louis XVI (*see* January 21) earlier in the year, Madame Roland had just enough time to finish her speech before the guillotine blade fell. Facing the Statue of Liberty on the Place de la Revolution, she cried, "O Liberty! What crimes are committed in thy name!" before becoming a crime statistic herself less than a minute later.

# NOVEMBER 9

❊ 1699: Hortense, duchess of Mazarin
† *Cause of Death: Drink*

The duke of Mazarin thought he was a tulip and had his servants "water" him every day. His wife Hortense, a buxom brunette known for several *liaisons dangereuses*, could not stand it and fled to Italy, and later to England, where she briefly became the favourite mistress of King Charles II. Given her intellectual acumen and sex appeal she also hosted a hugely popular salon where she became intimate in more ways than one with other men – and women – of the court.

When Charles died, she lived on a royal pension, most of which she frittered away on gambling and, according to the diarist John Evelyn, "the intemperate drinking [of] strong spirits". On her death, her floral husband took possession of her body and travelled with it the length and breadth of France, until finally agreeing that it would be best if she was planted somewhere.

## NOVEMBER 10

❀ 1793: Jean-Marie Roland, viscount de la Platiere
† *Cause of Death: Sword*

Having heard of Jeanne's execution (*see* November 8), Jean wrote a note. "As soon as I learned that they had murdered my wife, I would no longer remain in a world stained with enemies." He then positioned the note carefully on his chest, took out his sword, and dramatically secured it in place.

## NOVEMBER 11

❀ 1917: Liliuokalani, queen of Hawaii
† *Cause of Death: Stroke*

> I live in sorrow
> Imprisoned
> You are my light
> Your glory, my support

These are words from Liliukalani's famous song "The Queen's Prayer" written in March 1895, while she was under house arrest. The American authorities, who had already taken over control of the islands a couple of years earlier, were keeping her prisoner in her bedroom following a rebellion in which she was implicated, and she passed the time composing and playing the ukulele. After a few months they allowed her to move to Washington Palace, Honolulu's most prestigious address, in exchange for her abdication.

In confined splendour she lived out her days, a reluctant American citizen, demanding justice, receiving visitors and composing songs. Not all of them are sacred. One is about a quail, another celebrates her "granny", while a third, entitled "Wiliwiliwai", is addressed to a lawn sprinkler, with the chorus:

> Say there, say there
> You revolving object
> When, oh when
> Will you slow down?

## NOVEMBER 12

❉ 1567: Anne, duke of Montmorency
† *Cause of Death: Soldier of Fortune*

*Robert Stuart, killer of Anne, duke of Montmorency.*

In the overture to the Battle of Saint-Denis, Robert Stuart, a Scottish mercenary with the Huguenot army, rode up to Anne and demanded surrender. In reply, Anne picked up his sword, swivelled it round and broke three of his teeth with the hilt. Stuart bashed Anne's head in.

## NOVEMBER 13

❉ 1143: Fulk, king of Jerusalem
† *Cause of Death: Bunny Rabbit*

Fulk came a cropper while engaged in the Crusaders' equivalent of a Sunday drive. He was out with his wife Melisende on a gentle canter through a quiet suburb of Acre, when a rabbit broke cover, spooking both horse and rider. The unfortunate Fulk fell off and crashed heavily to the ground. His misery was then compounded when his saddle followed suit, sliding off his steed and crashing heavily onto his head.

## NOVEMBER 14

❉ 565: Justinian, Roman emperor
† *Cause of Death: Flea*

The carnage brought about by the bubonic plague that roared through the Byzantine Empire – at least twenty five million people lost their lives – meant that sixth-century Constantinopolitan octogenarians were a rarity, but by closeting himself in his palace and seldom setting foot out of the city, Justinian the Great ensured that he was one of the lucky few. His courtiers, unused to having a doddery old man in their midst, treated his sudden fascination in the minutiae of Church law (scouring dusty tomes to calculate the correct date for Epiphany, etc.) with good humour. They were less amused, however, when he announced that he was going on a pilgrimage to a small church in Anatolia … and they were coming along too.

It was a one-way journey. The "Black Death" that he had until then escaped, lurked in the fields around the church, and the aged emperor was felled by a flea carrying the deadly *Yersinia pestis* bacterium.

## NOVEMBER 15

✣ 1712: **James, duke of Hamilton, and Charles, Baron Mohun**
† *Cause of Death: Duelling Swords*

Hamilton went to great lengths to curry favour with Queen Anne, including naming his unlucky third son Anne in her honour, and was rewarded for his loyalty by being appointed Ambassador to France. Before he left England, however, he was tidying up some loose ends in the London law courts when he bumped into Charles, Lord Mohun, a nasty, aggressive man with whom his family had a running feud. Mohun was drunk. They argued. Mohun challenged him to a duel. Hamilton agreed.

William Morris (a humble groom, and not the pioneer of the British Arts and Crafts Movement) happened to be walking his horses towards Hyde Park when he saw four gentlemen squaring off against each other in a clearing. Morris testified that two of the men, whom he later learned to be Hamilton and Mohun, then set upon each other like savage beasts.

The fifty-four-year-old duke, though chubby and out of condition, had experience of duelling as well as the secret weapon of being ambidextrous. Suddenly switching his sword to his left hand, he caught the younger Mohun momentarily off guard, and struck what turned out to be a fatal blow to the chest. Mohun staggered backwards but, as he did so, somehow managed to slash his opponent's right arm, severing an artery. Now it was Hamilton's turn to stagger, in his case to a tree against which he collapsed, correctly exclaiming, "I am killed!" Within hours, ghoulish souvenir hunters had stripped the tree of its bark for macabre mementos of one of the bloodiest and most ferocious of all English duels.

# NOVEMBER 16

## ❀ 1272: Henry III, king of England
† *Cause of Death: Natural Causes*

Lovingly composed in different-coloured inks and dated March 23, 1263, an obituary in the annals of Tewkesbury Abbey extols Henry III's virtues, accentuating his sagacity, piety and political deftness. Basing their work on little more than hearsay, the monks had jumped the gun. Henry was very much alive, and it wasn't for a further nine years that the king, in the words of Raphael Holinshed, began to "wax somewhat craxsie".

The Gloucestershire monks were right on the money, however, when they wrote that the king was a deeply religious man. When Henry knew his "heavenly birthday" was soon approaching, he made for Westminster Abbey with all speed in order to sit alongside the tomb of his hero, Edward the Confessor, near to which he was himself interred a few days later.

# NOVEMBER 17

## ❀ 1558: Mary I, queen of England
† *Cause of Death: Cancer*

During her last year of life, Mary was treated her with indifference by her male colleagues. In early 1588, when she announced that she was pregnant, a sardonic cardinal of Lorraine commented that, since her husband Philip of Spain had been away from court for eight months, they wouldn't have to wait long to see if she was right. She wasn't. What she took for a baby was in all likelihood the emergence of ovarian cancer. Depressed and in great pain, the queen took to her bed, from which she comforted the women attending her, saying that she was having some lovely dreams in which angelic children plucked harps and sang sweet songs.

No one noticed her actual moment of death, although romantics would have us believe that her final sight on earth was the elevated host during Mass in her chambers. Philip, not exactly top of any list of romantics, had stayed abroad during her illness, and when he was told that she had died, wrote that he "felt a reasonable regret for her death".

# NOVEMBER 18

❁ 1305: John II, duke of Brittany
† *Cause of Death: Wall*

The crowds that amassed for the papal coronation of Clement V in Lyon were unruly and uncontrolled. As the pope passed by, a wall collapsed under the weight of the cheering spectators, Clement lost his balance and (a portent of a disastrous reign to come) the crown fell from his head. Things may have been uncomfortable for Clement, but they were worse for John who was leading the pope's horse at the time and was crushed to death under the rubble. Clement also came to a rather sorry end. He died after eating a bowl of crushed emeralds that he had been told might relieve his indigestion.

❁ 1851: Ernest, duke of Cumberland and king of Hanover
† *Cause of Death: Old Age*

The gutter press of the day pounced on salacious stories that Cumberland murdered one of his valets, raped one of his courtiers and slept with his one of his sisters. The serious papers showed more tact but no less opprobrium. When the eighty-year-old king died, the obituary in *The Times* began: "The good which may be said of the Royal dead is little or none."

# NOVEMBER 19

✤ 1825: Alexander I, tsar of Russia
† *Cause of Death: Sea Air*

Apart from a touch of housemaid's knee, contracted from kneeling in prayer on the cold stone floors of countless churches, Alexander was in fine fettle. His wife Elizabeth, on the other hand, was quite poorly and, on medical advice not to subject themselves to the ravages of another St Petersburg winter, the couple headed for the warmer climes of the small provincial outpost of Taganrog on the Sea of Asov. By all accounts, the sea air worked wonders for the empress. Not so for Alexander, who unexpectedly fell prey to "the bilious remittent fever of the Crimea".

# NOVEMBER 20

✤ 1591: Sir Christopher Hatton, English nobleman
† *Cause of Death: House*

With its three storeys, palatial staterooms and 123 windows (when glass was a rare commodity) Holdenby House in Northamptonshire was the largest private house in England. Hatton built it with one express purpose: to entertain Queen Elizabeth I. And he vowed never to spend a night in it until she was his guest. With dreams of his royal visitor, he spared no expense, going so far as to move an entire village so Elizabeth's view of the countryside would not be spoiled. The queen was touched by such a grand gesture, but never set foot across the threshold. In fact, she made it her business to ensure that Hatton repaid the £18,000 he had borrowed from the Crown to help with its construction.

Historian Thomas Fuller writes that her demand for full and immediate recompense not only broke his heart but also "cast him into a mortal disease". Financially and emotionally bankrupt, Hatton retreated to his rooms in London, where even a visit from Elizabeth herself could not halt his rapid decline. This was neither the place nor the manner in which he had hoped to play host to his sovereign.

## NOVEMBER 21

❀ 1969: Edward Mutesa II, king of Buganda
† *Cause of Death: Drink*

Sir Edward Frederick William David Walugembe Mutebi Luwangula Mutesa ("Freddie" for short) was found dead in his London apartment boozed up to his eyeballs. The police were confident that the one-time king of the Buganda region of Uganda, then Uganda's first president, then political exile, had deliberately drunk himself to death. Mutesa's supporters offer a different scenario. They suggest that ruffians in the employ of Milton Obote, Freddie's arch-rival, forced vast amounts of vodka down his throat.

## NOVEMBER 22

❀ 1774: Robert, baron of Plassey
† *Cause of Death: Penknife*

Suffering specifically from the agony of gallstones but more profoundly from a deep *Weltschmerz*, the man commonly known as "Clive of India" took his own life. How, precisely, is unclear. Lady Mary Coke heard that he collapsed after overdosing on medicine for a bowel problem. Horace Walpole wrote that, against his doctor's strict orders, he took two doses of laudanum "with fatal effects". Most fashionable at the moment is the belief that the founder of the British Empire in India slit his own throat. A lady visiting the house apparently approached him in his study and asked whether he would mend her pen. "To be sure" he replied and, taking a penknife from his waistcoat pocket, sharpened the quill. A short while later, a servant found he had taken the same penknife to his jugular.

## NOVEMBER 23

❀ 1407: Louis, count of Valois
† *Cause of Death: Burgundy*

Assassins on the payroll of the duke of Burgundy stalked Louis through the streets of Paris and set upon him as he was mounting his horse. Two sword blows expertly sliced through him just below the shoulders, rendering him armless, harmless, and soon lifeless.

## NOVEMBER 24

✱ 1830: Bungaree, Australian aboriginal "king"
† *Cause of Death: Old Age*

Colonial Australia's embarrassing relationship
with its indigenous population finds its way
into these pages in the form of Bungaree,
a natural entertainer with a winning smile
and the gift of the gab. Won over by his
coquettish manners and excellent grasp of
English, white Sydney society hailed him
as leader of the "Township Aboriginals",
and pressed him into giving public
demonstrations of boomerang throwing. The
well-meaning but naive Governor Macquarie
went so far as to dub him "King of the
Blacks" (and gave him a plaque to prove it)
and established him, together with principal
wife "Queen Gooseberry" and other wives
– "Askabout," "Onion", "Pincher", "Boatman" and "Broomstick" – on a nearby
farm. The venture failed, however, as did Bungaree's heart, after a life of being
misjudged, misused and misunderstood.

## NOVEMBER 25

✱ 1120: William Atheling, duke of Normandy
† *Cause of Death: Pilot Error*

When the captain of a brand new vessel called *The White Ship* requested the honour
of transporting Prince William back across the Channel to England, King Henry
I happily agreed. It is said that he never smiled again.

William and his mates were whooping it up when news came of their revised
travel plans, and to maintain the party mood, they sent several cases of wine
ahead of them. Spirits were running high. A group of priests who came to
bless the voyage were humiliated and sent packing, and by the time the boat
set sail, everyone – pilot included – was three sheets to the wind. Within
minutes of leaving port, the ship foundered on a rock and capsized. Howls of
despair were misinterpreted by those on land as howls of joy, and all hands

were lost, with the exception of Berold, a butcher from Rouen who had gone on board solely to collect some debts and had somehow got caught up in the festivities.

## NOVEMBER 26

✤ 1252: Blanche, queen consort of France
† *Cause of Death: Hay*

*From the ridiculous . . .*

En route to the Abbey of the Lys, Blanche of Castile fell into a bale of hay.

*. . . to the sublime*

Back in the Louvre in Paris, the queen donned the habit of a nun and lay down on a bed of straw. Conscious that her defective heart would pack in for good at any moment, she begged everyone for forgiveness, received the last sacraments and gently "fell asleep".

✤ 1818: Keppitipola, dissawa of Uva
† *Cause of Death: Blade*

A signal moment during the imperial conquest of what was then Ceylon was the execution of Keppitipola, perhaps the most noble of all rebel chiefs. Moved by his "propriety of behaviour" while in confinement, the British granted his final request of praying in a local temple. There, the dissawa gave the senior monk his upper tunic ("the only thing I have left to give") and washed his face and hands as a sign of purification, before walking calmly to his beheading on Kandy's Bagambara Green.

The head then went on a journey. A medical officer brought it back to Britain and donated to a museum in Edinburgh where it remained on display for over a century. Eventually, on the request of the government of Sri Lanka, it was shipped back to Kandy, and to this day islanders venerate the relic of a man who was as distinguished in death as he was in life.

❀ 1950: Edward, duke of Devonshire
† *Cause of Death: John Bodkin Adams?*

The duke died in the presence of his doctor. Nothing unusual in that, except the doctor in question was the suspected serial killer John Bodkin Adams, a GP thought to have helped well over a hundred of his patients to an early grave. Had Edward died a few months later, his family would not have had to sell off vast tracts of land and truckloads of precious heirlooms to pay crippling death duties.

## NOVEMBER 27

❀ 1779: Thomas, Lord Lyttleton
† *Cause of Death: A Ghost that would not be Bilked*

If Lyttelton is known for anything, it is his death, an account of which was written by his uncle some ten weeks after the event.

Thomas came down to breakfast one morning and nonchalantly declared that he had a curious dream in which a bird appeared before him and then suddenly morphed into a "Woman in White". The woman told him to prepare to die. He had replied that he hoped it wouldn't be for a couple of months at least, but the woman had insisted that it would be in three days.

The first day, as he dressed to go to the House of Lords, he made his staff agree that he looked marvellous and full of pep. On the evening of the second day, he told a Miss Amphlett not to look so melancholy as he had lived two days and "God willing he would live a third!" On the third morning he joked to some ladies that he believed he "should bilk the Ghost" and, after a busy day and hearty supper, went to bed. As he undressed he talked cheerfully to his servant and asked him to make sure that the rolls for breakfast were of a good quality. As his servant helped him remove his waistcoat he suddenly clutched his side, fell onto the bedspread and expired without even a groan.

## NOVEMBER 28

❀ 1290: Eleanor of Castile, queen consort of England
† *Cause of Death: Quartan Fever*

Not helped by the freezing temperatures that year, Eleanor died of quartan fever, a sister of malaria, in Harby, near Lincoln, and a distraught King Edward I began a sombre funeral procession back to London. At every place where the party stopped for the night on their journey south, he erected a memorial cross in his wife's honour. Of the twelve crosses, three still remain. The final monument, situated alongside the River Thames in London, is no more, and a bustling railway station now occupies the space where Charing Cross once stood.

## NOVEMBER 29

### ✿ 1314: Philip IV, king of France
† *Cause of Death: Boar*

De Molay's prophecy (*see* March 18) came true. While hunting near the town of Poissy, Philip was mauled to death by a wild boar less than nine months after the Grand Master of the Templars had spat out his curse.

### ✿ 1330: Roger Mortimer, earl of March
† *Cause of Death: Rope*

Mortimer's execution was a masterpiece of humiliation. For ordering the murder of King Edward II (*see* February 20) and carrying on with Queen Isabella, he was first made to put on the very same black tunic he wore at Edward's funeral, and then dragged on an ox hide by two horses from the Tower of London to Tyburn Hill. There, what was left of the tunic and his other clothing was ripped off him and, naked before God, he was then forced to listen to Psalm 52, including the words "Your tongue is like a sharp razor, you worker of treachery. You love evil more than good and lying more than speaking the truth." Finally, hoist by a piece of thick rope (and his own petard), he swung before his former subjects for two days and nights until some Franciscan friars were allowed to cut him down and bury him.

### ✿ 1988: Isabella, countess of Thurn, and Ludwig, prince of Hanover
† *Cause of Death: Drug Overdose and Gunshot*

A double tragedy for the House of Hanover. Ludwig came across his wife Isabella, dead from an overdose of cocaine. He rang for an ambulance, picked up his hunting rifle and shot himself in the head.

# NOVEMBER 30

❀ 1863: Kamehameha IV, king of Hawaii
† *Cause of Death: Broken Heart*

Wracked with guilt over the death of his son Albert (*see* August 27), weighed down by affairs of state and debilitated by chronic asthma, the previously hale and hearty monarch plunged into a vortex of glum, alcoholic depression ... and there was nothing anybody could do about it. Certainly there was nothing his wife, Queen Emma, could do to save him when his already shallow breathing stopped for good. Her attempt at mouth-to-mouth resuscitation was a heroic but ultimately futile act.

# DECEMBER

## DECEMBER I

❋ 1135: Henry I, king of England
† *Cause of Death: A Surfeit of Lampreys*

The lamprey is a hideously ugly eel-like creature with a great big sucker for a mouth. Gourmands wax lyrical about its flavour, but warn that it is fatty and hard to digest. Strange as it may seem, this was Henry's favourite food even though they always disagreed with him. Henry of Huntingdon writes that while Henry was staying at a hunting lodge in France, he wolfed down a whole bowl of them – expressly against his doctors' orders – and, as usual, fell ill. But this was no mere tummy upset. The "surfeit" of lampreys caused a "sudden and extreme disturbance" in his stomach and an "evil humour [cooled him] to a fatal degree".

## DECEMBER 2

❋ 1547: Hernán Cortés, marquis of the Valley of Oaxaca
† *Cause of Death: Pleurisy*

When Cortés the great conquistador finally returned from the New World, the Spanish didn't exactly bend over backwards to show their gratitude. They treated their old hero, in fact, with an indifference bordering on callous disregard. One day, when he saw the royal carriage passing his house, he ran outside and grabbed the straps, yelling for the emperor's attention. "Who is this man?" asked Philip. "I am the man," gasped Cortés, "who brought to Your Majesty more kingdoms than your father left you towns." Cortés was swatted away and the coach swept on. A nation's neglect, the guilt over his part in the execution of Aztec emperor Cuauhtémoc (*see* February 26), and acute shortness of breath made his last days an absolute misery.

## ✸ 1723: Philip II, duke of Orleans
† *Cause of Death: Mystery*

Obscene pamphlets detailing the antics of the champagne-swilling regent to Louis XV appalled and delighted the gossips of the day. Did he really have his favourite daughter, the charmingly silly Marie-Louise, pose nude for some etchings? Did she die at the tender age of twenty-four giving birth to his child? And what was his relationship with two other ladies of the court, one of whom was described as a "black little raven" with "knowing wiles"?

The English were similarly thrilled and shocked. When Philip visited London, bookmakers took one look at him and offered odds that he would be dead within three months. How he managed to live until forty-nine is a mystery, as is the precise cause of his death, since during his post mortem his pet dog leapt up on the slab, ran away with his heart, and ate it.

# DECEMBER 3

## ✸ 1894: Robert Louis Stevenson, Scottish nobleman
† *Cause of Death: Cork*

There was a modicum of blue blood in Stevenson's veins thanks to his mother's ancestry (she was descended from the first baronet of Minto) but there was hardly any red-bloodedness in the author, who spent much of his childhood and not a little of his adulthood being nursed back to health from one illness or another.

Retiring in his forties to the Samoan Island of Upolu, Stevenson refused to be an invalid again. "I wish to die in my boots," he wrote. "No more land of counterpane for me. To be drowned, to be shot, to be thrown from a horse — ay, to be hanged rather than pass again through that slow dissolution." He confided to his wife Fanny that he expected to succumb one day to consumption (tuberculosis), but in fact he died while helping her prepare supper. The effort of pulling a stubborn cork out of a bottle of wine one evening brought on a cerebral haemorrhage and he fell like a sack of potatoes onto the kitchen floor.

# DECEMBER 4

❋ 1944: Roger Bresnahan, duke of Tralee
† *Cause of Death: Heart Attack*

As his plaque in the American Baseball Hall of Fame records, Bresnahan was "one of the game's most natural players and might have starred at any position". Indeed the "Duke of Tralee" — so nicknamed because people (incorrectly) thought he was born in Tralee, Ireland — played all nine positions at the major-league level. He was best known as a catcher, however, most notably for the New York Giants between 1902 and 1908. When his sporting career ended, the duke returned to his native Toledo, Ohio, and spent his final days as a salesman for the city's Buckeye Brewing Company.

# DECEMBER 5

❋ 1082: Ramon Berenguer II, count of Barcelona
† *Cause of Death: Twin*

Long ago, a Spanish count had twin sons. He gave one of the boys the name of "Ramon Berenguer", but the public, thinking this was a bit of a mouthful, called him "Towhead" instead, on account of his white-blond hair. The other boy, the count called "Berenguer Ramon", and the public, perhaps confused by the transposition of names, didn't give him any nickname at all.

The boys never got on, and twenty or so years of mutual loathing finally culminated in Berenguer killing Ramon while they were out hunting in some woods. Had not Ramon's pet falcon enjoyed a bird's-eye view of the killing, the identity of his master's murderer might never have been known. At Ramon's funeral, the bird flew into the church and swooped about crazily, upon which the choir suddenly and involuntarily began singing the telltale words "Cain killed Abel! Cain killed Abel!" The public took the hint and finally gave Berenguer a nickname — that of "The Fratricide", "The Killer of his Brother".

❀ 1908: Helena, Comtesse de Noailles
† *Cause of Death: Old Age*

For much of her life, the eccentric Helena refused to drink anything but water in which pine cones had previously been boiled, while in her last few years, the octogenarian countess enjoyed a diet consisting almost exclusively of champagne and milk. She left her vast inheritance to her daughter on the condition that she never wear lace-up shoes.

## DECEMBER 6

❀ 2001: Sir Peter Blake
† *Cause of Death: Water Rat*

A band of Brazilian pirates got more than they bargained for when they boarded the *Seamaster*, a 119-foot schooner moored at the mouth of the Amazon River. Instead of some terrified tourists, they came across Blake and his crew having a few beers, celebrating a successful three-month expedition upriver. Sir Peter – perhaps the greatest ocean sailor of his age – and his muscle-bound mates offered spirited but ultimately futile resistance against the bandits, who were known locally as the "Water Rats". And Blake himself paid the ultimate price when one of the rats pumped two bullets into his back when he saw him clambering up from below deck with a rifle in his hand.

## DECEMBER 7

❀ 43 BC: Cicero, Italian nobleman
† *Cause of Death: Philippic*

Cicero had been a witness, but not a party, to the assassination of Julius Caesar (*see* March 15) – an event that proved to be the catalyst not only for his finest, but also his final, hour. With the dictator dead, Rome's greatest orator felt the time was ripe to launch a series of speeches demanding the restoration of the Republic. The speeches – known as Philippics – were brilliant; Cicero used biting wit and impassioned argument not only to press his political case, but also to denounce Mark Antony, a man whom he felt had personally wrecked the empire. His second philippic, in which he describes his enemy as "the cause of war, the cause of mischief, the cause of ruin", proved to be his death warrant. Antony and his fellow rival for power, the teenage Octavian, hammered out something of a power-sharing deal, and drew up a joint "hit-list" of people they wished to be rid of. For Antony, there could only be one name at the top.

Plutarch describes Cicero's execution in some detail. When Cicero realised that all attempts to flee were futile, he had his servants set down the litter in which he was travelling and allowed the imperial henchmen to catch up. He then "looked steadfastly at his murderers" and stretched his scraggly, chicken-like neck out from the litter. His head was swiftly separated from the rest of his body, and despatched, with his hands, to be nailed to the rostra in the Senate as a deterrent to potential dissenters. Before it was, however, Antony's wife Fulvia took it and placed it on her lap. She spat on it, forced open the mouth and, taking a pin from her hair, repeatedly jabbed the tongue that had so skilfully inveighed against her husband.

# DECEMBER 8

❀ 1626: Sir John Davies, poet
† *Cause of Death: Wife*

Sir John's wife was as mad as a box of frogs. One day while working on a commentary on the Book of Daniel, she apparently heard the voice of the prophet himself entrusting her with psychic powers, and to corroborate her claim, she pointed out that an anagram of her name – Eleanor Davies – was "Reveal O Daniel!" That this was not an anagram (one "l" too many and an "s" too few) didn't matter. The words "Daniel" and "Reveal" were there and that was good enough for her.

With her new clairvoyant powers, Eleanor began to pester people with messages of doom. One unfortunate target of Eleanor's attention was a Mrs Brooke, who became so distraught that her husband told Eleanor that if she did not stop badgering his wife he would "scratch a mince pie out of her". The argument ballooned into a public scandal, and prompted an embarrassed Sir John to burn Eleanor's prophecies – "an act", according to biographer Hans Pawlish, "that can hardly be viewed as a disservice to the reading public." Eleanor, in retaliation, predicted her husband's death within three years, and for three long years Davies had the unenviable experience of sharing a house with a mad wife dressed in mourning – for him.

At supper one evening, Eleanor suddenly burst into tears. Sir John asked what was wrong and she replied that she had foreseen his death within three days and that "these are your funeral tears". Sir John did indeed suffer a stroke and die within seventy-two hours, so perhaps Eleanor really was a prophetess. Or perhaps Davies just wanted to be rid of the woman.

## DECEMBER 9

### ✿ 1165: Malcolm IV, king of Scotland
† *Cause of Death: Paget's Disease*

Malcolm died when just 24 years of age, and some modern scholars attribute his early demise to osteitis deformans, more commonly known as "Paget's Disease", a condition in which the bones become enlarged or twisted. They wouldn't have known this back in the twelfth century, but a diet rich in local salmon (a splendid source of vitamin D) and milk from Highland cattle (excellent for calcium) would probably have helped the young monarch. Plenty of sunshine would also have been beneficial, but this was Scotland after all.

## DECEMBER 10

### ✿ 1865: Leopold I, king of Belgium
† *Cause of Death: Old Age*

Worried by news of her uncle's rapid decline, Queen Victoria arranged for her personal physician Dr Jenner to travel to Brussels and send daily bulletins on his condition. His reports, of a fragile twig of a man on a diet of broth every two hours and brandy every hour, reminded her "too painfully of beloved Albert's terrible illness" and worried her all the more. When Jenner and other medics confirmed that death was imminent, the king's daughter-in-law, Marie-Henriette, came to his side.

"Do not leave me," he pleaded.

"Sire," she responded, "do you regret the sins you have committed? Do you regret the scandals you have caused?"

The king immediately nodded, "Yes."

"And in the name of the love you bear the memory of the Queen," she continued, "would you not wish to draw closer to her and be converted to the religion that was hers?"

The Protestant king appeared to reflect momentarily on his own faith and that of the devoted and devout Catholic wife who had served him and country so well, before her death fifteen years before. He then raised his head from the pillow, parted his lips and firmly rasped, "No!"

Still holding Marie-Henriette's hand, the old monarch then whispered the name "Charlotte" a few times (no one quite knows who he was talking about) and permanently lost consciousness.

## DECEMBER II

### ❈ 1282: Llewellyn, prince of Wales
† *Cause of Death: Ambush*

Merlin's prophecies strike again (*see* November 8). The seer had once said that "when money should be round, a Prince of Wales should be crowned in London", so when Edward I introduced circular silver coins in Wales, many considered this a harbinger that their prince Llewellyn was to become king of England. They were wrong. One twilight, following a day of fierce fighting in the Wye Valley, Llewellyn was wending his weary way home, when a gaggle of English soldiers ambushed him and ran him through with their lances. They then cut his head off and sent it to London where it was put on public display, "crowned" with willow and ivy. So maybe Merlin was right after all.

### ❈ 1718: Charles XII, king of Sweden
† *Cause of Death: Button?*

While visiting the trenches during his war with Norway, Charles literally put his head above the parapet and paid the price. A rather fun if fanciful theory has it that the deeply unpopular Charles was actually shot by one of his own men using a bullet fashioned from a button stolen from his uniform. Recent level-headed research suggests, however, that the idea is just plain silly, and that the bullet did indeed emanate from a Norwegian musket.

## DECEMBER 12

✾ 1758: Francoise d'Issembourg d'Happencourt de Grafigny,
French noblewoman
† *Cause of Death: Aristide's Daughter*

Of all Francoise's many plays, *La Fille d'Aristide* was her last and her worst. The
abbot of Voisenon said, "She read me her play, I thought it bad, she thought me
unkind. The play was put on, the public died of boredom and she of grief."

## DECEMBER 13

✾ 1521: Manuel I, king of Portugal
† *Cause of Death: Indolence*

The chronicler Damiao de Gois writes how the dynamic Manuel was always on
the go, revelling in the frenzied busyness of an increasingly prosperous nation. He
reserved his greatest energies, however, for overseas expansion, "having discovered,
conquered and subjugated all the maritime provinces from the Strait of Gibraltar
to the seas of Arabia, Persia ... all the way to China." On the domestic front,
meanwhile, he energetically forged diplomatic links with ambassadors at his
court from "European kingdoms ... the Supreme Pontiff, and from many kings
and rulers of Africa and Asia". Nor was he a slouch on the even more domestic
front, producing "six sons and three daughters ... all gifted with beauty, good
dispositions and virture".

Given this picture of a high-octane monarchy, it seems wholly out of character
that he should die of "a sort of lethargy" when only fifty-two.

## DECEMBER 14

✾ 1542: James V, king of Scotland
† *Cause of Death: A Bad Year*

Culminating in the rout of his forces at Solway Moss, 1542 was an *annus horribilis*
for James, and he decided it was to be his last. "Where do you plan to spend
Christmas?" asked his courtiers, "so we can make the necessary preparations."
"You choose. I don't care," he answered morosely, "for before Christmas Day
you shall be without a master, and Scotland without a king." He was right. At

Falkland, he took to his bed with a high fever, and when news came that his queen had given birth to a baby girl and not a boy as he had hoped, he sighed deeply and pegged out.

## ✱ 1855: Charles Sibthorp, English nobleman
† *Cause of Death: Speech*

Quite unintentionally the funniest Member of Parliament of his time, Charles de Laet Waldo Sibthorp was a bewhiskered ultraconservative fop who detested anything that smacked of progress. His speeches in the House, in which he denounced railways and the newfangled "water closet", were hugely entertaining, but lightweight. His last speech in the Commons really was his last speech. Having suggested that Lord John Russell had misappropriated some public funds, he sat back down, had a stroke, and died.

## ✱ 1878: Alice Maud, princess of the United Kingdom
† *Cause of Death: Kiss*

When all but one of her children developed diphtheria, Alice dropped everything to care for them, and thanks to her incessant care and devotion, they all survived. All, that is, except the youngest – little Marie – who was simply too weak to withstand the ravages of the disease. For several days, Alice kept the news of Marie's death away from the other children, but finally she had to tell them that their baby sister had not gone on holiday (as she had previously stated) but had in fact passed away. On hearing the news, nine-year-old Ernie collapsed in a heap. To comfort him, Alice picked him up in her arms and tenderly kissed him, contracting the disease herself. Exhaustion from her selfless consideration of others rendered her defenceless, and she joined Marie within the week.

# DECEMBER 15

**❀ 1854: Kamehameha III, king of Hawaii**
† *Cause of Death: Drink*

The "white man's plague" of smallpox descended upon Hawaii in May 1853, and since the islanders had no natural resistance, they fell like flies. Kamehameha was one of the first to be vaccinated by a "haole" doctor, but six thousand of his subjects, including his favourite paramour, perished. The king was appalled at the loss of life and took to the bottle. Even for a big man his intake was phenomenal – a missionary called Mrs Amos Starr Cooke wrote in her journal that he was continuously drunk – and a year and half later he perished from alcoholism, a disease that remains to this day something of an epidemic in Hawaii.

# DECEMBER 16

**❀ 1945: Fumimaro Konoe, Japanese prince**
† *Cause of Death: KCN*

A prince of the royal line of Fujiwara, Konoe wasn't a natural warmonger, but will always be known as the prime minister whose cabinets successively oversaw the outbreak of the Sino-Japanese War and the start of the Second World War. Following Japan's surrender, he was commanded to turn himself in to the allies, but rather than face the ignominy of a public trial and possible execution, Konoe committed hari-kari by swallowing some potassium cyanide pills.

# DECEMBER 17

**❀ 1833: Kaspar, German "nobleman"**
† *Cause of Death: Dagger*

The enigma that is Kasper Hauser stretches from the circumstances of his birth to the manner of his death. When a young man of about sixteen, he was found in a square in Nuremberg clutching a note that claimed he had lived his entire life in isolation and suggested that he was of noble stock (in 2002, the Institute for Forensic Medicine of the University of Münster analysed DNA from his clothing, and concluded that he may well have been the son and heir of the Grand Duke Karl of Baden).

Five years later he was found staggering from a stab wound to the base of his heart. Hauser himself swore that a stranger had pounced upon him, but there are many who think the wound was self-inflicted, and many others who argue that he was bumped off to ensure his true origins remained a mystery.

# DECEMBER 18

✾ 1966: Tara Browne, Irish nobleman
† *Cause of Death: Lorry*

John Lennon picked up a copy of the *Daily Mail* and read that London socialite Tara Browne had died in a high-speed car crash in South Kensington. This inspired him to write the lyrics for the Beatles song "A Day in the Life".

"He blew his mind out in a car," Lennon wrote, while in fact Browne had ploughed his Lotus Elan into the back of a parked lorry. The songwriter was closer to the target, however, when he stated that, "He didn't notice that the lights had changed." Browne was quite possibly under the influence of mind-expanding drugs.

The remainder of Lennon's verse highlights the Swinging Sixties' fixation with celebrity even at times of horror: "A crowd of people stood and stared," he penned. "They'd seen his face before. Nobody was really sure if he was from the House of Lords."

# DECEMBER 19

✾ 1075: Edith, queen of England
† *Cause of Death: Old Age*

Edith died a rich woman – lonely, sad and friendless maybe – but rich, and for someone whose entire family had either been killed or thrown into exile during the Norman Conquest, this was quite an achievement. Semi-legend has it that during the last weeks of what was a long and painful illness, Edith denied any and all accusations of adultery by confirming that (despite a twenty-year marriage to Edward the Confessor) she was as chaste as the day she was born. She is buried near, but not alongside, her husband in Westminster Abbey.

# DECEMBER 20

❋ 1765: Louis, dauphin of France
† *Cause of Death: Pulmonary Tuberculosis*

Everyone was really impressed by the manner in which Louis met his end. The nobility were impressed with the natural grace and true grit he displayed in his daily audiences with them. Horace Walpole, on a visit to France, was impressed with the regularity with which Louis, who looked like "a spectre and cannot live three months", told his wife-cum-nurse how much her loved her. And even the cynical Richelieu was impressed "that one could be so peaceful and serene at the gates of death". The courtiers at Versailles were more impressed by his death than his dying, as it meant they could start partying again.

❋ 1961: Sir Earle Page, Australian politician
† *Cause of Death: Lung Cancer*

If a week in politics is a long time, forty-two years must be an eternity, but that is the length of time that Page held the same seat in the Australian Parliament. To many, the former prime minister's defeat in the 1961 general election was something of a shock. But not to Page: he died before he knew the result.

# DECEMBER 21

❋ 1992: Albert King, "King of the Blues"
† *Cause of Death: Heart Attack*

Of the four blues "kings" – Freddie, B.B., Earl and Albert – it was Albert who was the most unorthodox. His unique style of playing the guitar "upside down" – although left-handed he played with the strings set up for a right-handed musician, with the low E string at the bottom – meant that he bent a blues note by pulling, rather than pushing the string, producing an individual sound described as "falling off a cliff and bouncing back up". The "King of the Blues" suffered a massive coronary while in Memphis and at his funeral Eagles guitarist Joe Walsh played a rendition of "Amazing Grace". Presumably a performance of one of King's best-loved songs, "Everybody wants to go to heaven / But nobody wants to die", would have been a trifle gauche.

# DECEMBER 22

## ❀ 69: Vitellius, Roman Emperor
† *Cause of Death: Sword*

Disguise isn't easy when you're emperor. Your face is on the coinage for a start. Vitellius tried to evade capture by donning filthy rags and hiding in a large smelly kennel. Unfortunately, the dogs didn't recognise the authority of their visitor and bit large chunks out of him, and his yelps alerted some soldiers who seized him, laughed at his pot belly and then dragged him to the Gemonian Steps, where he underwent the ritual of torture, dismemberment and decapitation meted out to so many of his imperial forebears.

# DECEMBER 23

## ❀ 1588: Henry, duke of Guise
† *Cause of Death: Daggers*

The duke, who had been ordered to Henry III's chateau at Blois without explanation, was nervously munching on some prunes called "Brignoles", when he was summoned to see the king. Still holding the small box of fruit in his hand, he stooped down and started to make his way along the low passageway that linked his room to the royal quarters. Suddenly no fewer than eight henchmen launched themselves upon him and stabbed him repeatedly. Unable to extract his sword which had become entangled in the folds of his cloak, Henry turned to his only available weapon, his prune-filled "comfit-box", and lobbed it pathetically at one of his assailants.

   With arms outstretched like Frankenstein's monster, the duke somehow managed to stagger into the king's chamber, only to crumple onto the floor in a bloody heap. At this juncture, King Henry nonchalantly strolled into the room and saw his rival slumped lifeless at the bottom of his bed. "My God, how big he is!" he remarked. "He seems bigger dead than alive."

## DECEMBER 24

### 1749: John, earl of Crawford

† *Cause of Death: That Thirtieth Opening*

At the Battle of Krotzka in July 1739, Crawford's favourite black horse was shot underneath him. As he was mounting a fresh horse, a musket ball ripped into his left thigh, shattering the bone, and when he was eventually scraped off the battlefield, doctors declared that the wound was "mortal though not immediately fatal". Their diagnosis was spot on, although they probably didn't think the process would take a decade. Crawford spent the following ten years alternating between baths and battles, but eventually, after twenty-nine agonising "re-openings" of the wound, died when yet again, the bones came apart. Horace Walpole insists that the wound was not the cause of death but the bucket-load of laudanum he took to stave off the pain.

## DECEMBER 25

### 820: Leo V, Byzantine emperor

† *Cause of Death: Escaped Convict*

With guards posted at the doors of the cathedral, Leo was praying alone before the altar in the Hagia Sophia. Little did he know that his rival Michael the Amorian had escaped jail and, disguised as a priest (except for the dagger in his hand and chains still on his wrists), was padding down the nave. Just as Michael and his men reached the chancel step, the emperor broke away from his meditation and grabbed whatever came to hand to defend himself. These turned out to be a large wooden cross and an incense burner, and although neither was manufactured with fighting in mind, he swung the thurible and jabbed the cross to good effect. Eventually, though, he was overpowered and fell to his knees, one last prayer on his lips.

*A thurible.*

# DECEMBER 26

## ❋ 1476: Galeazzo Maria Sforza, duke of Milan
† *Cause of Death: Vanity*

It was bitterly cold morning and Bona, the duchess, begged her husband to stay home, but Galeazzo said he was determined to hear Mass at the Church of St Stephen on the saint's feast day. Bona replied that if he must go, he should wrap up warm and, in such violent times, remember to wear his breastplate. Sforza again refused to listen, saying it made him look fat. On the church steps, a man knelt before him and held out his cap as if asking for money. Galeazzo leaned over to hear the man's petition, upon which the "beggar" sprang up and plunged his dagger into the duke's unprotected chest.

*The murder of Galeazzo Maria Sforza.*

# DECEMBER 27

## ❋ 1734: Lee Boo, prince of Pelew
† *Cause of Death: Smallpox*

Shipwrecked on a remote island in the Pacific, the crew of *The Antelope* thought they were going to be eaten. The inhabitants of Pelew (modern-day Palau) were known to be cannibals, and Captain Wilson and his crew feared they would be lunch. Luckily, the local chief offered, rather than considered, them food, and gave them as many trees as they needed to reconstruct their vessel. In fact, the chief was so impressed with the sailors' courtesy, ingenuity and shipbuilding skills that he asked his visitors whether they would take his second son Lee Boo away with them, so he could become a learned Englishman.

And so it was that the twenty-year-old prince found himself a few months later in the unprepossessing district of Rotherhithe in southeast London in the grips

of the equally unprepossessing pox. Lee Boo held no grudges, however, and his dying wish was for the following message be taken in due course to his father: "Lee Boo take much drink to make smallpox go away, but he die: that the Captain and Mother very kind – all English very good men."

## DECEMBER 28

❋ 1694: Mary II, queen of England
† *Cause of Death: Smallpox*

When King William III was told that his wife was diagnosed with smallpox and "the very worst and most dangerous sort", he burst into tears and declared that from being the happiest, he was now "the miserablest creature upon earth". Until her inevitable death, he sat by her bed and watched helplessly as the small pustules expanded into large menacing spots. One blotch, situated "above the region of heart" concerned the doctors most of all, and they did everything in their power, including administering theriac, a drink containing honey, opium and dried viper, to stop it increasing. But they lost the battle, and Mary lost her life, and William lost the only thing he truly loved.

## DECEMBER 29

❋ 1986: Harold, earl of Stockton
† *Cause of Death: Old Age*

Former British prime minister Harold Macmillan, famous for his remark to the electorate that "You never had it so good", never had it so bad than in late 1986. By then he was a grand old man of ninety-two, with a lengthy political career on which to reflect. "Sixty-three years ago," he mused, "the unemployment figure [in my constituency] was 29%. Last November … 28%. A rather sad end to one's life."

# DECEMBER 30

## ❋ 1460: Richard, duke of York
† *Cause of Death: Swords*

The grand old Duke of York, he had ten thousand men. Well, actually, those in the know think that it was more like five thousand. He marched them up to the top of the hill at Sandal Castle in Wakefield and then marched them down again to face a far superior Lancastrian force. Outnumbered and outmanoeuvred, Richard of York gave battle in vain, and, together with nearly half his troops, fell in the field.

Military historians consider the Battle of Wakefield to be a significant event in the Wars of the Roses. Children worldwide, meanwhile, unwittingly remember it as the derivation behind a nursery rhyme and a mnemonic for the order of the colours of the rainbow.

# DECEMBER 31

## ❋ 192: Commodus, Roman Emperor
† *Cause of Death: Narcissus*

Commodus's Curriculum Vitae, like so many of the emperors before him, was studded with brutality, butchery and bloodshed. Likewise, a group of his closest companions couldn't stand the barbarity any longer and plotted his murder. Plan A was for Marcia, his favourite mistress, to persuade him to drink a goblet of poisoned wine, and it worked like a dream, until the unaccommodating Commodus was violently sick and vomited up its contents. Plan B had therefore to be put into operation.

It came in the shape of Narcissus, the emperor's personal wrestling partner, who thundered into his private chambers while he was in the bath, bore down on him like a rhinoceros, and snapped his neck like a twig.

## ❋ 1510: Bianca Maria, empress of Austria
† *Cause of Death: Snails?*

Beautiful she may have been, and at needlework she may well have had no equal, but Maximilian I found his second wife intolerable and treated her with complete disdain. Some commentators say she died of "chagrin" at such treatment, while others put her death down to a weak digestion brought on by eating her favourite food of snails. And these were no common or garden snails. These, writes historian William Coxe, were Austrian snails, lovingly fattened up for the table to a size that would "pall the appetite of an English ploughman".

*A snail.*

# CAUSE OF DEATH

1 of the 101 — July 8
23 Blows — March 15
27,860 Bloody Eye Sockets — October 6

A

A Certain Welsh Beer? — January 7
A Ghost that would not be Bilked — November 27
A Surfeit of Lampreys — December 1
AIDS — February 2
Alderman — August 12
Alzheimer's Disease — June 12
Ambush — December 11
American Independence — May 11
An Abbot's Amorous Advances — April 19
Angelic Omen — October 28
Ant — April 6
Apoplexy — January 8
Argument — June 9
Aristide's Daughter — December 12
Arrow — August 2
Arrow and Sword — October 14
Assegai — June 1
Axe — January 16, January 19, January 30, February 12,
    February 13 (x 2), May 27, June 14, July 15, August 9,
    November 26

Bad Manners — July 4
Barbary Macaque — October 25
Barbiturates — August 5

The BBC? — October 25
Being Caught with One's Trousers Down — January 17, April 8
Bertrade — July 29
Big Shiny Badge — March 29
Bite — August 15
Blood Clot — February 6
Bloodless Coup — May 12
Blow to the Head — July 24
Blue Naked People — April 23
Blunderbuss — June 22
Boar — November 29
Boil — April 27
Bolsheviks — July 17
"Brain Fever" — August 27
Brake Failure? — September 14
The British — April 13
Broken Heart — November 30
Browning — October 26
Bug — March 31
Bullet — March 18
Bunny Rabbit — November 13
Burgundy — November 23
Business — September 19
Button? — December 11

Camels — July 20
Cancer — March 28, July 10, September 13, September 29, November 7, November 17
Cannon — August 3
Cannonball — February 5
Car Crash — January 15, August 31
Catalogue — April 18
Charcoal Burners — February 1
Chest Infection — June 27
Chesterfields and Grouse — February 9
Chicken — April 9
Cirrhosis of the Liver — August 13
Class Consciousness? — January 18

Cleric? — June 11
Coach Crash — July 13
Cocktail — November 5
Coiffure — October 15
Cold Bath — February 6
Cold Dip — January 11
Comma — August 3
Congestive Heart Failure — August 20
Cork — December 3
Cossack — May 16
Cricket Ball — March 20
Crow Dog — August 5
Cubicularius — September 15
Cuckoldry? — May 3
Curiosity — March 13
Curse of the Mummy? — April 5

Dagger — February 19, April 16, December 17
Daggers — January 24, September 28, December 23
Danish Hospitality — April 14
Defenestration — May 29, August 16
Depression — July 6, December 14
Desire for Glory — August 11
Dial — July 12
Disappointment — September 17
Disguise — October 2
Doctors — February 6
Dodgy Electrician — March 5
Double-Crossing — April 12
Dream — September 22
Drink — January 15, January 31, November 4, November
   9, November 21, December 15
Dropsy — January 3, March 2, August 17
Drowning — June 10
Drug Overdose — June 10
Drug Overdose and Gunshot — November 29
Duelling Swords — November 15
Duodenal Cancer — January 7
Dysentery — July 7, November 8

Ear — July 21
Edward? — May 21
Eel — August 17
The Enemy Within — October 8
Erosion of a Nation — May 7
Escaped Convict — December 25
Excess — January 28, May 31, July 2, July 26, July 27
Excessive Bathing — June 23, September 13
Exhaustion — August 7

Falcon — March 27
Falling down the Stairs — January27
Fat — July 22
Feathers — September 9
Fever — July 11, August 21, September 21,
    September 25, October 18, November 6
Fifteen Degrees — August 25
Figs? — August 19
Final Request — August 26
Firing Squad — June 19
Fish — April 2
Fish and Folly — October 4
Flames — March 18, July 16
Flea — November 14
"Frenchman" — August 23
Fruit and a Woman Scorned — June 21

Gallantry — April 27
Game of Darts? — May 15
Gangrene — September 1
Gaol Fever — November 1
Garotte — August 29
Gastric Haemorrhage, etc. — June 26
"Gastric Problems" — March 24
Gatecrasher — May 26
Gift of God — March 15, May 18
Gluttony — May 23, June 8, July 21
The Good Life — January 20, September 15

Gordon — February 7
Gout — February 4, August 14
Greed — October 29
Greenberry Hill? — October 12
Grief — August 10, September 20, October 31
Guards — July 5
Guillotine — January 21, October 16, November 8
Guilt — May 30
Gunshot — October 9

Hackbut — January 23
Halberd and Spear — January 5
Hammer — September 23
Handgun — February 24
Hay — November 26
Heart Attack — May 6, June 3, June 4, August 25,
    October 25, December 4, December 21
Helicopter Crash — February 9
High Visibility — August 4
Hit-List — September 18
Holy Javelin? — February 3
Holy Water — April 2
Horseplay — February 23
House — November 20
Humiliation — February 16, August 8

Illicit Gardening — July 7
"Immense Efforts" — February 26
Inappropriate Military Uniform — June 18
Incompetence — March 14
Indolence — December 13
Infernal Machine — July 28
Inflammation of the Colon — February 24
Influenza — January 14
Involuntary Euthanasia — January 20
IRA — August 27
Irrelevance — October 8

John? — April 3
John Bodkin Adams? — November 26
Jumping into Boat — September 24
Just Dessert — June 17

KCN — December 16
Killjoy — March 25
Kiss — December 14
Knot — March 1
Knout — June 26
KOOLS — February 15

Lack of Breakfast — March 17
Lack of Love — April 24
Lack of Protection — October 17
Lack of Publicity — June 16
Lack of Sun — January 12
Lack of Victory — April 22
Lamentations Chapter 5 — September 16
Lance — July 10
Lemon — April 10
Lèse Majesté — April 28
Letter Opener — August 12
Leukaemia — August 21
Lightning — September 2
Lintel — April 7
Liquid Lunch — April 20
Liver Cancer — January 14
Lobster — March 18
Lola Montez — February 29
Lorry — December 18
Lousy French Accent — July 6
Lowering — November 6
Lulu — November 3
Lung Cancer — December 20
Lupus — August 1
Lyon and Moretto? — April 19

Madness — January 19, July 9, October 5
Magic Formula — September 10
Malaria — January 9
Malmsey — February 18
Mangonel — June 25
Map — June 11
Margaret? — October 4
Mattress or Towel — September 8
Measles — July 14
Melancholy — October 7
Michael — April 11
Milosh Obilic — June 28
Mine — June 5
Mineshaft — January 2
Mob — September 3
Mole — March 8
Monk — August 2
Monsieur Vallot's "Luckless Grains" — September 10
More Bolsheviks — July 18
Morphew? — June 7
Morsel — April 15
Mullet — April 1
Mushroom — October 13, October 20
Musketeer — June 25
Mustang — July 5
Mystery — December 2

Naja haje? — August 12
Naked Lust — January 6
Narcissus — December 31
Natural Causes — January 22, January 25, May 8,
    November 16
Nightingale — June 1
Nightlife — February 27
The Nile — January 13
Northumberland — August 22
Nutcracker — May 20

Old Age — January 5, March 9, March 24, March 30, April 26, May 14, May 22, May 25, August 16, August 18, September 11, October 22. November 18, November 24, December 5, December 10, December 19, December 29
Omelette? — June 15
One Question too Many? — June 13
Orthodox Blessing — May 17
Ortolan — April 29

Paget's Disease — December 9
Pancakes and Milk — February 18
Pardon — March 12
Parsimony — October 5
Passive Smoking — March 21
Pavement — August 24
Pea Soup — February 26
Penknife — November 22
Peritonitis — June 30
Philippic — February 5, December 7
Picking Flowers — March 10
Pike — March 16
Pilot Error — August 28, November 25
Plague — October 11
Plane Crash — July 31
Pleurisy — December 2
Pneumonia — January 5
Pneumonia and Cirrhosis of the Liver — June 20
Poet — May 24
Polish — February 10
Polo — June 24
Pommel — September 9
Poor Medical Attention — January 28
Poor Penmanship — August 6
Porphyria — January 29
Publishing Venture — March 3
Pulmonary Tuberculosis — December 20

Quartan Fever — November 28
Quartermaster — October 10
Quinsy — April 21

Rainstorm — September 8
Rapier — June 3
Razor — April 30
Recklessness — May 9
Recruit — September 5
Red Hot Poker — February 20
Religious Devotion — March 4
The Road Less Travelled — October 30
Rope — January 3, February 26, May 2, October 3,
    November 29
Rope and Axe — February 3
Rope and Butcher's Knife — July 1
Rudder Lock — January 26
Rye Bread — March 20

S

Salute — September 6
Scarf — March 23
Scottish Maiden — June 2
Scramble — February 17
Sea Air — November 19
Sex — January 1, January 19, March 11
Shame — April 25
"Shingles" etc — August 30
Shipwreck — July 19
Sightseeing — March 26
Silk? — May 5
Six Bullets? — January 30
Sleeves — February 10
Slipping out of Neutral — July 25
Smallpox — January 29, May 10, December 27,
    December 28
Snails? — December 31
Snobbery — October 24
Snuff? — February 8

Soldier of Fortune — November 12
Something Saintly? — August 31
Son — June 1, October 27
Spanish Flu — February 16
Spark — May 4
Speech — December 14
Starvation — July 22, September 27
"Stenography" — April 17
Stick — March 22
Stomach Cancer — May 5
Stone — June 29
Strangury and Stone? — January 28
Stroke — January 4, February 11, May 13, November 6,
    November 11
Strychnine? — June 10
Submarine? — May 30
Summons — September 7
Swiss Cheese — March 7
Sword — October 23, November 10, December 22
Sword of Calais — May 19
Swords — January 15, September 12, December 30

That Fourteenth Semla — February 12
That Second Red Pill — September 26
That Thirtieth Opening —December 24
Tennis Balls — February 21
Things Left Undone which They Ought to Have Done
    — September 4
Throat Cancer — May 28
Thrombosis of the Lungs — March 6
Tile — June 6
Toadstool — February 14
Traffic Jam — May 14
Tsetse Fly — October 1
Tuberculosis — June 8, October 21
Tumour — July 30
Twin — December 5
Two Questions and a Blade — July 17

Uncle — February 22
Underwear — February 25
Uxorial Duty — March 19

Vanity — December 26
Varlet — February 28
Veil — September 15
Viper Wine? — May 1

Wall — November 18
Wanton Baggage — June 21
Wantonness — January 10
Water Rat — December 6
The Welland and Peaches — October 19
Wet Stockings — January 23
Whist — January 5
Wicked Stepmother — January 1
Wife — December 8
Will — September 30
Wine — April 4
Worthing? — November 2

Yams — September 10
Yorker — July 23

# INDEX

— A —

abbot,
    lecherous: April 19
    light-fingered: July 29
    vindictive: July 29
accountants, used as traffic bollards:
  June 16
aphrodisiac: May 1, September 26
archbishop,
    conspiratorial: January 23
    emulating a yo-yo: March 24
    unshaven: January 28
armagnac, drowned in: April 29
armour,
    fashioned from scrap metal: April 6
    forgotten: October 17
    green: August 4
authors:
    Elizabeth Barrett Browning: July 19
    Robert Browning: July 19
    George Byron: April 19, August 12
    Thomas Carlyle: July 19
    Agatha Christie: February 10
    Alexander Dumas: June 25
    Euripides: October 23
    Antoine de Saint-Exupery: July 31
    George Sand: July 19
    George Bernard Shaw: September 11
    Voltaire: October 20
    P. G. Wodehouse: May 25
    William Wordsworth: July 19

— B —

baby, three-legged: May 14
backbone, sawn in two: August 16
baptism,
    delayed: May 22
    under duress: August 29
bark, removed from tree as souvenir:
  November 15
Barry Manilow, allusion to: February 29
battle of,
    Bosworth Field: August 22
    Crecy: August 26, October 11
    Hastings: October 14
    Hattin: July 4
    Newbury: September 20
    Saalfeld: October 10
    Scanderoon: July 11
    Tagliacozzi: October 29
    The Boyne: September 16
    Wakefield: December 30
beard, setting light to one's own: March 5
bed-linen, struck on head with: February 23
Beatles (The): December 18
Beethoven, 3rd piano concerto of: October 10
beheading: January 16, January 18,
  February 3, February 12, February 13
  (x2), April 28, June 2, June 14, July 1,
  August 9, November 26
    particularly neat: January 30, May 19,
  July 17
    particularly messy: May 9, May 27,
  July 15,

binge drinking, April 4, May 31, June 26,
   October 28, November 25, December 15
binge eating, June 8, June 26, July 21,
   September 1
bird,
      budgerigar, homing: October 9
      chicken, tied to table leg: January 19
      cockerel, medicinal: November 6
      crane, pet: April 19
      crow, pet: April 19
      eagle, pet: April 19
      falcon,
         guano of: April 7
         lethal: March 27
         pet: April 19
         portentous: December 5
      flamingo, sacrificial: January 24
      goose, pet: April 19
      nightingale, lethal: June 1
      ortolan, eaten whole: April 29
      partridge, eaten whole: September 1
      pheasant, eaten whole: September 1
      peacock, pet: April 19
      quail, song about: November 11
      wren, torn apart: March 15
bishop, drunk: July 29
bomb,
      concealed in boat: August 27
      concealed in handkerchief: March 13
books of the Bible,
      Daniel: December 8
      Exodus: May 18
      Genesis: August 9
      Lamentations: September 16
      Leviticus: June 26
      Psalms: January 19, November 29
boomerang throwing: November 24
bread,
      rye: March 20, August 31
      white: March 24
breasts, extremely large: February 29
brick, magic: April 5
bride, inappropriate choice of: March 9
burial,
      alive: June 3

      in glass coffin: June 10
      in secret location: May 8
      upright, January 28
butt,
      head: September 29
      of Malmsey: February 18

────── C ──────

Cain and Abel: August 9, October 18,
   December 5
camel,
      flea-ridden: September 12
      military: October 21
cannibalism: January 24, June 11,
   December 27
cardinal,
      bungling: January 9
      sardonic: November 17
cards,
      get well: January 7
      playing: January 5, July 30
castanets, skill at playing: May 25
catapult, operated by all-female crew:
   June 25
Christmas, unhappy: January 4, December 15
cigarettes,
      banned: May 20
      *Camel*: July 20
      *Chesterfields*: February 9
      *KOOL Menthol*: February 15
club,
      Belgian Alpine: February 17
      Cirencester Park Polo: June 24
      Hell-Fire: May 31
coffee enema: November 7
coffin,
      as constant travel companion: January 12
      Egyptian: August 18
      lined with lead: February 16
      opened repeatedly: September 25
      square: August 1
      tried out for size: May 25
      undersized: September 9
      used prior to death: September 21

coincidence, extraordinary: March 5,
  May 14, October 12
conducting, over-enthusiastic: March 22
conspiracy theories: January 15, January
  30, May 5
corpse,
  burned: May 17
  cut in half: February 19
  desiccated: May 8
  handcuffed to briefcase: August 25
  posed for portrait: July 15
  preserved in honey: June 10
  pretending to be one: June 28
  steeped in herbs: August 31
  stench of: February 20
  thawed out, January 5
  thrown into river: April 3
  thrown out of window: August 24
court appointments.
  Grand Master of the Wardrobe: May 10
  Keeper of the Seal: July 6
  Lord of the Bedchamber: July 21
cow, as unit of currency: January 16
crown, portentous: November 18
crucifixion: July 27

——— D ———

day of death, disputed: January 28,
  January 31
defenestration: March 18, May 29,
  August 16
disguise,
  as American soldier: October 2
  as bandit: July 3
  as carter's apprentice: September 27
  as deserter: June 28
  as doctor: July 26
  as man: September 27
  as nun: May 25
  as peasant: December 22
  as priest: June 11
  as prince, August 13
  useless: March 29
divine retribution: February 3, March 20,
  April 15, June 7
doctors,
  bungling of, February 6, March 28,
    April 6, April 10, November 6
  hatred of: January 28
dog,
  bulldog, tick-infested: April 19
  German Shepherd, only companion:
    July 20
  Maltese Poodle, heir to millions:
    August 20
  Newfoundland, vicious: April 19
  Pug, portentous: May 28
Domesday Book: variation of: April 18
dream,
  pleasant: November 17
  unpleasant: November 27
dressing gown, death in: February 21,
  August 2, August 24
drink, alcoholic
  arrack: June 13, October 28
  beer: January 7, June 13, December 6
  canary sack: May 1
  gin: February 9
  vodka: January 10, November 21
  whisky: February 9
  wine (see under *wine*)
drink, non-alcoholic
  cherry water: February 6
  hot chocolate,
  comfort found in: July 30
  hasty: June 21
  morning: October 25
  papal: January 19
  milk,
    almond: June 15
    and champagne comprising entire
      diet: December 5
    fermented mare's: February 18
    from Highland cattle: December 9
  water,
    drunk at inappropriate moment:
      July 4
    previously containing pine cones:
      December 6

drum, made out of human skin:
  October 11
duelling,
    airborne: June 22
    terrestrial: May 12, November 15
dwarves, collection of: July 30

———— E ————

egg, portentous: March 11
Elton John: August 5
Epiphany, Feast of,
    calculation of date: November 14
    celebrated in an unorthodox fashion:
      January 6
espionage: May 14, August 5, October 2
executioner,
    apologised to: October 16
    brilliant: January 30, May 19, July 17
    incompetent: May 5, May 9, May 27,
      July 15
executioner's block,
    difficulty in locating: February 12
    ease in locating: February 13
    held down on: May 27
    last minute reprieve from: March 12
    momentary confusion on: May 19
    recently used: February 13

———— F ————

false teeth, ill-fitting: January 22
feet, roasted: February 26
final speech,
    cut short: January 21
    lengthy: June 14
    loquacious: June 19
    unintentional: June 29
finger of suspicion,
    on Swede: January 1
    on the French: January 30
fire tongs, unorthodox use of: February 21
fish,
    Ethiopian: October 4
    herring: February 12

Nile: April 2
salmon: December 9
sardine: September 11
white mullet: April 1
see also seafood
fondue: March 7
fruit,
    apricot: November 7
    grape: October 21
    lemon: August 30
    melon: June 17, June 21
    orange: June 21, August 30
    peach: October 19
    pear: August 30
    prune: December 23
    strawberry: June 21
frying pan, used as shield: April 6
funeral,
    active participation in one's own:
      September 21
    Eagle at: December 21
    falcon at: December 5
    hurried: September 9
    mayhem at: June 3

———— G ————

Gentleman in Black Velvet: March 8
ghost,
    family: February 25, May 25
    heralding death: February 25,
      November 27
goat, comparison with: January 5
graffiti, on throne: April 17
guillotine,
    conventional: January 21, October 16,
      November 8
    maiden: June 2
guitar, playing upside down: December 21

———— H ————

hand (severed),
    preserved in rum: August 12
hanging: January 3, February 3, February

26, May 2, May 5, June 16, July 1,
  October 2, October 3, November 29
hari-kari, *see* suicide
hat,
  nightcap: June 17
  odd-looking: January 8
  pointy: September 13
  top: June 16
head (severed),
  crowned with willow and ivy:
    December 11
  displayed in museum: November 26
  jiggled in front of friend:
    September 3
  nailed to rostra: December 7
  shoved in bag: February 12
  smashed against lintel: April 7
  stuck on pole: January 15, August 12,
    September 3
  used as paperweight: October 3
heart,
  blackened: January 7
  slung: August 25
  stolen and eaten by dog:
    December 2
horse,
  crushed under: March 19
  fall from: May 31, September 19,
    November 13
  inability to mount: July 21
  irresponsible riding of: April 12
  spooked: March 27, November 13
  wins at Newmarket: May 6
horses, burst into tears: March 15
housemaid's knee: November 19
Houses of Parliament,
  Commons: May 11, October 18,
    December 14
  Lords: February 5, May 31, November
    27, December 18
humour, royal attempt at: April 24
hygiene, lack of: March 24, July 9,
  September 13

—— I ——

identification of body by,
  dental records: May 4
  Edith the Swan-Necked: October 14
  mole: September 20
  scars: January 5
ie ie vine: May 8
Impressionist paintings, final look at:
  January 14
*in flagrante*, caught: January 17
indecent exposure, committed at wedding:
  May 31
inheritance,
  deemed insufficient: September 30
  missed by a year: March 3
  received, on condition of footwear:
    December 5
  received, vast: February 24

—— K ——

kebab, human: March 16
kissing,
  of nose: March 25
  of girls at random: July 24
knots, tying and untying: January 29

—— L ——

lamb, eight-legged: May 14
lawn sprinkler, song about: November 11
liquids, obsession with: May 5

—— M ——

Merlin, prophecy of: November 8,
  December 11
medical remedy, unorthodox,
  cockerel, placed on feet: November 6
  emeralds (crushed), eaten: November 18
  giant tortoise blood, bathed in:
    August 30
  mercury potion, drunk: September 10
  pigeon, placed on head: November 6

red pill, swallowed: September 26
ring of fifth-century saint, worn:
    August 30
stone from goat stomach (use
    unknown): February 6
wood, sawn by patient: March 2
meteorology, scoffed at: April 30
mistaken identity, uxorial: January 18
moon, assistance in murder: March 23
moustache,
    bushy, August 13
    curly: April 27
mouth-to-mouth resuscitation:
    November 30
muezzin, unfortunate call of: January 27
mule,
    bad-tempered: October 30
    clandestine use of hoof: June 10
music lesson, chagrin at delayed: June 20
musical,
    *South Pacific*: February 6
    *The King and I*: October 1
    *The Sound of Music*: May 30
mutton, eaten while standing up:
    January 29

——— N ———

napkin, placed on head: April 29
near-death experience, career-destroying:
    June 27
Nelson, Horatio: January 16, April 22
nipple, pinched: April 10
numismatics, love of: July 18
nun, pregnant: September 4

——— O ———

obituary,
    harsh: November 18
    published early: October 7, November 16
obscene literature, papal: August 14
obscenities,
    shouted at ladies-in-waiting: March 24
    shouted in public: January 31

oil lamp, portentous: March 6
onions, eaten raw: August 8

——— P ———

physique, enormous, May 7, May 23, June
    26, July 21, August 1, September 10
pirates, Amazonian: December 6
pleasure cruise, unpleasant: April 20
pond, garden, as trompe l'oeil: January 11
post mortem,
    denied: February 8
    on billiard table: May 5
    brief: August 5
    surprise at: June 4
pot belly: September 9, December 22
pots, rattling of: March 11
practical joke, backfiring of: February 10
prison conditions,
appalling: April 14, June 8, August 6
    passable: November 1
public school,
    Eton: June 1
    Harrow: January 10

——— R ———

rainbow, mnemonic for colours of:
    December 30
retirement scheme, regretted by employer:
    April 26
revenge,
    inability to buy, April 19
    sweet: January 16, February 28

——— S ———

saints,
    Aidan: March 29
    Anthony: August 31
    Augustine: May 26
    Bartholomew: May 30
    Edmund: August 17
    Fiacre: August 31
    Isidore: March 31

John the Baptist: July 1
Justus: September 21
Leoba: September 28
Mary Magdalene: July 22
Oliver: July 1
Peter: July 1
Simeon the Crazy: July 1
Stephen: December 26
seafood
   caviar: February 12
   eels: March 19, August 17
   lamprey: December 1
   lobster: February 12, March 18
   *see also* fish
seatbelts,
   failure to wear (and death in crash):
     September 14
   wearing of (and still death in crash):
     July 5
sex, encouraged to have with fiancé:
   January 29
sex appeal: August 5, November 6,
   November 9
sexual appetite, enormous: January
   1, January 10, January 19, February
   26, March 11, April 29, July 29,
   September 26
shipping forecast, BBC: April 30
sibling rivalry: January 13, February 4,
   December 5
signal, pre-arranged for one's own death:
   January 30, March 14
snake-charmer, Libyan: August 12
snow, as a preservative: April 9
snowdrop, as love-token: July 7
snuff-box, unorthodox use of: March 23
soap dish, unorthodox use of:
   September 15
soothsayer, unheeded: March 15
spectacles, left at home: May 14
spider, fed roast beef: October 9
sport,
   baseball: December 4
   bowls: September 8
   cricket: March 20, July 23

darts: May 15
football: July 23
jousting: June 21, July 10
tennis: February 21, April 4, November 6
stake, burned at: March 18, July 16
sticks, gnawed on: October 19
suicide,
   attempted
     blunt scissors: August 10
     eating rotten fish: September 11
     lying naked in snow: September 11
   successful
     airplane: July 31
     dagger: April 16
     drug overdose: July 12, August 5
     in battle: August 11, September 20
     knife: November 3
     penknife: November 22
     pin: April 22
     potassium cyanide: December 16
     revolver: April 13, October 8,
      November 6
     rope: April 25
     skipping rope: June 16
     stick: November 10
synaesthesia: April 27
synagogue, makeshift: November 1

—— T ——

tarantula, rubber: February 29
tax,
   attempted evasion of: August 20
   deemed excessive: November 3
   levied on ploughs: August 9
testicles, crushed: May 20
thermal underwear, invention of:
   August 21
three-card monte, expertise at: July 8
thumb, unorthodox use of: January 15
thurible, unorthodox use of: December 25
Tower of London:
   attempted escape from: March 1
   execution at: February 12, February 18,
    May 21

imprisonment in: September 27,
    November 29
inscription on cell wall, incomplete:
    February 3
torture at: July 16,
trial by ordeal, carried out by substitute:
    January 1
tulip, belief in being a: November 9

—— U ——

undertakers,
    bargaining with: October 5
    forced to use winch: May 23

—— V ——

vegetables,
    artichoke, eaten whole: September 1
    cabbage, as part of last supper,
        February 12
    parsnip, accepted by hermit: August 30
    pea, eaten whole in pod: September 1
    yam, enormous: September 10
Venus,
    excess of: April 9
    transit of: October 22
village, moved for aesthetic reasons:
    November 20

—— W ——

wedding night, busy: January 1
Westminster Abbey,
    access denied to: August 8
    burial in: August 31, December 19
    death in: March 20
    final prayers in: November 16
    funeral in: July 10, August 12
windmill, first design of: November 3
wine,
    bathing leg in: September 1
    Champagne: February 12, July 2,
        July 20, November 5, December 2,
        December 5,
    Madeira: February 18
    pomegranate: July 7
    viper: May 1
    yellow: October 28
women, fear of: February 24
wrestling,
    for one's life: March 15, March 23,
        December 31
    professional: September 29
    with bears: May 5